"Turn It Again"
Jewish Medieval Studies
and Literary Theory

"Turn It Again"
Jewish Medieval Studies and Literary Theory

Edited by
SHEILA DELANY

Wipf & Stock
PUBLISHERS
Eugene, Oregon

Wipf and Stock Publishers
199 W 8th Ave, Suite 3
Eugene, OR 97401

Turn It Again
Jewish Medieval Studies and Literary Theory
By Delany, Sheila
Copyright©2004 by Delany, Sheila
ISBN 13: 978-1-55635-442-7
ISBN 10: 1-55635-442-8
Publication date 4/27/2007
Previously published by Pegasus Press, 2004

Contents

SHEILA DELANY, Introduction — 1

WILLIAM CHESTER JORDAN, Jewish Studies and the Medieval Historian — 7

DANIEL BOYARIN, A Tale of Two Synods: Nicaea, Yavneh, and Rabbinic Ecclesiology — 20

MICHAEL CHERNICK, "Turn it and turn it again": Culture and Talmud Interpretation — 59

SUSAN EINBINDER, Jewish Women Martyrs: Changing Models of Representation — 97

ELLIOT R. WOLFSON, Ontology, Alterity, and Ethics in Kabbalistic Anthropology — 119

TOVA ROSEN, Sexual Politics in a Medieval Hebrew Marriage Debate — 145

BRUCE ROSENSTOCK, Alonso de Cartagena: Nation, Miscegenation, and the Jew in Late-Medieval Castile — 172

SONIA FELLOUS, Cultural Hybridity, Cultural Subversion: Text and Image in the Alba Bible, 1422–33 — 190

CHANITA GOODBLATT, Women, Demons and the Rabbi's Son: Narratology and "A Story from Worms" — 213

Contributors — 233

"Turn It Again"
Jewish Medieval Studies and Literary Theory

SHEILA DELANY

> *Only they who do not know where they are going
> will come to the promised land.*

This Hebrew proverb served well as a point of departure when I undertook the first version of this project, a guest-edited special issue of *Exemplaria* (12.1, 2000), the American journal of theory in medieval and early modern studies. The blend of serendipity and chutzpah the proverb recommends aptly fitted my condition as a novice in Jewish studies, fortunate in meeting, knowing, and studying with some of the scholars whose work is represented here. As an experienced medievalist on sabbatical leave in New York (1997), and as a Chaucerian looking for another Middle Ages than Chaucer's, I began to read medieval Hebrew literature in translation. What better place to do so than New York, with Columbia University's library, the Dorot collection at the New York Public Library, the voluminous resources of the Jewish Museum, the Jewish Theological Seminary, Hebrew Union College, and even the flagship Barnes and Noble Judaica section?

My impression was of an undersea city, a "lost Atlantis" partly destroyed and partly forgotten, but beginning slowly to surface—not least in the work of the contributors to this volume. But it soon became apparent that the fit between medieval scholarship and Jewish studies was not as seamless as I had imagined it would be. Many conventionally trained medievalists, I found, have virtually no idea of the monuments, extent, or influence of Jewish culture in their chosen period, any more than I did, and rarely think of Jewish culture as a source of data for their own work in various disciplines. Their—our—normative training has often been profoundly eurocentric and christiancentric. To the extent that medievalists are aware of the Jewish presence in the Middle Ages, their idea of

Jewish studies is often the Christian representation of Jews, not the self-expression of Jews.

By the same token, many Jewish studies scholars have little idea how medieval studies has benefited in recent decades from methodological and theoretical advances. Thus Jewish studies scholars often remain in a sense insulated in their field, unaware of the potential intellectual impact of their wonderful translating, editing, and chronicling—of which there is still by no means enough. The most obvious aim of this collection is to help bridge that gap: to display to medievalists the most sophisticated, provocative, and theoretically informed Jewish studies work currently available; and to suggest to Jewish studies experts some extensions and implications of their field.

Thus the work assembled here is not typical Jewish studies—at least not yet; it is at this point vanguard work, its premises, methods, and conclusions frequently deplored by more traditional scholars. To those outside the field, such a reception is puzzling, for it seems that the task is simple enough: just apply the methods and premises of current critical theory to Jewish literature. But it isn't quite so straightforward, because there is a more intimate and complex relation between theory and practice here than we conventionally trained medievalists are used to. This is not only because Judaism is, among other things, an ethical system devoted to the cultivation of ethical practice, working out over and over again always anew in every epoch the behaviors that can be considered consistent with Torah and with rabbinic teachings. It is also because of contemporary politics and social life as these touch Jews: assimilation, intermarriage, non-Jewish philosophies, above all the relations of Jews and Arabs, Judaism and Islam, Israel and the Middle East. Because there are institutions, movements, parties, wars, and nations, there are agendas, and it is difficult to produce a piece of scholarship in this field that doesn't have—or cannot be construed as having—an agenda with pragmatic application. This condition itself poses a theoretical problem: that of the possibility of theory in a charged situation in which any speculation or contribution (e.g., about the late date of a Talmudic text, or the profound and lasting influence of Islam on Jewish culture, or the nonhumane attitudes of some medieval Jewish authors) may be attached by some readers to a polarized position, read as political agenda rather than as valid scholarship. As editor of this collection I do have an agenda, outlined below, and of course scholars may well want to do certain kinds of work because of their politics. By me (to use a yiddishism) agendas are fine, as long as the scholarship is sound.

The theoretical approaches represented here are varied—postcolonial, Foucauldian, Freudian, ethical, feminist or gender-conscious, historicist, narratological/Barthesian—but even these by no means exhaust the possibilities. This is why I have borrowed Michael Chernick's title, an aphorism from *Pirke Avot* describing the Talmud itself—"Turn it and turn it again, for everything is in it"—for the general title of this collection. And, as richly various as are the disciplines and genres represented here, they can only hint at the fullness of a culture so incompletely known to many medievalists. Most of the pieces challenge long-established cultural and interpretive paradigms or bring together for the first time a particular old literature and modern methods of reading. Others document the often convoluted relation of Jews with Christian and Islamic cultures, a relation sometimes collaborative, sometimes subversive, sometimes—as Sonia Fellous's marvelous essay in cultural art history shows—both at once.

Beyond the material itself, though, and beyond the blended arena of theoretically informed medieval Jewish studies, I intend this collection to have social and professional use. In a practical sense I would like to help de-ghettoize Jewish studies, to attempt a mainstreaming or normalization of the field. By that I mean not only that more of us conventionally trained medievalists might offer courses in medieval Jewish literature, but that we might integrate Jewish material into any syllabus, just as we have already learned to integrate writing by women authors or immigrant or native authors into our poetry, novel, or period courses. We might include translated Hebrew poetry, secular or religious, in a course on medieval lyric, Hebrew or Yiddish romance in a course on romance, Talmud in a course on narrative, Jewish martyrology whether late-classical or high-medieval in a course on hagiography, the anti-Jesus *Toledot* in a satire course, and Jewish philosophy, travel account, chronicle, ethical treatise, animal fable, or other genres in the appropriate medieval courses. Some of this vast treasurehouse of material is beginning to be translated into English or other European languages; some has to be hunted out in earlier, forgotten, or out-of-print translations. There is a tantalizing amount of scholarship in modern Hebrew, and one hopes that translators will soon make it available to the international scholarly community.

This attempt at mainstreaming is far from being a new effort; rather, in a very small way, it participates in a long tradition. One might mention, as an especially illustrious predecessor, the great Cordovan scholar Moses Maimonides (1135–1204) who, in addition to his theological, medical, and legal treatises, produced a reconciliation of Jewish theology with Aristotelian philosophy, much as Catholic *auctores* did in the same era. Of course the establishment in neither religion welcomed these efforts to incorporate rationalism; the Hispanic rabbis burnt Maimonides's books much as French archbishops would soon afterward burn those of the Jewish scholar's adventurous Catholic counterparts.

In the modern era, Jewish studies appeared, or reappeared, when German students wanted to demonstrate the compatibility of Judaism with the rationalistic philological and philosophical spirit of the day. Their first journal was published in 1822, the *Zeitschrift für die Wissenschaft des Judentums*; fifty years later an institute, or *Hochschule*, was founded. In France, the *Revue des études juives* published its first issue in 1880. It continues to publish today. Currently, and for the last half-century, the United States, Israel, and (more modestly) France play the leading role in the field.[1]

Why, with such a history, is it necessary to do it again? I often asked myself this question when perusing volumes of *REJ* with its many articles, published over the course of a century and more, on Provençal Jewish romance, Hebrew lyric, and other medieval Jewish literature. Why did this work not become normative; why was it not integrated into curricula and into paradigms of medievalism? In his erudite survey of the modern scholarly tradition, William Jordan suggests some reasons and offers some prospects. I hope that his cautious optimism will be justified eventually.

For my part, a political gesture is also intended with this collection: a gesture of the socially limited academic type, to be sure, but that is for the moment the available ground. I have already referred to the eurocentric/christiancentric model that this collection can perhaps assist to its demise in some small way, by suggesting expanded options for teaching and for scholarship that may in turn affect the social attitudes of colleagues and students. Any example of Jewish studies would do this, of course, and I

---

[1] See Frank Alvarez-Pereyre and Jean Baumgarten, eds., *Les études juives en France: Situation et perspectives* (Paris, CNRS, 1990); also the fiftieth anniversary volume of *Revue des études juives* (1930).

believe the work displayed here does it in an especially effective way precisely because of, and through, its courageous iconoclasm. It does not always paint a pretty picture of medieval Jewish culture. Jews, we learn, have been misogynistic and misogamistic; they have demonized the non-Jewish other in the most fundamental ontological way; they have manipulated history in struggles for power against other Jews. What is the value of such portraits, scrupulously painted "warts and all"? The same, I suggest, as for any historical truth: that if we don't know it we can't hope to understand anything—ourselves, the future, the ways we are manipulated ideologically here and now. Part of that long-range truth is Jewish presence. To borrow the words of Hirsh Glik, "Mir seinen doh!" ("We're here.")[2]

Even more: by deconstructing the rose-tinted stereotypes of an always benign, always pluralistic and life-affirming Jewish culture—stereotypes shared by many modern Jews and Christians—this scholarship renders impossible every stereotype and thus helps to deprive anti-Semitism of one of its main props. False positive stereotypes do not, in the long run, serve a cause or group better than false negative ones. Historical truth is always a gesture, however modest, flung in the teeth of anti-Semitism (or racism or sexism), even in the relatively genteel or semicovert ways that anti-Semitism occurs in academic life.

Last but far from least in this brief introduction I want to express gratitude and appreciation to Al Shoaf and Mario Di Cesare. As founder and editor of *Exemplaria*, Al offered an ideal balance of freedom and expert guidance, from his warm reception of my proposal down to the meticulous production and circulation of the special issue. Mario has been similarly hospitable and prompt in his capacity as director of Pegasus Press, which publishes *Exemplaria*. And I must thank both Simon Fraser University and Canada's Social Science and Humanities Research Council for funding that enabled me to pursue Jewish Studies in Manhattan, surely one of the best places in the world to do so.

---

[2] Glik, living in the Vilna ghetto, wrote the Yiddish song "Zug nit keinmol" ("Never say....") for the Warsaw ghetto rising of 1943, and it quickly became the anthem of the Jewish partisan resistance movement. "Mir seinen doh" is its refrain.

Jewish Studies and the Medieval Historian

WILLIAM CHESTER JORDAN

The task that I propose is a difficult one—to describe and perhaps explain some ramifications of Jewish studies for medieval history. In order to do so, I will first sketch the emergence of Jewish studies as a field of scholarly inquiry, then concentrate on its impact in the area I know best: the study of political power in the Middle Ages. I believe that concentrating on these subjects will throw light on other topics and will offer some prophecy about the future relationship between Jewish studies and what is sometimes called general medieval history.

The "new Jewish studies," according to a recent issue of the *Chronicle of Higher Education*, "defies tradition and easy categorization." Indeed if the article in which this statement appeared is accurate, it may even be a little risky to speculate on the subject. At least, it was in Boston at the 1998 meeting of the Association for Jewish Studies. David Berger, the president of the Association and a distinguished scholar in the field, is quoted in the article as criticizing the address of one of his colleagues in a nice way, by saying that her particular take on the future of Jewish studies, which called for a kind of confessional or ideological commitment in the classroom, was "surely inappropriate." (A less courteous respondent deemed it "useless.")[1]

Although not endorsing the intemperate language of the unnamed respondent, I will have to agree on the point: if Jewish studies is perceived mainly as a form of cheerleading for an ethnic or confessional commitment to Judaism, it will have minimal impact on general medieval history.

One way to think about this is from the situation of African-American studies and its impact on general history. In the Fall of 1998 at Princeton University the Program in African-American Studies organized a series of fourteen weekly lectures on the theme, "What does African-American Studies offer the Traditional Disciplines?" Literature, Political Science, Critical Theory, Immigration Studies, Women's Studies, Philosophy, and many other disciplines were subjected to systematic scrutiny in order to determine what they had imbibed from African-American studies and

---

[1] Scott Heller, "The New Jewish Studies: Defying Tradition and Easy Categorization," *Chronicle of Higher Education*, January 29, 1999, A21–22.

what they might still learn. It should come as no surprise that the main problem in bridging the gap between African-American studies and other disciplines has been the feeling—very difficult to dispel—that even moderate practitioners are susceptible to using the field to celebrate an ethnic or racial consciousness. On the other hand, the very titles of the presentations in the series of lectures I mentioned suggest that there has been a fruitful dialogue between African-American Studies and other disciplines and that there is, at present and not least because of the siting of major African-American Studies programs in general institutions, no danger of a broad retreat to self-ghettoization, although that possibility always remains.

The Origins of Jewish Studies[2]

Certainly the founders of Jewish studies (*Wissenschaft des Judentums*) as a distinct field of modern scholarly inquiry saw institutional accommodation, that is, incorporation of Jewish studies into universities, as a necessary if not sufficient goal in the process of integrating the field with enlightened learning in general. But from the beginning this was an uphill battle. Very briefly, then, let me sketch the history of *Wissenschaft des Judentums*, for its history is crucial for an adequate understanding of the present state of Jewish studies and its relationship to general scholarship on the Middle Ages.

Wissenschaft des Judentums originated in post-Enlightenment Germany in tandem with political emancipation in the early nineteenth century. The idea among the pioneers of the field was to give scientific respectability to studies of Jewish culture. The chief practitioners, many of whom were among the first to benefit from the political emancipation of Jews in central Europe, were trained in or imitated the then-emerging approaches to the study of the past that we have come to call Germanic scholarship. This method stressed, first and foremost, careful research in archives—this was to be above all a documentary history; second, it demanded "objectivity"; and, third, it required a transparent prose style.

Jewish scholars (and almost all the earliest scholars in post-biblical Jewish studies were Jews by birth) were first encouraged to find texts in

---

[2] Although I have occasionally departed from the narrative line and emphases of Nahum Glatzer's account of the origins of Jewish scholarship, most of the framework of this section of my essay has been deeply informed by his "Beginnings of Modern Jewish Studies," in *Studies in Nineteenth-Century Jewish Intellectual History*, ed. Alexander Altmann (Cambridge: Harvard University Press, 1964), 27–45.

obscure places and to edit or inventory them in order to make their contents accessible to other scholars. The work of the bibliographer Moritz Steinschneider is legendary; his search for manuscripts through the libraries of Europe was pursued with obsessive dedication and thoroughness.[3] Meir Wiener, less well known nowadays, also published a major *Inventory of the History of the Jews of Germany during the Middle Ages* in 1862. He justified his work by "the extraordinary importance and significance of sources for a true representation of history."[4] (This pithy justification is otherwise embedded in a German sentence that goes on for 21 lines. Part and parcel of Germanic scholarship was its forbidding character.) In any case, Wiener's was a remarkable achievement, and the Inventory is still valuable. But the *Wunderkind* in this effort was Julius Aronius, who at 22 defended his dissertation on Anglo-Saxon sources and at 23 joined the "Historical Commission for the History of the Jews in Germany" in order to compile the *Inventory for the History of the Jews in the Frankish and German Empires*. Aronius literally worked himself to death by the age of 32, but his remarkable book is still the fundamental inventory of documents on medieval German Jewish history. The memorial notice that accompanied the original though posthumous publication of the book spoke of his as a "life wholly dedicated to *Wissenschaft*."[5]

The inventorying and publication in modern scholarly editions of important texts constituted the first step. Editions were the raw material for highly specialized monographs and articles. Since the weight of scholarly tradition as well as the prevalence of anti-Semitism made it almost impossible to get articles on post-biblical Jewish subjects published in general journals, it was necessary to found independent scholarly journals that unprejudiced scholars would be willing to cite because of the scientific quality of the work published. Almost like a refrain, the opening pages of these new scholarly journals stress their scientific character. The first issue of the *Monatschrift für Geschichte und Wissenschaft des Judenthums* (1851) declared that its mission was to have a deeper and "wider scientific (*wissenschaftlich-*

---

[3] See the biographical notice in *Encyclopaedia Judaica*, 16 vols. (Jerusalem: Keter, 1972), 15.375–76.

[4] Meir Wiener, *Regesten zur Geschichte der Juden in Deutschland während des Mittelalters* (Hannover: Hann'sche Hofbuchhandlung, 1862), iii, "die ausserordentliche Wichtigkeit und Bedeutung von Urkunden für eine richtige Darstellung der Geschichte."

[5] Julius Aronius, *Regesten zur Geschichte der Juden im fränkischen und deutschen Reiche* (Berlin: Verlag von Leonhard Simion, 1902), "ganz der Wissenschaft gewidmeten Leben."

er) tendency" than was typical of earlier periodicals devoted to Jewish subjects.⁶

What happened in Germany set the standard, but this desire leapt national borders. The initial issue of the *Jewish Quarterly Review* published in England in 1889 identified itself as "providing ... a medium in which scholars may register the results of their research, and theologians the results of their thoughts, [and which] may stimulate the few to work, think, and write, and the many to read."⁷ As late as 1903 the maiden issue of the annual of the *Jüdisch-Literarische Gesellschaft* in Germany continued to see the task as one of furthering "Wissenschaft des Judentums" and making it respectable and acceptable in the wider scholarly community.⁸

The truth is that, notwithstanding occasional expressions of respect that non-Jews gave in personal letters to scholars in the *Wissenschaft des Judentums* tradition, very few read extensively in the specialized literature on post-biblical Jewish studies. This is why great synthetic works were also deemed necessary. A scholar who did not have the time or inclination to dive into the detailed articles of the *Monatschrift* might open a good general book on Jewish history. And if he did so, it was hoped, he might think about his own work in a new light. One of the most famous works produced in this synthetic tradition was Heinrich Graetz's *Geschichte der Juden*, quite different from the highly specialized and narrowly focussed articles he submitted to and edited for the *Monatschrift*. On the title page of the Leipzig edition (1873) to the first chronological volume of his work, he advertised its rigorous tie to the sources; this was its badge of authenticity and, at least in part, a response to criticisms that his level of generalization was insufficiently grounded in original sources.⁹ On another level the carping was personal. Graetz was a difficult and contradictory man, who antagonized a great many people, especially in the Reformed

---

⁶ "Einleitendes," *Monatschrift für Geschichte und Wissenschaft des Judenthums* 1 (1852): 1, "mit erweiterter wissenschaftlicher Tendenz."

⁷ "Introductory," *Jewish Quarterly Review* 1 (1889): 2. For a very interesting recent treatment of Israel Abrahams, one of the founders of the *Quarterly*, see Elliott Horowitz, "Jewish Life in the Middle Ages and the Jewish Life of Israel Abrahams," in *The Jewish Past Revisited: Reflections on Modern Jewish Historians* (New Haven: Yale University Press, 1998), 143–62.

⁸ *Jahrbuch der Jüdisch-Literarischen Gesellschaft* 1 (1903): 3, "Wir wollen die Förderung der Wissenschaft des Judentums anstreben."

⁹ Heinrich Graetz, *Geschichte der Juden* 1 (Leipzig: O. Leiner, 1873), "aus den Quellen neu bearbeitet." Graetz actually started to publish the work in the 1850s, but he began with volume four.

Jewish community, and was not to have an easy career; he was not offered a position on the "Historical Commission for the History of the Jews in Germany" mentioned above.[10]

In Jewish studies, even great narrative reconstructions needed angels. In the preface to the English translation of his *History of the Jews* Graetz went out of his way to thank his patron, Frederic Moccata, "whose name," he said, "is a household word in every Jewish circle."[11] It was Moccata, the extremely wealthy scion of, ironically, a Reform family, who underwrote the appearance of Graetz's work in English as well as English translations of several works by the founder of Jewish scientific scholarship, Leopold Zunz.[12]

Practitioners of *Wissenschaft des Judentums* also saw the need for scholarly reference tools, like encyclopedias, that general scholars could use as a springboard for deeper study. Such enterprises, much like the great syntheses and narrative panoramas, depended on the pre-existence of source collections and of monographs and specialized articles. But after a half-century or so of work, the material was finally available for compilation, abridgement, and informed simplification in encyclopedias. So wrote the editors of *The Jewish Encyclopedia* when they launched their first volume in 1901.[13]

If the quality of research and its availability were the first consideration in making Jewish studies respectable, the second, closely related, was objectivity. It is fashionable now to question the possibility of objectivity. Every text has a sub-text; every author has a hidden agenda; deconstruction allows us to see the multiplicity of meanings both in an original source and in a historical work. Purist claims to objectivity are considered at best naive—at worst stigmatized as lies. None of this would have been

---

[10] A very informative, though not comprehensive, essay on Heinrich Graetz may be found in the introduction to Ismar Schorsch's volume of translations of selected essays by Graetz, *The Structure of Jewish History and Other Essays* (New York: Ktav for the Jewish Theological Seminary of America, 1975), 1–62. Schorsch entitled his study, "Ideology and History in the Age of Emancipation."

[11] Heinrich Graetz, *History of the Jews* (Philadelphia: Jewish Publication Society of America, 1891), 1:vii.

[12] *Dictionary of National Biography*, Supplement 2 (Oxford: Oxford University Press, 1912), 626. Zunz is treated in considerable detail in Schorsch, "Ideology and History" and Glatzer, "Beginnings of Modern Jewish Studies," but analysis of his work, which dealt with post-biblical literature, is not especially relevant to the focus of the present essay on studies of politics.

[13] *Jewish Encyclopedia* (New York and London: Funk & Wagnalls, 1901), 1:viii–ix.

accepted in the dominant scholarly world of Jewish studies in the nineteenth century. Moreover, on the question of objectivity hung a remarkable claim, namely, that the scholars of *Wissenschaft des Judentums* had liberated themselves from the confessional impulse that many of them associated with traditional Jewish learning. This did not mean that they necessarily lost respect for traditional ways of inscribing the Jewish experience (though some certainly did), but they carefully separated what they considered the scientific reconstruction of the history of Judaism and Jewish life from the confessional, sectarian, apologetic, and polemical work of traditional rabbis. This was why Moritz Steinschneider, no enemy of traditional Judaism as a mode of worship, still "opposed rabbinical seminaries as centers of scholarly research, fearing the introduction of the theological considerations into pure, objective scholarship."[14]

The maiden issue of *Jewish Quarterly Review*, to which reference has already been made, affirmed the dedication of its editorial board to publish on theology—all stripes—noting, however, that "the best exegetical criticism of our own day is absolutely without sectarian bias."[15] This statement notwithstanding, the articles that appeared were not indifferent on confessional matters. The lead article in the maiden issue itself was by Heinrich Graetz, who, while sympathetic to traditional Judaism (except its Polish version), could be devastating when he was trying to present Judaism "objectively" as a shaper of the highest Western values. His essay for the *Review* was entitled "The Significance of Judaism." After lauding what he regarded as the threefold contribution of Judaism to world civilization—humane ideals, monotheism, and religious rationalism—Graetz added: "Of course, Judaism contains an elaborate ritual besides these ideal principles, which, unfortunately, owing to the tragic course of history, has developed into a fungoid growth which overlays the ideals."[16]

Graetz's disagreeable sentiments here would not have been shared by, say, his contemporary Alexander Kohut, and even with Graetz they represent perhaps a phase in his feelings—or just a poor choice of phrase. Nonetheless, recent work has shown how strongly most claims of objectivity co-existed with a concerted ideological effort on the part of many scholars in the *Wissenschaft des Judentums* tradition to make Judaism respectable in the eyes of rationalistic often religiously skeptical scholars of Christian,

---

[14] *Encyclopaedia Judaica*, 15:375.

[15] Introductory, *Jewish Quarterly Review* 1 (1889): 2.

[16] Heinrich Graetz, "The Significance of Judaism," *Jewish Quarterly Review* 1 (1889): 13.

particularly Protestant, background. Anything that was "embarrassing" in Jewish ritual could be explained by late nineteenth-century rationalistic Jewish intellectuals as a response to the hostility of the Christian majority in the past which had forced Judaism to turn in on itself. Under the improving conditions expected by many late nineteenth-century scholars, despite what they regarded as occasional atavistic outbreaks of anti-Semitism, understanding and mutual respect would emerge, and these would help both traditions—Christian and Jewish—to divest themselves of their supposed anti-rational elements. Again, not everyone shared this viewpoint, certainly not the pessimistic Graetz, but it took events of the mid-twentieth century to utterly expose the utopian nature of the expectation.

Closely related to the insistence on objectivity was the desire for transparent prose. Individual sentences might be long and challenging —especially in German. Narrative or descriptive lines, however, were to be firm and straightforward; *Wissenschaft* scholars deliberately avoided the elliptical turns of phrase and metaphors of biblical, talmudic, and rabbinic prose. This made scholarly writing clear but terribly dull, the dullness itself becoming a kind of badge of authenticity and truth. There was also an extraordinary emphasis on detail, especially dates, in obvious reaction to traditional rabbinic scholarship which by eschewing dates created an image of a timeless unchanging Judaism. To the newer scientific scholars Judaism was alive, if not necessarily completely healthy, precisely because it did change and adapt; and it was their task to recover the history of those changes and adaptations. The *Jewish Encyclopedia* informed its readership that it would "accordingly cast light upon the successive phases of Judaism, [and] furnish precise information concerning the activities of the Jews."[17] Again, the hidden—sometimes not so hidden—agenda of many of these scholars, and the attitude that compromised their own objectivity, was their desire to show that the traditional approach was obsolete, even primitive, indeed an embarrassment, something that kept many Jews under obscurantist leadership and prevented the social acceptance that should have accompanied political emancipation.

Now, despite the hopes repeatedly expressed by *Wissenschaft* scholars that their document-based, positivist work in post-biblical Jewish studies would somehow transform general scholarship, this did not, by and large, turn out to be the case.[18] In Yosef Yerushalmi's words, "the cumulative

---

[17] *Jewish Encyclopedia*, 1:7.
[18] Gavin Langmuir, "Majority History and Postbiblical Jews," in *Toward a Definition of Antisemitism* (Berkeley: University of California Press, 1990), 21–41,

results of intensive Jewish scholarship were virtually without influence upon general historiography." And "postbiblical Judaica was never admitted to the universities as a recognized and distinct discipline." Outside of Germany, *Wissenschaft*'s homeland, it was the same. In the Ivy League, Yerushalmi points out, there were no chairs in Jewish studies before 1925—and the one established then, at Harvard, is the oldest not just in the Ivy League or America, but in the world.[19] Among general historians, none seemed to care about post-biblical, that is, medieval and modern, Jewish studies.

Jewish Studies and the Historians

In the essay just cited, Yerushalmi suggests that most general historical scholarship in the nineteenth and early twentieth centuries focussed on problems of high politics and state formation: power and its exercise. He conjectured that, apart from anti-Semitism, this might have rendered *Wissenschaft des Judentums*, with its emphasis on folkloric customs, theology, and the internal life of Jewish communities, uninteresting to generalists.[20] *Wissenschaft des Judentums* was a form of cultural studies, born before its time. In a scholarly book written in 1900 or 1910 Jews might be mentioned, if they were mentioned at all, with brief comments on their special legal status in the Roman Empire and during the Middle Ages or with equally brief comments on the movement toward emancipation in the Enlightenment and post-Enlightenment period of the eighteenth and nineteenth centuries. Except for such instances the history of postbiblical Jews was of little interest to historians of the state, and most distinguished historians of the time were historians of politics, administrative and financial institutions, and law—in a word, of the state.

As Yerushalmi observed, this description of the situation was accurate until the post-war period; in some ways, it remained accurate until my

---

provides a leisurely tour of the sources that make this point with regard to Anglo-American scholarship. For an exception, where conclusions from Jewish scholarship were taken up (and blisteringly refuted) by a "majority" historian—on the question of the reliability of Nachmanides's report of the Barcelona disputation of 1263—see Robert Chazan, *Barcelona and Beyond: The Disputation of 1263 and Its Aftermath* (Berkeley: University of California Press, 1992), 6.

[19] Yosef Hayim Yerushalmi, Introduction, in *Bibliographical Essays in Medieval Jewish Studies* (New York: Ktav for Anti-Defamation League of B'nai B'rith, 1976), 2:7–8.

[20] Ibid., 6.

generation was studying history in graduate school in the 1970s. Yet nothing could be further from the truth at present. Now, the position of the Jews seems to be at the very core of studies of medieval and, to some degree, modern European statebuilding and national identity formation. This development is a spinoff of a larger concern for what have been called "marginal" groups, itself perhaps a spinoff of the 1960s counterculture. Originally, that concern provoked a retreat from the study of the state, except among traditional Marxist historians or senior scholars, of whatever ideological persuasion, who simply refused to change. Most younger scholars of the 1970s preferred to study saints—especially odd ones—or lepers, or prostitutes, or other stigmatized outsider groups in the Middle Ages. Not many of my peers in the early 1970s thought I was doing anything interesting when I began to work on thirteenth-century French government and administration. Why wasn't I working on French vagabonds or women or heretics or better yet women heretics who were vagabonds?

Nevertheless, most historians eventually came to realize that in order to understand marginality, they had to define the center very carefully. A heretic was a heretic because someone in religious authority said he or she was. A prostitute was a prostitute because someone in legal or moral authority defined her sexual relations as licentious. A vagabond was a vagabond because a whole array of social authorities defined sedentary residence as good and unlicensed wandering as a threat to social order. The same authorities that made these decisions also defined the proper relation of out-groups to the "orthodox and worthy" members of society. Study of the state, which was along with the Catholic Church the most visible construction of authority in the Middle Ages, therefore came to include the study of vagabonds and dissenters of all sorts—including Jews.

Gavin Langmuir, the distinguished Stanford historian, was in many ways a seminal figure in this development. Trained as a legal and constitutional historian of medieval France, he came to the study of the Jewish policies of the French kings as a purely constitutional issue. Steadily he widened his horizon until he saw attitudes toward Jews infiltrating almost all aspects of medieval French life, and he has had almost a zealot's spirit in uncovering the prejudices against Jews and Jewish studies in the works of earlier general historians.[21] A radically austere rationalist from what he describes as "an atheistic family that nonetheless went to church," Langmuir has recently produced a challenging and controversial explanation of

---

[21] Langmuir's collected essays appeared in 1990 under the title Toward a *Definition of Antisemitism*.

the roots of anti-Semitism.²² In a simplified summary, it runs as follows.

According to Langmuir, every religion includes beliefs that are nonrational, that is, not susceptible of rigorous standards of proof. Some of these beliefs are intrinsically non-rational; others are nonrational only so long as there is no scientific way to test them. When the latter in the course of time become testable and are found wanting, it becomes irrational to continue to hold to them. But since such beliefs provide the religious person with a sense of self and place, they are not given up easily. The believer doubts them, but transfers his self-hatred or guilt for doubting onto those people who openly deny them. It would follow that the apparatus of state power could become a means of protecting the property and authority of those who depend on the threatened ideology embedded in the creed to justify their status and wealth in society.

Generalists working on England have not been far behind in appreciating the place of Jews in the critical transformations of medieval social and political life, though they have not necessarily adopted Langmuir's scheme. Robert Stacey is in the process of rewriting English legal and constitutional history by studying the state's attitude toward the Jews. Stacey has been centrally interested in conversion and the perceived need of state authorities to use considerable resources to try to achieve the conversion of the Jews in England in the Middle Ages. Using administrative and legal records that were well-known but underutilized, and other sources whose existence was virtually unheard of, he is putting together a history of the conversion impulse and the remarkable "House of Converts" in England—for converts and their descendants—that lasted from the mid-thirteenth century to the Renaissance, even though the Jews were expelled in 1290.²³

It is to a quite different cluster of scholars—those who write about the internal rhythms of Jewish life based on Hebrew sources—that we have to turn in order to capture other aspects of the experience of medieval Jews. Heirs to the tradition of *Wissenschaft des Judentums* but no longer defensive

---

²² Gavin Langmuir, *History, Religion, and Antisemitism* (Berkeley: University of California Press, 1990), 8.

²³ Robert Stacey's writings on Jews in the English medieval state are already extensive. A selection of the most important includes "1240–1260: A Watershed in English-Jewish Relations," *Bulletin of the Institute of Historical Research* 61 (1988): 135–50; "The Conversion of Jews to Christianity in Thirteenth-Century England," *Speculum* 67 (1992): 263–83; and "Crusades, Martyrdoms and the Jews of Norman England, 1096–1190," in *Juden und Christen zur Zeit der Kreuzzuge*, ed. Alfred Haverkamp (Sigmaringen: Jan Thorbecke Verlag, 1999), 233–52.

or apologetic about the history they explicate, these scholars have added to the repertory of subjects once studied. They know general constitutional and political history and thus can assess the extent to which state power affected Jewish behavior or was resisted. Moreover, influenced by the same trends that brought a marriage of studies of marginal groups and state power, they have felt impelled to blend their vision of Jewish history into powerful syntheses of general history. Although they write mercifully shorter sentences than their German predecessors, they wield equally strong technical skills. Most important, perhaps, the tentative foothold first established in the 1920s and 1930s in the universities has become a much stronger presence now, with at least twenty university presses (mostly of secular institutions) publishing series emphasizing Jewish studies.[24] It is impossible to ignore the avalanche of work that is appearing.

It would be tedious to list all the authors whom I could cite here, but a few have to be mentioned. These include Robert Chazan of New York University, Ivan Marcus of Yale University, Kenneth Stow of Haifa University, and Mark Cohen of Princeton. Chazan in a striking series of studies began by trying to set Jewish life in medieval France inside an agreed-upon narrative of general French history.[25] The result was uneven in that the stories seemed to be parallel rather than integrated. To an extent Chazan realized this, and his work over the last twenty years has attempted to mesh the two tales, although part of the difficulty of achieving this synthesis is that the two traditions have been so intractably focussed on different problems. It has been necessary for him to systematically unpack not only layers of prejudice but layers of mutual indifference in order to make progress at all.[26]

Ivan Marcus has taken a somewhat different approach. He has probed the inner tensions of Jewish social life in the twelfth and thirteenth centuries in order to show certain structural similarities between Jewish

---

[24] According to one recent count, there are at least thirty-four series devoted to publishing works in Jewish studies. Although a few of these appear under European imprints, most of the series are published by university presses in the United States. I owe this information to Professor Marc Saperstein of George Washington University (personal communication, 16 March 1999). The situation in Germany, where *Wissenschaft des Judentums* began, is less thriving; cf. Peter Schäfer, "Jewish Studies in Germany Today," *Jewish Studies Quarterly* 3 (1996): 146–61.

[25] Robert Chazan, *Medieval Jewry in Northern France: A Political and Social History* (Baltimore and London: Johns Hopkins University Press, 1973).

[26] Chazan's works are too numerous to list here. His current work aims again at a synthetic history of northern European Jewry and is near completion.

and Christian social and political history. His object has been to see the two cultures not as twins but rather as forces striving for similar goals. No neat pictures emerge from his brilliant work; everything is complex. What to some earlier scholars look like curious parallels between Jewish life and Christian life, Marcus sometimes shows were deliberate inversions, not mere curiosities. And he brings to bear profound reading in anthropology to explicate historical problems, so that certain aspects of Jewish behavior in the Middle Ages which in the past have resisted explanation appear under Marcus's analysis to turn on deep structural affinities or contrasts with Christian behaviors or symbolic systems.[27]

Few scholars have done as much as Kenneth Stow to probe the relationship of medieval Jewish life to the institutional power of the Catholic Church. Earlier historians, if they talked about this subject at all, usually dealt in generalities, retreated to arid discussions of theology, or simply blamed the Church for every atrocity. Stow was determined to look below the surface. The Church was the most complex governing institution in the Middle Ages. How could the relationship between such a multifaceted institution and the Jews be as simply defined as earlier historians had done? That, I think, was the motivating question in Stow's work. And so he reread documents of Christian and Jewish theology, the Catholic canon law and Jewish law, to deepen his understanding of what was at stake in everyday life. The consequence of that enterprise has been a radical re-interpretation of the relation of the Church and the Jews and, in Stow's view at least, a belief that educated Jews had a strong affinity for alliance with the papacy over and against secular state authorities.[28] Finally, a few words need to be said of Mark Cohen, whose goal has been to contrast Jewish life under medieval Christian and Muslim rule. Recognizing that modern scholars often distort the historical record for polemical purposes related to current Middle Eastern politics, Cohen has been determined to fight bad scholarship with truth—always, or almost always, a thankless task. His accomplishment, an intelligent assessment that stresses the more positive situation of the Jews under Islam, has been a powerful corrective

---

[27] Ivan Marcus's most important work with regard to the points made in this study is *Piety and Society: The Jewish Pietists of Medieval Germany* (Leiden: E. J. Brill, 1981), but he has done pathbreaking work that has taken him beyond questions of power and authority. See, for example, his *Rituals of Childhood: Jewish Acculturation in Medieval Europe* (New Haven: Yale University Press, 1996).

[28] Kenneth Stow's most comprehensive statement of his position to date is his *Alienated Minority: The Jews of Medieval Latin Europe* (Cambridge: Harvard University Press, 1992).

to much recent propaganda to the contrary.²⁹

I do not agree with every word these scholars have written, and with some of them I have significant scholarly disagreements. In some cases they also differ sharply among themselves. My point is merely to display the richness of the harvest—delayed, to be sure— for which the creators of *Wissenschaft des Judentums* so fervently hoped nearly two centuries ago. General historians read these works for their information and their stimulation; they integrate the findings in their own scholarly productions, whether to dispute or to confirm them. In a word, the integration of Jewish and Christian themes in medieval historiography proceeds. It would be a tragedy if the fruitful relationship were undermined by a deliberate return to provincialism and self-celebration in the classrooms or the scholarship of Jewish studies.

The Future

As an historian I feel more comfortable discussing the past than the future, but I do believe that the signs are strong that cross-fertilization continues in interesting ways. I hesitate to mention David Nirenberg's book on *Communities of Violence*, since he was my student and I do not want to claim any credit for his brilliant conceptualization of ritual violence among Jews, Christians, and Muslims in medieval Spain, a conceptualization which was uniquely his own.³⁰ I will conclude, though, by noting that, because the winds are favorable for continued integration, Peter Schäfer, now of Princeton, and myself are planning a new series, specifically designed to publish books that bring together the strengths of Jewish studies and of general history. The series will exist in large part as a thank-offering for the hopes and efforts of the pioneers of Jewish Studies and of those toiling tirelessly in their shadow over the last two centuries.

Princeton University

---

[29] Mark Cohen, Under Crescent and Cross: The Jews in the Middle Ages (Princeton: Princeton University Press, 1994). For the programmatic statement, see xv–xvii.

[30] The full citation is David Nirenberg, *Communities of Violence: Persecution of Minorities in the Middle Ages* (Princeton: Princeton University Press, 1996).

A Tale of Two Synods:
Nicaea, Yavneh, and Rabbinic Ecclesiology

DANIEL BOYARIN

For Chana Kronfeld

I begin with a kind of paradox or conundrum, a mystery that I might call the Yavneh Conundrum. Shaye Cohen wrote, in a now near-classic essay:

> A year or two before the church council of Nicea Constantine wrote to Alexander and Arius, the leaders of the contending parties, and asked them to realize that they were united by their shared beliefs more than they were separated by their debate on the nature of the second person of the Trinity. Let them behave like members of a philosophical school who debate in civil fashion the doctrines of the school (Eusebius, *Life of Constantine* 2.71). The council of Nicea ignored the emperor's advice and expelled the Arians. The sages of Yavneh anticipated Constantine's suggestion. They created a society based on the doctrine that conflicting disputants may each be advancing the words of the living God.[1]

Much of Christian and Jewish scholarship before Cohen had indeed portrayed Yavneh (Jamnia, supposed date 90 AC) very differently. As Cohen himself described it:

> According to the usual view, sectarianism ceased when the Pharisees, gathered at Yavneh, ejected all those who were not members of their own party. Christians were excommunicated, the biblical canon was purged of works written in Greek and apocalyptic in

---

I wish to express gratitude to Virginia Burrus, Catherine Keller, Chana Kronfeld, Lisa Lampert, Rebecca Lyman, and Dina Stein for reading earlier versions of this essay and commenting, as usual, sharply and usefully, and to Sheila Delany for patiently shepherding me through several rounds of revision of this article. Early oral versions have been delivered at the University of California at Berkeley and at Williams College, where I profited on both occasions from stimulating questions and discussion.

[1] Shaye J. D. Cohen, "The Significance of Yavneh: Pharisees, Rabbis, and the End of Jewish Sectarianism," *Hebrew Union College Annual* 55 (1984): 51.

style, and the gates were closed on the outside world, both Jewish and non-Jewish. Functioning in a "crisis" atmosphere, the rabbis of Yavneh were motivated by an exclusivistic ethic; their goal was to define orthodoxy and to rid Judaism of all those who would not conform to it. In this interpretation, the "synod" of Yavneh becomes a prefiguration of the church council of Nicea (325 CE): one party triumphs and ousts its competitors.[2]

Thus, considering "the Council of Jamnia" as a real historical, religious, political event, New Testament scholars have accredited to reaction against the activities of this conciliar body everything from the ire against Jews in the Gospel of John to Jesus's Sermon on the Mount in Matthew.[3] Cohen himself assiduously dismantled the exclusivist image of Yavneh, arguing, to paraphrase his statement above, that Yavneh, far from being a type of Nicaea, was a countertype. It was, for him, not a council in which an orthodoxy was established and heretics and Christians expelled but rather a pluralistic one in which there was "created a society based on the doctrine that conflicting disputants may each be advancing the words of the living God." Cohen's work has been largely adopted by scholars who have further unsettled the narrative of what supposedly took place at Yavneh, including especially the closing of the canon of the Hebrew Bible and the alleged expulsion of the Jewish Christians.[4]

In a cogent revision of the revision, however, Martin Goodman has compellingly shown there was, in many ways, after Yavneh, less "tolerance" of difference rather than more. It was, after all, during that time—after Yavneh—that the category of *minim* and *minut* (heretics and heresy) first appears on the Jewish scene.[5] Following Goodman, it would

---

[2] Ibid., 28.

[3] W. D. Davies, *The Setting of the Sermon on the Mount* (1963; rprt. Cambridge: Cambridge University Press, 1966), 256–315. "The majority opinion is that the First Gospel was composed in the final quarter of the first century AD," W. D. Davies and Dale C. Allison, Jr., *Matthew*, International Critical Commentary (Edinburgh: T. & T. Clark, 1988), 1:128. The chronology, accordingly, works if we assume the Council of Yavneh to have been a real event as recorded in rabbinic literature.

[4] Peter Schäfer, "Die sogennante Synode von Jabne: Zur Trennung von Juden und Christen im ersten/zweiten Jahrhundert n. Chr," *Judaica* 31 (1975): 54–64, 116–24; Günther Stemberger, "Die sogennante 'Synode von Jabne' und das frühe Christentum," *Kairos* 19 (1977): 14–21; Reuven Kimelman, "Birkat Ha-Minim and the Lack of Evidence for an Anti-Christian Jewish Prayer in Late Antiquity," in *Aspects of Judaism in the Greco-Roman Period*, ed. E. P. Sanders, A. I. Baumgarten, and Alan Mendelson, Jewish and Christian Self- Definition 2 (Philadelphia: Fortress Press, 1981), 226–44; 391–403.

[5] Martin Goodman, "The Function of Minim in Early Rabbinic Judaism," in

seem, then, that although we can accept Cohen's argument that the focal point for sectarian division over the Temple with the concomitant production of a *particular* kind of sectarianism (separatism from the "corrupted" Jerusalem center or conflict over hegemony there) had vanished with the destruction of the Temple, nevertheless the epistemic shift marked by the invention of rabbinic Judaism included the production of a category of Jewish "outsiders" defined by doctrinal difference. Jewish sectarianism had been replaced, on Goodman's reading, by Jewish orthodox and Jewish heretics: those who are Jews and say the wrong things and may, therefore, no longer be called "Israel."[6] It is not, then, that sectarianism had disappeared but that one group was beginning to achieve hegemony and could now plausibly portray itself as Judaism *tout court*, and thus more like Nicaea than Cohen had proposed, an act of radical exclusion and not one of inclusion and pluralism.

It can hardly be denied, nevertheless, that rabbinic texts frequently thematize and valorize sanctified and unresolved controversy. Rabbinic textuality, far more than other Jewish or Christian textualities, is marked, almost defined, by its openness to dissenting opinions, by its deferral of final decisions on hermeneutical, theological, halakhic, and historical questions, by heteroglossia. This characteristic of the literature is well thematized within the texts themselves, i.e., it is a self-conscious trait of rabbinic religion, just as much as doctrinal rigor is of fourth-century Christianity.

Talmudic tradition indeed fashions itself as a collective that avoids schism through pluralism, declaring: "these and these are the words of the Living God";[7] it displays tolerance, even appetite, for paradox and disagreement on issues even of fundamental importance for practice and belief. These are traits that contemporaneous late ancient ecclesial Christianity, with its history of constant schism and anathema, seems unwilling to foster. Gerald Bruns was, therefore, surely on to something when he wrote,

---

Geschichte—Tradition—Reflexion: Festschrift für Martin Hengel zum 70. Geburtstag, ed. H. Cancik, H. Lichtenberger, and P. Schäfer (Tübingen: Mohr Siebeck, 1996), 1.501–10. See also now Daniel Boyarin, "Reforming Judaism; or, Justin Martyr, the Mishna, and the Rise of Rabbinic Orthodoxy" (forthcoming).

[6] I am, of course, playing on the title of another essay of Cohen's here, Shaye J. D. Cohen, "'Those Who Say They Are Jews and Are Not': How Do You Know a Jew in Antiquity When You See One?" in *Diasporas in Antiquity*, ed. Cohen and Ernest S. Frerichs, Brown Judaic Studies 288 (Atlanta: Scholars Press, 1993), 1–45.

[7] Babylonian Talmud Eruvin 13b and Gittin 6b (see below). My translations throughout unless otherwise noted.

From a transcendental standpoint, this [rabbinic] theory of authority is paradoxical because it is seen to hang on the heteroglossia of dialogue, on speaking with many voices, rather than on the logical principle of univocity, or speaking with one mind. Instead, the idea of speaking with one mind ... is explicitly rejected; single-mindedness produces factionalism.[8]

There is a certain elasticity to the Rabbis' form of orthodoxy that must, then, be captured in our descriptions. Cohen's revisionary description of Yavneh can, thus, certainly not be dismissed.

We seem, ourselves, then, to have arrived at an aporia. How can these two seemingly contradictory propositions be reconciled? In this scholion, I hypothesize that these two descriptions are best diachronically emplotted: heteroglossia is the end-point of a historical process and not an essential or timeless description of the rabbinic formation. The social historian of Rome Keith Hopkins is, however, perhaps the only scholar who has so far even adumbrated, and that in a virtual aside, the point that this vaunted heteroglossia of Judaism is the product of a specific history and not a transcendental essence of rabbinic Judaism, *a fortiori* of Judaism *simpliciter*. Hopkins argues that, "unlike Judaism after the destruction of the Temple [in 70 AC], Christianity was dogmatic and hierarchical; dogmatic, in the sense that Christian leaders from early on claimed that their own interpretation of Christian faith was the only true interpretation of the faith, and hierarchical in that leaders claimed legitimacy for the authority of their interpretation as priests or bishops." Hopkins accounts for the rabbinic formation historically: "Admittedly, individual leaders claimed that their own individual interpretation of the law was right, and that other interpretations were wrong. But systemically, at some unknown date, Jewish rabbis seem to have come to the conclusion, however reluctantly, that they were bound to disagree, and that disagreement was endemic."[9]

I would emend Hopkins's formulation, however, in three ways. First, I would put forth that we can locate that "unknown date," if not precisely, surely more accurately than "after the destruction of the Temple," specifically towards the end of the rabbinic period (fourth and fifth centuries), at the time of redaction of the classic texts. Secondly, it may very well have

---

[8] Gerald Bruns, "The Hermeneutics of Midrash," in *The Book and the Text: The Bible and Literary Theory*, ed. Regina Schwartz (Oxford: Basil Blackwell, 1990), 199.

[9] Keith Hopkins, "Christian Number and Its Implications," *Journal of Early Christian Studies* 6.2 (1998): 217.

been much more prominent in Babylonia than in Palestine. Third, while Hopkins historicizes the process through which Judaic orthodoxy came to have a certain character, he reifies Christianity, as if it were always and everywhere (at least from "early on") "dogmatic and hierarchical." Our idea of early "Christianity" also has to be dynamized and historicized. The form of Christianity of which Hopkins speaks is as much the product of particular historical processes within Christianity as is the form of Judaism of which he speaks.[10] In neither case do we have a transhistorical essence, of course, and in both cases, I suggest, the processes that produced the differences are complexly intertwined. Indeed, the burden of my current project is to suggest that rabbinic Judaism and orthodox Christianity, as two hypostases of post-destruction Judaism, only find their separate and characteristic forms of discourse and textuality toward the end of late antiquity and not near the beginning.

As historians of Christianity have observed for some time now, "Nicaea" itself is largely the retrospective textual and then legendary construction of a primal scene of the triumph of orthodoxy. In a recent paper, Michel René Barnes has offered a sharp summation of the current historical consensus regarding the trajectory of trinitarian theology from Nicaea (325) to Constantinople (381) and the retrospective construction of Nicaea as founding moment by Athanasius, Bishop of Alexandria.[11] One of the strongest arguments for this description of Nicaea as virtually a constructed Athanasian representation is the fact, noted by several scholars in the last fifteen years or so, that "a careful reading of Athanasius's works reveals that it took [Athanasius] almost twenty years to come to this understanding of the significance of Nicaea, while he took almost another ten years to fasten upon *homoousious* as the sine qua non of Nicene theology.... The suggestion that that paragon of Nicene theology, Athanasius, did not always regard Nicaea as authoritative is breathtaking."[12] It is breathtaking because, until less than two decades ago, the prevailing scholarly consensus

---

[10] Richard Lim, *Public Disputation, Power and Social Order in Late Antiquity*, Transformations of the Classical Heritage 23 (Berkeley and Los Angeles: University of California Press, 1994) suggests that this form of Christian authority was the product of relatively late socio-historical processes, a point that I shall be further investigating in later chapters of the book in which this essay will eventually be incorporated—tentative title, *The Birth of the Study House: A Talmudic Archaeology*.

[11] Michel René Barnes, "The Fourth Century as Trinitarian Canon," in *Christian Origins: Theology, Rhetoric, and Community*, ed. Lewis Ayres and Gareth Jones (London: Routledge, 1998), 47–67.

[12] Ibid., 53.

was that Athanasius emerged immediately from a fully transparent and clear conciliar verdict on the orthodox faith at Nicaea as the "lonely and courageous" champion of that orthodoxy, prepared to defend it against the depredations of "Arian" opponents.

In a similar vein, Richard Lim has suggested that Nicaea, the Council, is a product of later legend-making.[13] In his very impetus, however, to demonstrate the "legendary" character of the fifth-century construction of a Nicaea that enshrined *homonoia*—total unity of opinion without discussion or dialectic—as the utopian pattern of Christian truth, Lim played down the role of prior textual practices in preparing the soil in which those legends could take root. These are the practices to which Barnes's analysis of Athanasius's role calls our attention, and which have been further explored by Virginia Burrus, as she examines the formative influence of Athanasius's literary corpus in producing the textual practices of fourth-century (and later) Christian orthodoxy, the modes of its discourse, its *habitus*.[14] Positioning her mediation in relation to Lim's claim that it is with the death of the last "eye-witness," Athanasius, that the "legends about Nicaea began to emerge,"[15] Burrus writes:

> Athanasius' death marked the *end* of a crucial phase in the *literary* invention of Nicaea; and, furthermore, the layered inscription of his 'historical' or 'apologetic' texts—resulting in his retroactive construction of a virtual archive for the council—contributed heavily to the creation of a documentary habit that was, as Lim and others have demonstrated, crucial to the success of the late antique council in producing 'consensual' orthodoxy.[16]

By substituting "end" for "beginning" and "literary" for "legendary," Burrus both supports Lim's argument and subtly shifts its terms. The implication of the "death of the eyewitness" and "legend" is that during Athanasius's lifetime, something like a "true" memory of the council was available, while Burrus implies that through the literary work of the eyewitness himself the "legend" of Nicaea was already being constructed. The implied oppositions of true and legendary, written and oral, are thus unsettled.

---

[13] Lim, *Public Disputation*, 182–216.

[14] Virginia Burrus, "Fathering the Word: Athanasius of Alexandria," in *Begotten not Made: Conceiving Manhood in Late Antiquity*, Figurae (Stanford: Stanford University Press, 2000).

[15] Lim, *Public Disputation*, 186.

[16] Burrus, "Fathering the Word," emphasis added.

Furthermore, Lim had emphasized that Nicaea, in contrast to other synods and councils, left no written record of its acts. Agreeing with him, Burrus shows, however, through close readings of the Athanasian dossier on Nicaea, that Athanasius, through the arrangement and redacting of materials documentary and otherwise, produced ex post facto virtual *acta* for "his" council. Burrus's reframing allows us to perceive that Athanasius may have made a contribution through this activity to the practice of the production of such archives and *acta* for other conciliar formations, as well as to the system of textual practices, in general, that constituted late ancient "patristic" orthodoxy. Nicaea, the Council—and not only (or primarily) Nicene doctrine—was "invented" through the writings of Athanasius. The point of overlap between Barnes and Burrus, and the point that I most need for my own narrative here, is to be found in the keen articulation of the extent to which Athanasius's literary exertions produce retrospectively a certain account of "Nicaea," an account which, as Burrus makes clear, was generative for the future history of Christian textual practices. Burrus thus focuses our attention on the particular form of textuality and the textual form of particular types of orthodoxy and their "habitus," a point that will provide special resonance in my own inquiry, in which the question of literary and legendary textual practices will also prove central.

The solution that I suggest, therefore, to the seeming aporia in descriptions of rabbinic Judaism as rigid and exclusivistic or as inclusive and elastic, is to realize that Yavneh itself, like Nicaea, is a legend, or rather, a series of changing legends of foundation. It must, however, be made clear that, even though it is a foundation myth, the idea of a Synod at Yavneh is hardly a "myth of Christian scholarship," nor is it the product of Spinoza's imagination, *pace* David Aune.[17] Both the early third-century Mishnah and the later Talmuds are full of material which suggests that Yavneh was *imagined* as a council by Jewish texts much before Spinoza.[18] Both the exclusivist and the pluralist version of Yavneh are encoded, then, within rabbinic literature itself. Both the early one of conflict and exclu-

---

[17] David Aune, "On the Origins of the 'Council of Yavneh' Myth," *Journal of Biblical Literature* 110.3 (Fall 1991): 491–93.

[18] To be fair, what Aune was referring to was the question of the canonization of Scripture at such a "synod," and I agree that there is little evidence for that, as there is also little evidence to suggest that the Christians were expelled at the "real" (i.e., imaginary) Synod of Yavneh, as already shown by Stemberger, "Synode"; Kimelman, "Birkat Ha- Minim." My student Robert Daum is preparing a dissertation on the corpus of Yavneh legends.

sion and the later one of "agreement to disagree" are versions of Yavneh. This will emerge when we read the different "myths" of the Council of Yavneh in the third-century tannaitic or fourth- and fifth-century amoraic contexts of their literary production, and not in the firstcentury context of their ostensible subject-matter, as the nineteenthcentury (and later) positivist historians had done. I would suggest also that, parallel to the scholarship on Nicaea, the portrayal of Yavneh in the rabbinic literature of the early third century underwent a reinterpretation in the second half of the fourth century to receive a normative status (of course we can hardly date this reinterpretation as specifically as Nicaea's normatization at Constantinople "in 381," nor assign agency to a particular author, a rabbinic Athanasius). In any case, that retold and ultimately definitive Yavneh-legend finally fits Cohen's description of the "creation of a society based on the doctrine that conflicting disputants may each be advancing the words of the living God."[19] The very phrase, however, that Cohen refers to here is never found in early sources but only in the two Talmuds of late antiquity. In the Palestinian Talmud we find it:

> It is taught, a heavenly voice went out and said, "These and these are the words of the Living God, but the Law is like the School of Hillel." Where did the voice go out? Rabbi Bibbi said in the name of Rabbi Yoḥanan, "In Yavneh the voice went out."[20]

I would, therefore, substitute for Cohen's prospective "creation," a retrospective and utopian "imagination." Cohen is right, I think, but the Yavneh that he describes is a product of the late myth-making discourse of the Talmuds.

In contrast to W. D. Davies's classic position that the "Sermon on the Mount" is "the Christian answer to Jamnia [Yavneh],"[21] it is possible to hypothesize that "Yavneh" was produced in the talmudic *imaginaire* as a sort of rabbinic answer to the conciliar formations of the Christian fourth century, themselves, as we have seen, the product of a certain *imaginaire* as well. One way of configuring this point would be to say that while the retrospective construction of Nicaea by Athanasius and his followers involved the production of an imaginary enemy, "the Arians,"[22] the retro-

---

[19] Cohen, "Yavneh," 51.
[20] Palestinian Talmud Yabmut (sic) 3b, chapter 1, halakha 6.
[21] Davies, *Setting of the Sermon on the Mount*, 315; and see Jacob Neusner, *Eliezer Ben Hyrcanus: The Tradition and the Man*, Studies in Judaism in Late Antiquity 3–4 (Leiden: Brill, 1973), 2.333–34.
[22] "'Arianism' as a coherent system, founded by a single great figure and sus-

spective construction of Yavneh in late-fourth-century (or even later!) rabbinic texts involved the denial of real enmity and the production of an imaginary and utopian comity. The Talmud, I suggest, is Yavneh's collective Athanasius.

Women's Bodies and the Rise of the Rabbis

If Nicaea was a belated Athanasian invention that helped produce a Christianity "in which dissent and debate were literally swept aside,"[23] Yavneh as a "grand coalition" in which everybody in Jewish antiquity who wasn't an outright "heretic" was a Rabbi, and all opinions were equally "Torah," was an equally belated talmudic invention. This late moment of literary crystallization was the juncture at which the "agreement to disagree" was raised to a theological and hermeneutical principle of the highest order, indeed to a divine institution. Just as the story of Nicaea "gives rise to the 318 conciliar 'fathers,' and also to their only begotten credal Word,"[24] the story of Yavneh gives rise to the father Rabbis and their only begotten Oral Torah.

Moshe Halbertal has written:

> The idea that expertise in the text is a source of authority—an idea that gives rise to the centrality of the scholar in the Jewish hierarchy—defines an important feature of text-centeredness. Such expertise may become the main source of authority, and then priests and prophets are replaced by scholars. The leading role of the scholar constituted a revolutionary, postbiblical conception of religious authority within Judaism, challenging other conceptions.[25]

---

tained by his disciples, is a fantasy—more exactly, a fantasy based on the polemic of Nicene writers, above all Athanasius," Rowan Williams, *Arius: Heresy and Tradition* (London: Darton, Longman & Todd, 1987), 82. Also, "the term 'Arian' seems to have been Athanasius' own coinage and his favoured appellation for his opponents (unless he could call them 'Ariomaniacs'). Apparently it was only in 341, however, that the Eastern bishops learned that they were being called 'Arians'," Joseph T. Lienhard, S.J., "The 'Arian' Controversy: Some Categories Reconsidered," *Theological Studies* 48 (1987): 417. This, moreover, according to Barnes, represents the consensus of present-day scholarship on the trinitarian controversies ("Fourth Century as Trinitarian Canon," 47).

[23] Lim, *Public Disputation*, 227.
[24] Burrus, "Fathering the Word."
[25] Moshe Halbertal, *People of the Book: Canon, Meaning, and Authority* (Cambridge: Harvard University Press, 1997), 6.

What Halbertal apparently misses here is the extent to which the revolution was not only in the transfer of power from priests and prophets to scholars but also in the particular role that the concept of Oral Torah played in locating all religious authority in the hands of one community of scholars, the Rabbis, and one institutional locus, the House of Study (bethammidrash). This epistemic shift begins, to be sure, with the Mishnah at the end of the second century,[26] just as the process that Athanasius and his Nicaea were to bring to fruition began, in some sense, with Justin and Irenaeus in the second century as well. Athanasius's "ἐκ Πατερων εἰς Πατερα" ("from Father to Father")[27] is strongly reminiscent of the Mishnah's succession list which represents the Oral Torah received by Moses on Sinai and codified by the Fathers in the mishnaic tractate called "Fathers" at "Yavneh."[28] But just as Christian orthodoxy received its definitive formation in the fourth century, so too the social form, i.e., the heteroglossic regime of power/knowledge of rabbinic orthodox Judaism, was formulated much later than the Mishnah. The codified dissensus, the "agreement to disagree," was as efficient a mode of power for the achievement of "consensual orthodoxy" for rabbinic Judaism as were the creeds and councils of orthodox Christianity. Yavneh and Nicaea can thus also be said to represent a twin-birth of orthodoxies.[29] Late rabbinic literature more than once produces selfdescriptions in which the notion of irresolv-

---

[26] Boyarin, "Reforming Judaism."

[27] *De decr.* 27, cited in Burrus, "Fathering the Word."

[28] It would be interesting to attempt to determine when the Tractate is first called *Avot*, "Fathers," particularly in respect to the fact that it was Athanasius who seemingly first referred to the bishops of Nicaea as "Fathers." The comparison between Athanasius's language and the idea of Tractate Avot is, at any rate, compelling:

> Since those who attended Nicaea are in a conspicuous sense the transmitters and agents of the divine "tradition" or "παράδοσις," that is, of the "teaching" or "διδασκαλία" that is handed down from "Fathers to Fathers," they themselves are designated with this title, which is surely the highest that Athanasius has to bestow. And the more conscious Athanasius is of the fact that the Nicene faith in its positive formulation is the divine "παράδοσις," the more exclusively are the council's attendees designated by this title.

Hermann Josef Sieben, *Die Konzilsidee der alten Kirche* (Paderborn, Munich, Vienna, Zurich: Ferdinand Schöningh, 1979), 39, Burrus's translation ("Fathering the Word"). For a reading of the "Fathers" text, see Boyarin, "Reforming Judaism."

[29] With "Esau," Nicaea, the slightly elder of the two. The figure is drawn from Alan F. Segal, *Rebecca's Children: Judaism and Christianity in the Roman World* (Cambridge: Harvard University Press, 1986).

able controversy over central issues is made an emblem of the pattern of Jewish truth. This is occasionally thematized within the texts in the form of divine approbation of the undecidability of a given point of interpretation or law.

The following text, from circa fourth-century Babylonia, is both scandalous and revealing. The text explores a biblical locus: "And his concubine went astray" (Judges 19:2). Two Rabbis, in interpreting the story, try to discover what caused the concubine's husband's anger that had driven her out of the house:

> Rabbi Eviathar said, "He found a fly on her." Rabbi Yonathan said, "He found a hair on her."
> Rabbi Eviathar met up with Elijah [the prophet], and said to him, "What is the Holy Blessed One up to?"
> He said, "He is studying [the story] of the concubine of Gibeah."
> "And what does He say about it?"
> He said to him: "[God says,] 'Eviathar my son says thus, and Yonathan my son says thus.'"
> He [Eviathar] said to him [Elijah], "God forfend: Is there doubt before Heaven?"
> He [Elijah] said to him, "These and these are the words of the Living God. He found a fly and did not get angry; he found a hair and got angry."
> Rav Yehuda said: "The fly was in the cup, and the hair was in that place [her vulva]. The fly is disgusting, but the hair is dangerous."[30]
> Rav Hisda said: "A man should never produce fear within his household, for behold the concubine of Gibeah; her husband produced fear in the household, and there was a massacre of tens of thousands in Israel."[31]

This rabbinic narrative deals with one of the most horrifying of biblical stories, the so-called "Concubine of Gibeah" in Judges 19–21. In this story a wife or concubine leaves her husband and is eventually violated and

---

[30] An interesting bit of sex lore is alluded to here. Women were apparently expected to shave their pudenda, and the presence of even one hair was understood to represent a danger of cutting off of the penis during intercourse (cf. Rashi ad loc., referring to Deut. 23:2).

[31] BT Gittin 6b.

murdered. The story is a savage narrative of the most appalling violence toward a woman. It results in civil war, but for the Rabbis it conveys the domestic moral that a husband should not display anger towards his wife, for if he does, she may run away, with the appalling personal and public consequences of the story of Judges 19. The Rabbis debate what the fault was that the husband found with her that made him so angry that the concubine was afraid and ran away from him. According to one of the Rabbis, he had found an unwanted fly, and according to the other, he had found an unwanted hair. The remarkable thing about the rabbinic text is that it seemingly encodes radical undecidability in the biblical narrative itself.

Let us follow this process with the text. In the first move, when Elijah, the mediator of divine knowledge, is asked what God himself has to say on the question that the Rabbis are debating, the text informs us that all he does is quote his "sons," the Rabbis: "Eviathar my son says thus, and Yonathan my son says thus." According to the Rabbis, even God, the author of the Book, can only say with certainty that there are various interpretative possibilities; he can only repeat the tradition of interpretation that is extant in the Bet-Hammidrash (rabbinic House of Study). As if in panic at its own suggestion that the text is inhabited by such radical undecidability that even God can only "teach the controversy" and not resolve it, the narrative then opts for harmonization of the two views: The husband found both fly and hair.

In the spaces among the original level of controversy, the level of the narrative of God's doubt, and then the level of the retraction of that narrative, we can read a little historical allegory of the history of rabbinic Judaism. At the first stage of the talmudic story, there is controversy; at the second stage, undecidability; at the third, harmonization. Stories such as these have been taken up in much contemporary writing on rabbinic Judaism as encoding either radical undecidability in the theoretical sense or radical pluralism in the social sense. No one, scholars suggest, can exercise control over interpretation according to the rabbinic system of midrash, for the Rabbis allegedly understood that no textual interpretation is ever definitive, even that of the Author himself.[32] Somewhat less lyrically, but with equal idealism, we sometimes find this structure described as a radical democratization of interpretation within the rabbinic polity.[33]

---

[32] Susan Handelman, "Fragments of the Rock: Contemporary Literary Theory and the Study of Rabbinic Texts—A Response to David Stern," *Prooftexts* 5 (1985): 73–95.

[33] This is no more a democratization, *pace* Halbertal (*People*, 7), than the

Neither of these two constructions, however, pays attention to the fact that interpretative authority is located exclusively in the rabbinic Study House. Far from representing a utopian moment of ludic interpretative freedom, on my construction, the project of a hermeneutic parable like this one is rather to advance the rabbinic program of exclusive control over the religious lives of Jews and to secure the interpretation of the Torah for their institution, the House of Study, in whose controversies all truth and authority lie.[34] The key, I think, to a more nuanced and differentiated description of rabbinic Judaism than the relatively unhewn ones offered so far has been provided not by a historian, but by a literary critic, David Stern, who discussed the vaunted "undecidability" (or protodeconstruction) of language promulgated in midrash, the "derridean" interpretation of rabbinic culture.[35] Stern's close reading of rabbinic texts suggests that their pluralism, even such a limited and internal pluralism, is a product not of the rabbinic schools or teachers but of later redactors of rabbinic texts.

In a famous derasha (rabbinic sermon) analyzed by Stern, the problem of polysemy is explicitly confronted in social terms of univocity (of the community, not the text!) and difference:

> [What does the phrase] "the masters of assemblies" [mean]? These are the disciples of the wise, who sit in assemblies and study the Torah, some pronouncing unclean and others pronouncing clean, some prohibiting and others permitting, some declaring unfit and others declaring fit. Should a man say: "Since some pronounce unclean and others pronounce clean, some prohibit and others permit, some declare unfit and others declare fit, how then shall I learn

---

medicalization of childbirth is, simply because "everyone" can become a gynecologist. Halbertal explicitly refers to the fact that all men (!) had theoretical access to the House of Study as "democratic," not noticing that the stringent controls which the institution placed on interpretation, legitimate and illegitimate, represent an even more general set of exclusions of all who do not accept the rabbinic program than just the exclusion of women, which he duly and fully remarks.

[34] I should add, perhaps, that I mean by this to ascribe nothing sinister to the Rabbis, although the effects on some Jews (especially women) might well have been very deleterious, as the subject-matter chosen for this hermeneutic parable itself might hint. It is not inapposite for me to mention that I am one of the scholars whose former opinions I am revising here; cf. my *Intertextuality and the Reading of Midrash* (Bloomington: Indiana University Press, 1990), especially 33–37.

[35] David Stern, *Midrash and Theory: Ancient Jewish Exegesis and Contemporary Literary Studies*, Rethinking Theory (Evanston: Northwestern University Press, 1996), 15–38; David Stern, "Midrash and Indeterminacy," *Critical Inquiry* 15.1 (Autumn 1988): 132–62.

Torah"? Therefore Scripture says: All of them "were given by one shepherd." One God gave them, one leader (i.e. Moses) proclaimed them from the mouth of the Lord of all creation, blessed be He, as it is written, "And God spoke *all* these words" [Exod. 20:1; my italics]. Therefore make your ear like the hopper and acquire a perceptive heart to understand the words of those who pronounce unclean and the words of those who pronounce clean, the words of those who prohibit and the words of those who permit, the words of those who declare unfit and the words of those who declare fit.[36]

Stern notes that, though the student despairs at the possibility of studying Torah owing to the multiplicity of interpretations, there is really no cause for such despondency, for "although the sages' opinions may contradict each other, they all are part of Torah, part of a single revelation."[37] This notion is then correlated with the alreadyquoted famous talmudic statement that a heavenly oracle declared, with respect to the contradictory opinions of the two "Houses," of Hillel and of Shammai, that "these *and* these are the words of the Living God."

The conclusion of such a discourse is powerful and tendentious support for rabbinic hegemony:

> [T]he citation of multiple interpretations in midrash is an attempt to represent in textual terms an idealized academy of Rabbinic tradition where all the opinions of the sages are recorded equally as part of a single divine conversation. Opinions that in human discourse may appear as contradictory or mutually exclusive are raised to the state of paradox once traced to their common source in the speech of the divine author.

---

[36] BT Ḥagiga 3a–b, trans. Stern, *Midrash and Theory*, 19.

[37] Stern, ibid., 20. That this fear was not an idle one can be shown from the following quotation from the antirabbinite Karaite text:

> I have set the six divisions of the Mishna before me. And I looked at them carefully with mine eyes. And I saw that they are very contradictory in content. This one mishnaic scholar declares a thing to be forbidden to the people of Israel, while that one declares it to be permitted. My thoughts therefore answer me, and most of my reflections declare unto me, that there is in it no Law of logic nor the Law of Moses the Wise.

Leon Nemoy, *Karaite Anthology, Excerpts from the Early Literature*, Yale Judaica 7 (New Haven: Yale University Press, 1961), 71; and see Halbertal, *People*, 46. Although this early medieval tradition is surely later than our talmudic text, it eloquently indicates the sort of polemic (and not merely psychomachia) that our text might be responding to.

Stern, however, argues that this theology of language was not the operative ideology within the House of Study itself but is a purely literary phenomenon. Nor does it represent the social reality of human language use; it is a theological representation of the divine language. It is here, at the level of theology of language encoded in the redaction of the rabbinic texts themselves, in their very textuality and not in the practice of the House of Study, that the derridean moment is produced:

> This representation, however, is a literary artifact.... The phenomenon we witness in multiple interpretation, in other words, is in actuality a literary impression given by the redaction of Rabbinic literature, the result of a common choice made by its anonymous editors to preserve minority as well as majority opinions, the varieties of traditions rather than single versions.[38]

Stern introduces an important distinction here. In the literary redactional textuality of the documents, the reader is implicitly informed that what is in human eyes a contradiction is in God's eyes a unity. But this "unity" does not represent, according to Stern, any historical reality. Rabbinic literature records bitter and sometimes violent strife between the various groups that constituted "Judaism" after the destruction of the Temple, even if we leave out of the picture the excluded *minim* (heretics): gnostics, Sadducees, and Jewish-Christians. As he emphasizes, in the century following the founding of Yavneh, far from a "grand coalition," we find rather a scene of constant combat "to consolidate Palestinian Jewry under the form of the specific religious vision that eventually came to be known as Rabbinic Judaism.... The task of unification was not accomplished easily, indeed, the endemic divisiveness that was a source of tragic factionalism in Palestinian Judaism as well as a source of its individualism and creativity was never entirely eradicated."[39] Stern shows compellingly that the very narrative context within which the above homily is recited in the Babylonian Talmud refers not to a world of idyllic pluralism but rather to one in which "conflict [is] a malignant presence and its resolution [is] the violent exercise of power, as indeed it sometimes was in Rabbinic society."[40] The redactors of the rabbinic texts chose, however, to enshrine multiple views as being of equal validity:

In making this choice, the Rabbinic editors did not act without

---

[38] Stern, ibid., 33.
[39] Ibid., 34.
[40] Ibid., 37.

precedent; indeed, they followed in a venerable tradition of early Jewish literature that included such other sacred "compromise texts" as the Pentateuch, in which separate documentary sources are combined into a single composition as though their agenda and ideologies were compatible (which eventually they are made out to be).... *The difference between these earlier texts and the Rabbinic midrashim is simply that in the latter, editorial policy was elevated to the order of exegetical ideology, to the conception of polysemy as a trait of sacred Scripture. Here, for the first time, editorial pluralism has become a condition of meaning.*[41]

Stern draws a distinction between earlier Palestinian and rabbinic literature by indicating that it is only within the latter that we find polysemy not only enacted but thematized, lifted up, as it were, as a theological principle.

I would argue, however, that we have to separate out diachronic layers (and not merely "traditions" and "redactions") within rabbinic literature. The production of what Stern calls "sacred 'compromise texts'," can be located in other Palestinian Jewish texts (including the Mishnah, with its harmonization of the schools of Rabban Gamaliel and Rabbi Yoḥanan ben Zakkai,[42] and the Gospels as collected in the New Testament Canon). But the "elevation [of editorial policy] to the order of exegetical ideology," indeed, "the conception of polysemy as a trait of sacred Scripture" seems peculiarly a characteristic of the Babylonian Talmud, as witnessed by the very texts that Stern analyzes.[43] The distinction between these two cate-

---

[41] Ibid., 34, emphasis added.

[42] Boyarin, "Reforming Judaism." Halbertal (*People*, 45) points out that in another respect,

> The Mishnah, edited at the end of the second century by Rabbi Yehudah the Prince, is the first canon of its kind known to us, a canon that transmits the tradition in the form of controversy: the House (school) of Shammai said one thing, the House of Hillel said another, and so on.... By contrast, in the earlier canon, the Bible, debates are either repressed, concealed, or harmonized.

While I think that Halbertal's point is well taken, and does reveal how the Mishnah lies as it "ought" to at the rudimentary beginning of the textual practice that would culminate in the Babylonian Talmud, we cannot ignore also the ways that the Mishnah functions also precisely as the Bible does, e.g., in this very tacit merger between the *diadochoi* of what were clearly rival schools, the Gamlielites (= Pharisees) and the Yoḥanines (= Scribes).

[43] Stern's "polysemy" is not precise here; we need to distinguish between mere multiplicity of meaning, as in "The Torah has seventy faces," a concept found early

gories is that while in the earlier Palestinian texts, incompatible views are set side by side, as in the Pentateuch itself, in the Babylonian Talmud it is a matter of principle that all the views, however incompatible, are *right*—"all have been given by the same shepherd"—as long, of course, as they are expressed by Rabbis.

Another way that I might articulate this difference would be to say that if for the earlier Palestinian Rabbis undecidability seems to be the product of the limitations of human knowing, for the Talmuds, and especially the Babylonian in its late redactorial stage, it would seem to be a condition of language itself, so that the idea that even God cannot know the truth of the text can at least be entertained—or alternatively, that our very ways of posing questions about meaning are irrelevant for the divine Logos. At the same time, the borders of the social body in whose hands it is given to determine the parameters of radical doubt—the walls of the House of Study, as it were—are being constructed and firmly shored up, as we shall see, through a process of "domestication" of figures who might otherwise be found outside these walls, figures such as Rabbi Eli'ezer or the early pietists.[44]

What I am proposing, then, is a foucauldian genealogy of a "derridean" episteme, for the textual practice of the redactors of the Babylonian Talmud was very effective. Owing to the overwhelming impact of the Babylonian Talmud, this pattern of truth becomes the intellectual legacy of medieval rabbinic Judaism everywhere. The nexus between textual habits of Palestinian Jews and the canonized, theologically sanctioned undecidability of the Babylonian Talmud, as symbolized by the legends of "Yavneh," is analogous to the hypothesized causal connection between Athanasius's production of a textual *habitus* and the textual practices of the "consensual" orthodoxy of the late fourth and fifth centuries, as symbolized by the legends of "Nicaea." What is needed here—and will be forthcoming in future chapters of my book—is a study of the subtle interanimations between the oral and the written, the documentary and the legendary, in

---

and in Palestine, and the much more radical theologoumenon of the Babylonian Talmud that even mutually exclusive and contradictory views are all part of God's speech. In an expanded version of this essay, I will deal more extensively, *deo volente*, with the context of this passage as part of the legend of Yavneh in which it is set in the Talmud. For the nonce, it is important merely to note that that is its context there.

[44] William Scott Green, "Palestinian Holy Men: Charismatic Leadership and Roman Tradition," in *Principat: Religion (Judentum: Paälastinisches Judentum)*, ed. Wolfgang Haase, Aufstieg und Niedergang der Römischen Welt 19.2 (Berlin: Walter de Gruyter, 1979), 619–47.

the invention of ecclesial Christian and rabbinic Jewish orthodoxies.

§ § §

It should be clear by now that, far from representing a democratic dispersal of power, the narrative of rabbinic heteroglossia is, on my view, a technique for the concentration of power in the hands of the Rabbis and their characteristic institution, the House of Study. Rabbinic Judaism is, on this conjecture, the end-product of an extended history of struggle for hegemony by a particular version of religious authority that locates it exclusively in the hands of a male elite devoted primarily to the study of Torah, that is, the preservation and development of their particular traditions and modes of interpretation. Paying close attention to these narratives will help us uncover the "significance[s]" of Yavneh. This history can be read, as it were, between the lines of various talmudic narratives. It is no accident, I suggest, that this struggle is enacted in no small measure as a contest for control over sexuality and at that a struggle between the Rabbis, a.k.a. the Torah, and women:[45]

> Rabbi Yoḥanan the son of Dahavai said: "The Ministering Angels told me: 'Why are there lame children? Because they [their fathers] turn over the tables [have intercourse with their wives on top]. Why are there dumb children? Because they kiss that place. Why are there deaf children? Because they talk during intercourse. Why are there blind children? Because they look at that place'...."
>
> Rabbi Yoḥanan said: "These are the words of Rabbi Yoḥanan the son of Dahavai, but the Sages say, 'Anything that a man wishes to do [together] with his wife, he may do, analogously to meat that comes from the shop. If he wishes to eat it with salt, he may; roasted, he may; boiled, he may; braised, he may. And similarly fish from the store of the fisherman.'"

Rabbi Yoḥanan—not the same as Rabbi Yoḥanan the son of Dahavai—dissents from the halakha that the angels had communicated through that former Yoḥanan, and next:

> Amemar said: "Who are the Ministering Angels? The Rabbis, for if you say literally, *Ministering Angels*, then how did Rabbi Yoḥanan say that the law is not like Rabbi Yoḥanan the son of Dahavai? After all, angels certainly know embryology!"

---

[45] All the following is BT Nedarim 20 a–b.

Amemar cannot believe that Rabbi Yoḥanan would dissent from truly prophetic authority and has reinterpreted that authority, therefore, as being a metaphorical representation of "normal" rabbinic authority. So then:

> And why does he call them "Ministering Angels"? Because they are excellent like the Ministering Angels.

Through his reinterpretation of the "angels" as a metaphorical representation of "our Rabbis," Amemar transforms the conflict in this text from a contest over power between different forms of authority, different modes of power/knowledge, into a normal rabbinic controversy within the same kind of episteme, the realm of Torah, the Rabbis themselves. He does this by converting the "angels" of the earlier text into ordinary Rabbis. The use of "the Sages" and "the Rabbis" here marks this subtle shift, since both designate the same group. It should be emphasized, however, that Amemar only renders explicit what was implicit in Rabbi Yoḥanan's dissent, wherein the latter already transformed the angelic knowledge into an ordinary rabbinic opinion of Rabbi ben Dahavai.

The narrative continues with "actual cases," precedents that both illustrate and buttress the point made in the preceding section and indicate, on my reading, one of the important matrices of this sociocultural conflict:

> A certain woman came before Rabbi, and said to him: "Rabbi: I set him a table, and he turned it over." He said to her: "My daughter, The Torah has permitted you; and I, what can I do for you?"
>
> A certain woman came before Rav. She said to him: "Rabbi, I set him the table, and he turned it over." He said: "How is the case different from fish?"

Quite understandably, this has usually been read by scholars as a sort of rudimentary rabbinic *scientia sexualis*, or at least, *ars erotica*, and one that is, moreover, particularly obnoxious in its disregard for women's sexual rights over their own bodies. At first glance, it seems as if a wife is being compared to a fish. I shall not be disregarding this element if, at the same time, I suggest that there are even more compelling political forces at work, and that the text represents part of a rabbinic project of takeover and disenfranchisement of all sources of traditional religious authority among Jews, including the traditional authority of women's traditions. It is thus not an accident, I would suggest, that so many of these crucial narratives of struggle over power and authority are connected with sexuality, because they are implicated in struggles against sites of women's traditional power/

/knowledge. The struggle for rabbinic authority is, I suggest, in part, a struggle for control of women's bodies and sexuality.

Now we must engage in some lexicography. The term "turning the tables" can most likely be identified as vaginal intercourse with the woman on top.[46] Most interpretations of the narratives of the two women who come to the Rabbis complaining of having set the table which the husband overturned and the Rabbi's refusal to intervene understand this as rabbinically sanctioned marital sexual abuse.[47] The full context, however, suggests another interpretation. This is, I suggest, a text primarily about the acquisition of rabbinic power and their struggle with other forms of Jewish authority, and not principally "about" sexuality at all. According to Rabbi Yohanan the son of Dahavai, one of the sexual practices proscribed by the "angels" is precisely the activity that the two women claim their husbands desired. Moreover, according to this "angelic" eugenics, intercourse in this position produces damaged children. My assumption is that this nascent angelic embryology represents a form of popular Jewish pietistic practice of sexual hygiene, one that would have been the province of women as well as men. The complaint of these wives is not that their husbands wish to engage in a painful or distasteful form of sex but that they wish to engage in intercourse that the old mores of the Jews considered improper and dangerous to the fetus. The responses of Rabbi and Rav do not, therefore, counsel submission to abuse, in order to indicate that the wife is either the husband's sexual property or a "consumable," but rather assert the sole authority of "Torah" over any other kind of religious

---

[46] In the past scholars, including me, have wavered between this interpretation and identifying it as anal or dorsal vaginal intercourse. The standard lexica understand it as anal intercourse, although traditional commentaries do not. There is no philological or contextual support for that interpretation, however, and, in the context of our text, where it is understood to lead to conception, anal intercourse can hardly be comprehended. There is, moreover, another very common term for the latter. While it is possible to see why "turning the tables" could metaphorically suggest anal penetration i.e., turning the woman who has "set the table" over, however as an image of the bottom becoming top it also makes great sense. Indeed, in English we use this very metaphor to refer to a reversal of dominance, even, moreover, in sexual contexts. See also Michael L. Satlow, *Tasting the Dish: Rabbinic Rhetorics of Sexuality*, Brown Judaic Studies 303 (Atlanta: Scholars Press, 1995), 239, and especially Rachel Biale, *Women and Jewish Law: An Exploration of Women's Issues in Halakhic Sources* (New York: Schocken Books, 1984), 137–39. Biale also compares BT Gittin 70a, where it is stated that "she above and he below is the way of brazenness."

[47] Typical, if judicious in his formulation, is Satlow, who writes, "From this passage, it is again not clear what activity is being performed. Clearly, though, these women do not like it," Satlow, *Tasting the Dish*, 240.

leadership, whether angelic or traditional, including traditional women's power/knowledge.[48] If the Torah does not prohibit an activity, no other

---

[48] This interpretation is supported by the continuation of the Nedarim text:

> *And I will remove from you the rebellious ones and the criminals* [Ezekiel 20:39].
>
> Said Rabbi Levi: "These are nine categories: Children of fright; children of rape; children of a despised woman; children of excommunication; children of exchange; children of strife; children of drunkenness; children of one whom he has divorced in his heart; children of mixture; children of an audacious wife."
>
> Indeed? But did not Shĕmuel the son of Nahmani say that Rabbi Yohanan said: "Any man whose wife approaches him sexually will have children such as were unknown even in the generation of Moses...."
>
> That refers to a case where she arouses him [but does not explicitly and verbally request sex].

It is hard to credit an interpretation of the text that leads us at one moment to assume that the Rabbis are saying that a wife has *no* control over sexual practice, and a few lines later indicates, using the same language of eugenics, that unless there is love and harmony between the couple their progeny will be rebellious criminals.

Furthermore, as indicated by my translation, the phraseology in Hebrew, "anything a man wishes to do [together] with his wife," does not suggest objectification of the wife's body. While in English, "do with" is ambiguous, in Hebrew, a different preposition would be used for the instrumental meaning. Finally, as Lisa Lampert has noted to me, part of the point is that women are responsible for cooking in that culture. Just as the "Torah" would make light of women's customs and taboos with respect to food that are not enshrined in the rabbinic high religious law, so also with respect to sex. Given the control that women had over the preparation of food, the Rabbis' statement to the wives is most plausibly read as: You have the fish, you are permitted to cook it in any fashion by the Torah, and not: You are the fish; your husband is permitted to cook it in any fashion according to the Torah. Lampert remarks (in a letter, April 1999):

> The talmudic discussion of the level of intimacy implied by wives serving food and drink and Bynum's arguments about food preparation as a key site of control for women seem to come into play here. The erotic and food could be linked or at the very least, they are both, to some degree, under women's control. I think just remembering that these rabbis probably were not cooking for themselves helps me to see your point much more clearly, since I do think one's first impulse, given the feminist focus on the objectification of women's bodies, is to want to see a parallel between the wife and the meat, which leaves out the importance of what women quite often do control in a culture, the food.

My point here, I would emphasize, is surely not to "defend" the Rabbis in any sense but to arrive at a more exact interpretation of the regime of power/knowledge that they are setting up here, and it does not, I remain convinced, operate by ceding power over women's bodies to individual non-rabbinic men but by retaining all such power in the hands of the Rabbis themselves (the "Torah"), thus maintaining control over the non-rabbinic husbands as well as the wives and abrogating the authority of traditional sexual mores of both men and women.

source of authority has any jurisdiction over Jewish behavior according to the Rabbis; neither angels nor popular, including women's, culture. The metaphor of the fish does not refer to the wife's body but to intercourse itself; since the Torah permits sex in general and does not prohibit any specific form of it, just as a kosher fish may be cooked in any fashion desired, therefore, women's and other popular traditions of interdiction are immaterial. You may have intercourse on top, says the male Rabbi to the woman, because the Torah, i.e., the Rabbis say that it is permitted, your women's customs notwithstanding. The irony is, of course, palpable and the cloaking of control as license conjures up Foucault, as well as feminist critiques of the "sexual revolution."[49] Women on top in intercourse, but not in discourse.

The interpretation of "Torah" in this context as referring to rabbinic power is supported and specified by another puzzling talmudic text having to do in part with sexuality:

> We have learnt in a baraita Rabbi 'Aqiva said: "Once I followed Rabbi Yehoshua' into the privy and I learned from him three things. I learned that one does not eliminate standing but sitting; I learned that one does not eliminate facing east to west but north to south, and I learned that one does not wipe with the right hand but with the left."
>
> Ben Azzai said to him: "Were you indeed so brazen-faced with your teacher!?"
>
> He said to him: "It is Torah and I must learn it."
>
> We have learnt in a baraita Ben 'Azzai said: "Once I followed Rabbi 'Aqiva into the privy and I learned from him three things. I learned that one does not eliminate facing east to west but north to south, I learned that one does not eliminate standing but sitting; and I learned that one does not wipe with the right hand but with the left."
>
> Rabbi Yehudah said to him: "Were you indeed so brazenfaced with your teacher!?"
>
> He said to him: "It is Torah and I must learn it."
>
> Rav Kahana entered and lay down beneath the bed of Rav. He heard that he was talking and laughing and having sexual intercourse. He said, "The mouth of Abba [Rav's name] appears as if it

---

[49] This interpretation is a revision, if not quite a retraction, of my reading in *Carnal Israel: Reading Sex in Talmudic Culture* (Berkeley and Los Angeles: University of California Press, 1993), 109–20.

has never tasted this dish [i.e., has never had intercourse (Rashi)]." He [Rav] said to him, "Kahana, get out; this is not proper behavior!" He [Kahana] said to him, "It is Torah, and I must learn it."[50]

To my mind, the crucial moment in this story is the three Rabbis' "defense" of their strange behavior in the statement that there is nothing that escapes from the purview of Torah. Torah here is not the written word, not Scripture, but the behavior of the Rabbi/master. The rabbinic project is to subsume everything under the control of Torah, that is, under the lineage of spiritual fathers and sons of which the rabbinic tradition and its *paradosis* consists, a married version of the celibate paternal relations of bishop to bishop in the contemporaneous Christian polity.[51] This interpretation is significantly strengthened by the doubling of the first sequence. Surely Ben 'Azzai could have learned what he had to learn via the report of his teacher Rabbi 'Aqiva of his observation of Rabbi Yehoshua''s practice. Why, then, does the text insist that Ben 'Azzai embarrassed his teacher in the same way? By these means, the text inculcates the motif that Torah involves observing the behavior of the Master as well, and therefore, can only be acquired within the confines of the rabbinic institution. The very contradictions between such an idolized homosociality and heterosexual relations are thematized in this story as well.

This interpretation, however, does not render the text any less "sexist"; in fact, if anything it is more male-dominant in its implications, precisely because of the power/knowledge nexus that it institutes, one in which all control is arrogated to the "Torah," i.e., to the community of rabbinic scholars. Even if we do not have here, on my reading, a tale of cruel indifference to sexual abuse of wives by husbands, we have an even more powerful grab by a male elite of control of all traditional and religious knowledge and power. This is accordingly one of the founding moments of rabbinic Judaism, defined as a Judaism in which a group called Rabbis are the only religious virtuosi.

One could read the later Rabbi Yirmiah's intervention (interpreting the angels as rabbis) as a further step in the same process of the denial of all power/knowledge outside of the rabbinic collective. The issue here is finally, not what kind of sex Jews will engage in but who gets to decide: angelic (i.e., mantic) authorities, women's tradition, or the "Torah" (the Rabbis). This seems to me a plausible construal of the text in that it

---

[50] Berakhot 62a.
[51] Burrus, "Fathering the Word." For the rabbinic version, see Boyarin, *Carnal Israel*, 205.

renders the actual "cases" illustrations of the principle articulated by Rabbi Yoḥanan, and that persona together with Rabbi and Rav are surely central figures in the narrative of the rabbinic rise to domination. Deploying in this text precisely these three crucial culture heroes in the struggle against alternative sources of authority indicates the centrality of the narrative here encoded in telling the story of the rise of the rabbinic episteme. Nothing I am saying here, of course, diminishes the salience of the fact that here, as so often,[52] this battle between men for power is being carried out across the discursive bodies of women. The story of the concubine of Gibeah is, perhaps, then not so inept a figure for this struggle, since that story itself within the biblical context is also a narrative of shifting modes of authority played out across the body of a woman.[53]

The Rabbinization of Eli'ezer

The intervention of Rabbi Yirmiah provides a significant connection to another well-known Babylonian talmudic narrative that can be read as a figure of the two Yavnehs: a first stage in which rabbinic authority was produced through acts of exclusion not entirely dissimilar from the heresiology of contemporaneous Christianity and then a second stage of self-fashioning of rabbinic culture itself as one that permitted and even celebrated diversity within its borders. My next text is a fictionalized or legendary biography of one of the central figures of the Yavneh period and the Yavneh events, Rabbi Eli'ezer the Great. The Babylonian Talmud tells an elaborate story of Rabbi Elie'zer's exclusion from the community of the Rabbis over an issue of authority.[54] Rabbi Eli'ezer refused to accept the

---

[52] See on this Virginia Burrus, "The Heretical Woman as Symbol in Alexander, Athanasius, Epiphanius, and Jerome," *Harvard Theological Review* 84 (1991): 229–48; Kate Cooper, "Insinuations of Womanly Influence: An Aspect of the Christianization of the Roman Aristocracy," *Journal of Roman Studies* 82 (1992): 150–64.

[53] See Mieke Bal, *Death & Dissymmetry: The Politics of Coherence in the Book of Judges*, Chicago Studies in the History of Judaism (Chicago: University of Chicago Press, 1988). In a later chapter of the present research, I plan to do a more thoroughgoing analysis of the role of gender and sexuality in the production of rabbinic authority per se and thus explain why so many narratives of the construction of authority and power involve sexuality in their thematic matter. Indeed, the story of Rabbi Eviathar is cited in the Talmud in order to buttress his opinion on a matter of divorce law. It strains the bounds of credulity to imagine that this is mere accident.

[54] There is an important parallel in the Palestinian Talmud which shows the apparent "raw materials" of tradition from which the Babylonian story was made. The Palestinian version is either missing entirely or much less emphasizes the themes

will of the sages in a halakhic matter; he was cursed, sentenced to complete isolation, and removed from the rabbinic and even the Jewish community for this relatively minor malfeasance. I suggest that rather than the point of halakhic disagreement, in this narrative it was instead the manner of Rabbi Eli'ezer's self-authorization, via quasiprophetic or magical means, that so enraged the Rabbis:[55]

> On that day, Rabbi Eli'ezer used every imaginable argument, but they did not accept it from him. He said: "If the law is as I say, this carob will prove it." The carob was uprooted from its place one hundred feet. Some report four hundred feet. They said to him: "One does not quote a carob as proof...." A voice came from heaven and announced: "The law is in accordance with the view of Rabbi Eli'ezer." Rabbi Yehoshua' stood on his feet and said "it [the Torah] is not in heaven."[56]

On the original halakhic question, Rabbi Eli'ezer initially tried to support his position using the "normal" rabbinic modes of rational argument, the very modes of argument (*tĕšuvot*) which might be said to define rabbinic rationality. When that failed, however, he didn't accept defeat but rather turned to another source of authority: miracles and heavenly oracles, a form of authority that, in my view, it was the essence of rabbinic Judaism to contest.[57]

---

that I am highlighting in my reading of the Babylonian text. In a longer version of this discussion, I will treat these differences in detail and argue that they strongly support the construction offered here. See meanwhile Neusner, *Eliezer Ben Hyrcanus: The Tradition and the Man*, 2:411–16. For the Palestinian version of the excommunication story, see Palestinian Talmud Mo'ed Qatan 3:1, 81 c–d. As pointed out by Neusner, this Palestinian text is "the fragments of a story before they have been put together into a smooth and coherent account" (Neusner, *Eliezer Ben Hyrcanus*, 1:425). There are several stories of Rabbi Eli'ezer's death preserved in rabbinic literature. The only one that makes explicit reference to the excommunication tradition is the Babylonian Talmud's, although the closest parallel version to it in the Palestinian Talmud ambiguously alludes to it. The PT story is found at Shabbat 2:7, 5b.

[55] Christine Trevett has remarked analogously: "The matters at issue between the earliest New Prophets and the developing Catholic tradition ... concerned not heresy but *authority*." Christine Trevett, "Gender, Authority and Church History: A Case Study of Montanism," *Feminist Theology* 17 (January 1998): 14.

[56] BT Baba Metsi'a 59a–b.

[57] To forestall any superfluous demur based on misunderstanding, I am *not* claiming that the Rabbis were more rational than their opponents among the Jewish leaders. Their own modes of authorizing themselves, notably divination through the reading of Torah, as in some forms of midrash, are hardly from our perspective less magical than divination via carob trees, but this is for another day. The point is that

As in the story of Rabbi Yoḥanan the son of Dahavai (above), it is not so much the content of Rabbi Elie'zer's dissent that is anathematized but his appeal to mantic and even prophetic modes of authority, while the Rabbis are struggling to establish their own sole control via the institution of Torah. Rabbi Yehoshua''s statement, frequently taken as an instance of a sort of proto-deconstruction, in fact, once again, in this Babylonian version, represents an instance of precisely that complete rabbinic take-over (not, of course, a hostile one) of religious life and practice. Not even God, not even the angels can compete with the Rabbis and their Torah. The Torah is no longer in heaven; it is on earth in the possession of the rabbinic institution. As Rabbi Yirmiah glosses Rabbi Yehoshua''s statement: "Since the Torah has been given on Mt. Sinai, we no longer listen to heavenly voices, for you have already written in the Torah: 'Incline after the majority' [Exodus 23:2]." Rabbinic Judaism represents a particular episteme of power/knowledge, and the shift into rabbinic Judaism is analogous in structure to the transfer of authority over women's health from midwives and female practitioners to male doctors in the Hellenistic, high-medieval, and Victorian periods; it is a transfer of authority and of control over discourse.

In this story, as in the previous one of the undecided interpretation of the Gibeah narrative, we find Rabbi Yirmiah as the final arbiter: this suggests a connection between the two tales and a possible approximate dating (or at least a terminus post quem) for these discursive developments. In both we find the same theme, namely an explicit inscription of the victory of the Rabbis over the power/knowledge of God himself, as sanctioned by the mediating figure of Elijah the Prophet, a divine abdication of authority in favor of the House of Study and the Oral Torah of the Rabbis:

> Rabbi Natan met Elijah [the Prophet] and asked him, "What was the Holy Blessed One doing at that hour?" He said to him, "He was laughing and saying, 'My sons have defeated me; my sons have defeated me.'"[58]

It is hard to imagine a more unambiguous and audacious account of an epistemic shift than this one. As in the story of Rabbi Eviathar above, a divine voice is made the guarantor that divine voices have nothing to say

---

their own divination was thematized as "Oral Torah" as well but not the divinatory methods of opponents or dissenters.

[58] BT Baba Metsi'a 59a–b.

in the religious lives of Jews anymore; only the Rabbis, once more designed the sons of God, and their Torah serve that function. Only the majority decision of the Rabbis has power and authority, and only their knowledge is relevant.

The consequences for dissent from such a majority could be quite horrifying, for the Rabbis developed shunning and exclusion as powerful means of control. The following case is illuminating. According to the Mishnah 'Eduyot 5:6, Rabbi 'Aqabya ben Mehalelel was excommunicated and his coffin was stoned after his death, owing to a disagreement on whether or not female freed slaves were subject to the ritual of the errant wife (*Soṭah*) or not; once more a struggle for male power is fought over the body of a woman and her sexuality. The stoning of the coffin of Rabbi 'Aqabya ben Mehalelel, whether historically "true" or merely legendary, is surely more than a mere disciplinary measure but rather it related dire exclusion from the community.[59]

The consequences for Rabbi Eli'ezer were nearly as dire as those for 'Aqabya. According to the Talmud's version of this story, Rabbi Eli'ezer was then punished by an extremely harsh version of excommunication, a highly unusual practice in cases of halakhic disagreement: "On that day, all the objects that Rabbi Eli'ezer had declared clean were brought and burned in fire. Then they took a vote and excommunicated him." The Babylonian Talmud here preserves a memory, I would suggest, that Eli'ezer was not an "orthodox" member of the rabbinic party or even a tolerated dissident. Rabbi Eli'ezer, to put a point on it, is treated as a heretic:[60]

---

[59] This represents precisely the parallel of the "false prophet" heresiology documented by Alain Le Boulluec in Justin and plausibly derived by Justin according to Le Boulluec from an older Jewish model; see Alain Le Boulluec, *La notion d'hérésie dans la littérature grecque II–IIIème siècles* (Paris: Études Augustiniennes, 1985), 65 and 33–34. "For just as there were also false prophets in the time of the holy prophets that were among you, so there are among us also many false teachers"; Justin, *Dialogus cum Tryphone* 82 (and passim), ed. Miroslav Marcovich, Patristische Texte und Studien 47 (Berlin: Walter de Gruyter, 1997), 212; trans. A. Lukyn Williams, *Justin Martyr: The Dialogue with Trypho*, Translations of Christian Literature (London: SPCK, 1930), 174. Indeed, as we learn from a tannaitic source in the Babylonian Talmud Sanhedrin 89b, the prescribed punishment (at least according to some authorities) for a false prophet is stoning, precisely the punishment meted out to 'Aqabya, suggesting that that new character, the Jewish heretic, just like his Christian compatriot, is indeed the genealogical scion of the false prophet who must be "utterly extirpated from your midst" (Deut. 13:6).

[60] Dina Stein, "Folklore Elements in Late Midrash: A Folkloristic Perspective on Pirkei de Rabbi Eliezer" (Ph.D. dissertation, Hebrew University, 1998), 173–81, makes the point that Rabbi Eli'ezer is precisely the type of the internal other, the

> It has been related: On that day, they took all of the things that Rabbi Eli'ezer declared pure and declared them polluted. And they took a vote about him and "blessed him" [*a euphemism for dire curse and anathema*]!
> They said: "Who will go tell him?"
> Rabbi Aqiva said, "I will go tell him, for if someone who is not blameless should go and tell him, he might destroy the entire world."

If someone less saintly than Rabbi Aqiva were to inform Rabbi Eli'ezer of his excommunication, the latter's powers of magic would be sufficient to destroy the entire world:

> What did Rabbi Aqiva do? He wore black clothes, and wrapped himself in a black cloak [signs of mourning], and went and sat before [Rabbi Eli'ezer] at a distance of four cubits [thus signalling the latter's excommunication].
> Rabbi Eli'ezer said to him: "Aqiva—what is different about this day?"
> He said to him: "My teacher, it seems as if the members of the fellowship are dissociating from you."
> He [Eli'ezer] also tore his clothes and removed his shoes, and slid down and sat on the earth [further signs of mourning]. Tears rolled out of his eyes, and the world suffered the loss of a third of the olive crop, a third of the wheat crop, and a third of the rye crop.
> And there are those who say that even the dough in the hands of a woman was spoiled [through over-rising].
> It is taught: It was so great that day that every place where Rabbi Eli'ezer's eyes fell was burned, and also Rabban Gamaliel was travelling in a ship. A mighty wave came to sink it. He said, "I believe that this is only because of Eli'ezer the son of Hyrcanos." He stood on his feet and said: "Master of the Universe, you know that everything I did was not for my own glory and not for the glory of my father's house, but for your glory, *in order that there would not be many controversies in Israel.*" And the sea rested from its fury.[61]

At this stage in the story we have a dramatic rendition of the conflicts of the early stages of the formation of rabbinic Judaism. Rabban Gamaliel

---

heretic, as opposed to the apostate who leaves the community entirely. (Stein's thesis is in Hebrew with English abstract.)

[61] BT Baba Metsi'a 59a–b.

says that he excommunicated Rabbi Eliʻezer with the most dire form of anathema, one that renders him as if a dead man, in order to protect Israel from controversy. In other words, the initial stages of the process that would lead to the vaunted "grand coalition" and anti-sectarianism of "Yavneh" involve the most extreme acts of exclusion, both of Eliʻezer and of ʻAqabya. Cohen seems to accept almost en bloc the terms of the rabbinic literature itself when he writes that "two categories of people could not be incorporated into the Yavnean coalition: those who insisted upon a sectarian selfidentification, and those who refused to heed the will of the majority."

Cohen attempts to soften the implicit self-contradiction in his argument by claiming that "[t]hese sectarians were denounced, not excommunicated." However, Rabbi Eliʻezer himself was certainly excommunicated. ʻAqabya too was certainly excommunicated. Cohen argues: "Whatever the truth of these amoraic stories, they reflect the essential problem of the Yavnean period: the creation of the society which would tolerate, even foster, disputes and discussions but which could nonetheless maintain order. Those rabbis who could not play by the new rules were too great a danger to be punished with just a curse. They were expelled." In the end, Cohen also admits, as it were, that this is only a rabbinic construction: "This rabbinic ideology is reflected in Justin's discussion of the Jewish sects: there are Jews, i.e., the 'orthodox' and there are sects, among them the Pharisees, who scarcely deserve the name Jew."[62] Reading critically, we hardly see here the inclusiveness and tolerance that most scholars now identify as the legacy of Yavneh. We find rather the production of an exclusivistic institution of orthodoxy not unlike, mutatis mutandis, the story of Nicaea, in order, like that invention, to prevent "the proliferation of controversy in Israel."[63] To be sure, the narrative registers some ambivalence about the treatment of Rabbi Eliʻezer—the boat does almost sink—, but in the end, Rabban Gamaliel's argument for authority and stability and centralized power/knowledge is affirmed, "in order that there would not be many controversies in Israel." Those who will not conform to the new rabbinic program of the sole authority of the House of Study are thrown out of Israel.

How then shall we explain the final form of rabbinic Judaism in which we find the opposite? —namely that "opinions that in human discourse may appear as contradictory or mutually exclusive are raised to the state of

---

[62] Cohen, "Yavneh," 49.
[63] Cf. Lim, *Public Disputation*.

paradox once traced to their common source in the speech of the divine author," that is, the form of ecclesiology that we today associate with the Rabbis and that Cohen ascribed to Yavneh. The Talmud itself dramatizes an answer. In the continuation of the Babylonian talmudic narrative found in Tractate Sanhedrin, in contrast to the unfortunate 'Aqabya ben Mehalelel of the thirdcentury Mishnah,[64] Rabbi Eli'ezer of the fourth/fifth-century Talmud is fully rehabilitated at the end of his life. This story can be read, I suggest, as a virtual historical allegory of the retrospective construction of catholic Israel on the part of the later Rabbis and especially (but not exclusively) the Babylonian Talmud:

> It is taught: When Rabbi Eli'ezer was sick, Rabbi Aqiva and his colleagues went in to visit him. He was sitting in his canopied bed, and they were sitting in his anteroom....
> When the sages saw that his mind was clear, they went and sat down four cubits from him [thus indicating that, according to this text, Rabbi Eli'ezer is still excommunicate]. He said to them: "Why have you come?"
> They said to him: "To learn Torah we have come."
> He said to them: "And until now, why have you not come?"
> They said: "We didn't have time."
> He said to them: "I will be amazed if they die a natural death."
> Rabbi Aqiva then said to him: "What about me?"
> He said: "Yours is more severe than all of them."
> He [Elie'zer] took his two arms and placed them on his heart and said: "Aiih to these two arms that are like two Scrolls of the Torah rolled up. I have learned much Torah, and I have taught much Torah. I have learned much Torah and I didn't diminish from the teaching of my masters even as much as a dog licks from the sea. I have taught much Torah, and my disciples have not diminished from my teaching so much as the brush in its case.[65]
> "And not only that but I teach three hundred laws in the matter of leprosy, and no one ever asked me a question about them, and in the planting of cucumbers, and no one ever asked me about them,

---

[64] Interestingly, 'Aqabya as well receives a sort of post-mortem rehabilitation in the Mishnah itself, when Rabbi Yehuda insists that it was not he to whom this happened but someone else entirely, some (otherwise) unknown Rabbi, and it was the tomb of this unknown Rabbi that was stoned.

[65] On this passage, see discussion in Jacob Neusner, *Why No Gospels in Talmudic Judaism?* Brown Judaic Studies 135 (Atlanta, 1988), 52; Stein, "Folklore," 166–67.

except for Aqiva ben Yosef. Once he and I were walking on the way. He said to me: 'Teach me their planting.' I said a word and the field was full of cucumbers. He said to me: 'Rabbi, you have taught me their planting; now teach me their uprooting.' I said another word, and they were all gathered into one place."

The [sages then] said to him: "A ball, a slipper, and a cameo [that are made of leather and filled with wool]."

He said to them: "They are pure."

And his soul left him in purity.

Rabbi Yehoshua stood on his feet and said: "The vow is released. The vow is released!"

On the going out of the Sabbath, he met Rabbi Aqiva on the way [in the funeral procession] from Caesarea to Lydda. He was smiting his flesh until the blood flowed to the ground. [Rabbi Aqiva] opened his eulogy and said: "'My father, my father, the chariot of Israel and its cavalry' [2 Kings 2:12]. I have many coins and no banker to change them."[66]

Rabbi Elie'zer is reincorporated into the rabbinic community just before his death "in purity." It is not his views on halakha that have changed but the manner of his discourse. He has been rabbinized. We can read this shift within the narrative, at the moment when Rabbi Eli'ezer turns from magic planting and harvesting of cucumbers to answering the Rabbis' purity question. Thus the story becomes a mini-historical allegory of the shift in the social status of dissent from the second/third-century to the fourth/fifth century context.

As Jacob Neusner has pointed out,[67] older traditions of Rabbi Eli'ezer hardly mention his commitment to the study of Torah as the central act of Jewish piety,[68] while here, the disciples come to "learn Torah," and the "much Torah" that Eli'ezer has learned and taught are now central to his self-image.[69] According to the Tosefta,[70] Rabbi Eli'ezer never said a

---

[66] BT Sanhedrin 68a.

[67] Neusner makes the excellent point that in the earlier documents, Eli'ezer is never rabbinized, never depicted as making the study of Torah as central to his piety. He is, moreover, never depicted in the earlier stages of the tradition as a disciple of Rabbi Yohanan ben Zakkai, but rather as a representative of the old Pharisaic cultic practices. These, too, have been displaced in the production of rabbinic authority, of the House of Study as the sole locus of power, as our story represents it; see Neusner, *Eliezer Ben Hyrcanus: The Tradition and the Man*, 2:301.

[68] Jacob Neusner, "The Formation of Rabbinic Judaism: Yavneh (Jamnia) from A.D. 70 to 100," in *Principat: Religion (Judentum: Palastinisches Judentum)*, 36.

[69] My student Gerald Roth has pointed out a similar development with respect

word that he had not heard from his teachers, fitting perfectly Josephus's description of the Pharisees who follow their traditions and do not argue with their elders.[71] Study of Torah and the practice of producing new interpretations must have been the province of another tributary group in the stream that became rabbinic Judaism, and our story dramatizes in narrative the historical confluence of these two tributaries.[72] Moreover, we see a shift in the very nature of Rabbi Eli'ezer's personality. From a mantic who relies on prophetic signs, oracles, and magic, Rabbi Eli'ezer is transformed within the space of the story into a proper talmudic sage,[73] converted into a Rabbi.[74] Rabbi Eli'ezer, historically perhaps a problematic and dissident Pharisee, has been thoroughly domesticated. What is narrated in the text as a story of transgression and repentance can be reread historically as the story of appropriation into rabbinic orthodoxy of a "heterodox" strand of Pharisaic Judaism.

---

to Pinhas ben Ya'ir, another early charismatic, who in the early sources produces an ascetic rule in which "diligence leads to cleanliness, cleanliness to purity, purity to sexual abstinence," and finally via resurrection one proceeds to "Elijah,"—prophetic vision (Mishnah Sotah 9:15). In the Babylonian Talmud's version of this, the list begins with Torah (absent entirely from the early version) and ends with the resurrection—no prophecy (BT Avoda Zara 20b).

[70] PT Yabmut (sic) 3:1; ed. c. 250 A.C.

[71] Flavius Josephus, *Books XVIII–XX*, vol. 9 of *Jewish Antiquities*, ed. and trans. L. H. Feldman, Loeb Classical Library (Cambridge: Harvard University Press, 1965), 10–11.

[72] Boyarin, "Reforming Judaism."

[73] It is perhaps not inapposite to mention that at approximately the same time there was a struggle against the "New Prophecy" of the Montanists or Kataphrygians as well. It is fascinating that the leadership of this group was always referred to by its enemies as "Montanus and the women," e.g., by Eusebius; Hugh Jackson Lawlor and John Ernest Leonard Oulton, trans. and eds., *Eusebius, Bishop of Caesarea, the Ecclesiastical History and the Martyrs of Palestine* (London: Society for Promoting Christian Knowledge, 1927), 161 (5.16.20–22). I am not, however, claiming a strong connection between these events, just a certain suggestiveness to the coincidence.

[74] This interpretation is consistent as well with the argument made by Kalmin that the Babylonian Talmud so thoroughly "rabbinizes" such figures as the charismatic, antic, wonder-working holy men Honi Hame'agel and Hanina ben Dosa that it actually has them studying Torah and thus "forgetting" that they were, in their Palestinian origin, an antithetical force and factional opposition party to nascent rabbinic Judaism; Richard Kalmin, "Christians and Heretics in Rabbinic Literature of Late Antiquity," *Harvard Theological Review* 87.2 (April 1994): 158. See also Green, "Palestinian Holy Men: Charismatic Leadership and Roman Tradition"; Sean Freyne, "The Charismatic," in *Ideal Figures in Ancient Judaism: Profiles and Paradigms*, ed. George Nickelsburg and John Collins (Chico, Cal.: Scholars Press, 1980).

Adversus Minaos

An important constituent of my gloss here is the notion that there is reason to think that Rabbi Eli'ezer was figured, in the Palestinian rabbinic literature of the mid third century, as a Jewish Christian, a *min* (heretic) or at any rate as a rabbi who came dangerously close to sympathetic intercourse with such *minim*. In one early (mid-third-century) Palestinian story, Rabbi Eli'ezer is arrested by the Romans on suspicion of being a Christian, referred to as *minut* in the story. This is the excerpt:

> It happened to Rabbi Eli'ezer that he was arrested for sectarianism [*minut* = Christianity],[75] and they took him up to the platform to be judged.
>
> The ruler said to him: "A sage such as you having truck with these matters!?"
>
> He said to him: "I have trust in the judge."
>
> The ruler thought that he was speaking of him, but he meant his Father in Heaven. He said to him: "Since you trust me, I also have said: 'Is it possible that these gray hairs would err in such matters?' [*Dimus* = *Dimissus!*] Behold, you are dismissed."[76]

Having tricked the Roman, he then confesses to his fellows that he has, indeed, had improper friendly religious conversation with a disciple of Jesus; indeed, on my reading, that he had been "arrested by *minut*," i.e., found heresy arresting, and not only arrested for *minut*—the Hebrew phrase allows for both meanings.[77] It is important to observe the shifts in reference of the term "min" itself chronologically as well as geographically. In its first appearances in the Mishnah (early-third-century Palestine),

---

[75] This identification is explicit in the continuation (not cited here), in which Rabbi Eli'ezer refers to his intercourse with a certain James, the disciple of Jesus. Jerome knows that the term *min*, "sectarian" is a name for Jewish Christians, as we see from his famous letter to Augustine; Jerome, *Correspondence*, ed. Isidorus Hilberg, CSEL 55 (Vienna: Verlag der Osterreichischen Akademie der Wissenschaften, 1996), 381–82. This letter was written about 404; Ray A. Pritz, *Nazarene Jewish Christianity: From the End of the New Testament Period Until Its Disappearance in the Fourth Century* (Jerusalem: Magnes Press, 1992), 53.

[76] Tosefta Hullin, 2:24. M. S. Zuckermandel, ed., *Tosephta: Based on the Erfurt and Vienna Codices, with Lieberman, Saul, "Supplement" to the Tosephta* (Jerusalem: Bamberger & Wahrmann, Publishers, 1937), 503.

[77] For much longer and more detailed discussion, see Daniel Boyarin, *Dying for God: Martyrdom and the Making of Christianity and Judaism*, The Lancaster/Yarnton Lectures in Judaism and Other Religions for 1998 (Stanford: Stanford University Press, forthcoming), chapter 1.

there is no evidence that Christians are being referred to, while in the Tosefta (mid-third-century Palestine), it is nearly certain that at least some references, including this story about Rabbi Eliʿezer are precisely about Christians in the Galilee.[78] This would be not inconsistent with the assumption, recently being made by sociologists of religion, of an exponential growth in the number of Christians throughout the Empire, precisely between the beginning of the third century, when the Mishnah was edited, and the mid-third when the Tosefta came into being.[79]

However, there is a further shift in the fate of the term *min* that is even more significant to my point here, for it will help us to understand why it was safe, as it were, for the Rabbis of the Babylonian Talmud to adopt such an expansive and elastic notion of Jewish orthodoxy. As Richard Kalmin has observed: "Th[e] notion of the powerful attraction that *minut* ('heresy') and Christianity exerted on rabbis and their families is found almost exclusively in tannaitic collections such as the Tosefta, but also in tannaitic sources in the Babylonian Talmud that have toseftan parallels. Statements attributed to later Palestinian and Babylonian amoraim in both Talmuds, in contrast, reveal no hint of this notion."[80] This argument can be further substantiated by observing that the Babylonian Talmud almost systematically "forgets" what the meaning of the term *min* is. There are two effective pieces of evidence for this proposition.

The first comes simply from the continuation of the Babylonian Talmud's version of the narrative about the arrest of Rabbi Eliʿezer. In the earlier Tosefta and the Palestinian midrash, this text appears without a sequel, but in the Talmud we find the following continuation:

> Our Rabbis have taught: When Rabbi Elʿazar the son of Perata and Rabbi Ḥanina the son of Teradyon were arrested for sectarianism [*minut*], Rabbi Elʿazar the son of Perata said to Rabbi Ḥanina the son of Teradyon: "Happy art thou who hast been arrested for only

---

[78] This point was made to me by my student, Henry Millstein. In a later, expanded version of this text, I will further treat the question of interaction between the usages of the term *minim* and the histories of the gradual separation of "Christianity" from "Judaism," as well as the much discussed question of the so-called "Curse of the Minim" (Kimelman, "Birkat Ha-Minim"). For the nonce, let it be said that even if there were such a curse and even if it did refer to Christians—both questionable points but *non liquet*—that would only demonstrate how much sociopolitical work had yet to be done to distinguish "Jews" from "Christians," and hardly that a final separation or a parting of the ways had taken place and was securely in place.

[79] Hopkins, "Christian Number."

[80] Kalmin, "Christians and Heretics," 160.

one thing. Woe unto me who have been arrested for five things." Rabbi Ḥanina the son of Teradyon said to him: "Happy art thou who hast been arrested for five things and will be rescued. Woe unto me who have been arrested for one thing and will not be saved, for thou hast busied thyself with Torah and with good deeds, while I only busied myself with Torah." — This is in accord with the view of Rav Huna who said that anyone who busies himself with Torah alone is as if he had no God.

In contrast to Rabbi Eli'ezer, where it is explicit that the *minut* involved is Christianity, these two Rabbis clearly are under no suspicion whatever of Christianity. Their fictive arrest is clearly during the Hadrianic persecutions of the early second century (not under Trajan in the second half of the first) and has to do with the public teaching of Torah, forbidden by Hadrian for political reasons. And yet the Talmud refers to it as an arrest for *minut*. The term *minut* has clearly shifted meaning for the Babylonian Talmud. No longer Jewish heresy, it now refers to the binary opposition between Jewish and Gentile religion. Judaism is *minut* for the Romans; Roman religion and Christianity are *minut* for Jews. This semantic shift changes the interpretation of Rabbi Eli'ezer's arrest in the Talmudic context as well.[81] It is unthinkable to this Talmud that Rabbi Eli'ezer had been under suspicion—much less somewhat justifiable suspicion—for association with *minim*, and therefore the text has to make it a code name for arrest for being Jewish, for teaching Torah, i.e., *minut*, heresy, from the point of view of the Roman order, not from the point of view of Judaism.

On my view, we have evidence then that by the time of the editing of the Babylonian Talmud, and perhaps at that geographical distance from the center of contact, Palestine, Christianity had receded sufficiently into the distance from rabbinic Judaism, was sufficiently definable as a separate "religion," that it no longer posed a threat to the borders of the Jewish community. It is in the Babylonian Talmud that early Palestinian Judaism comes to be represented as a "a society based on the doctrine that conflicting disputants may each be advancing the words of the living God." With

---

[81] In the early Palestinian version of the narrative, there is not a hint of the term *minut* involved with respect to the arrest and martydom of these Rabbis; see Louis Finkelstein, ed., *Sifre on Deuteronomy* (1939; rprt. New York: Jewish Theological Seminary of America, 1969), 346; and, for discussion (in Hebrew), Daniel Boyarin, "A Contribution to the History of Martyrdom in Israel," in *Festschrift for Prof. H. Z. Dimitrovsky*, ed. Menahem Hirschman, et al. (Jerusalem: Magnes Press, 1999).

the borders of unanimity secured, there are no more (at least in theory) internal others.

We now have an explanation for the well-known fact that, in the Babylonian Talmud, the term *min* no longer refers to a difference within Judaism, an excluded heretical other, but has come to mean gentiles and especially gentile Christians as well. Judaism has been reconfigured as a grand coalition of differing theological and even halakhic views *within the strictly defined borders of rabbinic Judaism*, and it is this reconfigured Jewish polity with no heresies and no heresiologies that is exhibited in Cohen's and Bruns's phenomenologies. Once more, as in the period of the second Temple (up until 70 A.C.) and before, the excluded other of Judaism is the Gentile and not the heretic within. A story, previously read in a very different context by historians, bears out this suggestion:

> Rabbi Abbahu used to praise Rav Safra [a Babylonian immigrant to Caesarea Maritima] to the *minim* that he was a great man [i.e., a great scholar]. They released him from excise taxes for thirteen years.
>
> One day they met him. They said to him: "It is written: 'Only you have I known from all of the families of the earth; therefore I will tax you with all of your sins' [Amos 3:2]. One who is enraged,[82] does he punish his lover?"
>
> He was silent, and didn't say anything to them. They threw a scarf on him and were mocking him.
>
> Rabbi Abbahu came and found them.
>
> He said to them: "Why are you mocking him?"
>
> They said to him: "Didn't you say that he is a great man, and he could not even tell us the interpretation of this verse!"
>
> He said to them: "That which I said to you has to do with Mishnah, but with respect to the Scripture, I didn't say anything."
>
> They said to him: "What is it different with respect to you that you know [Scripture also]?"
>
> He said to them: "We who are located in your midst, take it upon ourselves and we study, but they do not study."[83]

Following the principle set out by Saul Lieberman—that talmudic legend may be read as useful information for the history of the time and place of its production and not the time and place of which it speaks[84]—there is

---

[82] My translation here follows the interpretation of Rashi ad loc.

[83] BT Avoda Zara 4a.

[84] Saul Lieberman, "The Martyrs of Caesarea," *Annuaire de l'Institut de Philologie*

no way that this story, only attested in the Babylonian Talmud, ought to be taken as representing Palestinian reality. Moreover, it can be demonstrated that it almost definitely does not do so, simply by virtue of the fact that the genre of encounters between Rabbis and *minim* is very rare in Palestinian sources and very common in Babylonian texts, as Kalmin has recently shown.[85] Almost always these Babylonian narratives relate the confrontation between a Palestinian sage and a *min* of whatever variety.

A story such as this may tell us something, therefore, about Babylonian reality in the fourth or fifth century.[86] In that time and space, this text explicitly testifies, Christians were no longer an internal threat to the integrity of the religious life-world of the Rabbis: "They [the Babylonians] do not study Bible, because you [the Christians] are not found in their midst." This is not, however, to be taken as a sign that Christianity did not have powerful effects on the historical development of Judaism in Babylonia (and the reverse),[87] but only that with the borders clearly established, it was now, I conjecture, more functional to expand the definition of in and out, rather than to shut it down—just in time, that is, to confront the so-called "Karaite schism" of the early Middle Ages.[88]

Yavneh and Nicaea Revisited

The talmudic production of a Council of Yavneh and the effects of its *Nachleben* in the real world can be usefully compared to the Athanasian production of the Council of Nicaea and its effects in the real world. There are, however, significant differences as well. These legendary narratives have their correlates finally in distinct forms of textuality and formations of canon. Burrus writes,

> Sorting through the complicatedly intercalated writings either authored or ghostauthored or edited and published by the bishop of Alexandria [Athanasius], we observe Nicaea and its frozen Logos being produced as the cumulative effect of a series of very deliberate

---

et d'Histoire Orientales et Slaves 7 (1939–44): 395.

[85] Kalmin, "Christians and Heretics."

[86] Cf., e.g., Lee I. Levine, *The Rabbinic Class of Roman Palestine in Late Antiquity* (New York: Jewish Theological Seminary of America, 1989), 87; and see as well Lieberman, "The Martyrs of Caesarea," 398.

[87] Daniel Boyarin, "Martyrdom and the Making of Christianity and Judaism," *Journal of Early Christian Studies* 6.4 (Dec. 1998): 577–627.

[88] See above, note 37. This point will be further developed elsewhere, *deo volente*.

textual acts of self-defense, by which the armoured body of the bishop was also conceived.[89]

In the even more complicatedly intercalated pseudospeech of the Rabbis as edited and published in the Babylonian Talmud, a similar body, that of the Rabbi, was being conceived. If, in Burrus's words, "the Alexandrian Father conceives Nicaea as the 'ecumenical' council of the Fathers who begat the immortal body of the written word," then the Talmud conceives Yavneh as the ecumenical council of Fathers who transmitted the immortal (but ever-growing and shifting) body of the Oral Torah. Just as Athanasius promulgated "the strikingly close identification of the divinely begotten Word with the written texts that now incarnate 'Nicaea',"[90] so too did the Talmud closely identify its own founding text, the Mishnah, and their own commentaries on it, with the divinely given Oral Torah.

Yavneh was projected back into the first century, Nicaea only into the beginning of the fourth. Nicaea is a textual story that begins its life with eye-witnesses to a real event which then gives rise and gives way to legends; Yavneh is an event whose very existence is always already shrouded in legend and folk-tale but which then becomes the foundation-myth for a distinctly textual and literary culture.[91] Both are myths of foundation of an orthodoxy.[92] The Talmud itself, however, is a different kind of text from either the Athanasian corpus or the monovocal "Church Fathers" that the late ancient Christian orthodoxy produced.[93] Exploring that distinction, and querying how much of a difference it made, will be

---

[89] Burrus, "Fathering the Word."

[90] Ibid.

[91] As such, even more than to Nicaea, the legend of the founding of Yavneh as preserved in the Talmud (BT Gittin 56a–b) is strikingly similar to the equally fabulous tale of the retreat of the Jerusalem Christians in the same circumstances to Pella, as pointed out recently by Galit Hasan-Rokem, *The Web of Life—Folklore in Rabbinic Literature: The Palestinian Aggadic Midrash Eikha Rabba* (Tel Aviv: Am Oved, 1996), 201 (in Hebrew).

[92] Barnes, "Fourth Century as Trinitarian Canon," 62. The differences in textual and literary as well as political structure between these two orthodoxies remain salient and will be explored in another part of the present project.

[93] See Patrick T. R. Gray, "'The Select Fathers': Canonizing the Patristic Past," *Studia Patristica* 23 (1989): 21–36; Mark Vessey, "The Forging of Orthodoxy in Latin Christian Literature: A Case Study," *Journal of Early Christian Studies* 4.4 (Winter 1996): 495–513; David Brakke, "Canon Formation and Social Conflict in Fourth-Century Egypt: Athanasius of Alexandria's Thirty-Ninth *Festal Letter*," *Harvard Theological Review* 87 (1994): 395–419; J. Rebecca Lyman, "The Making of a Heretic: The Life of Origen in Epiphanius *Panarion* 64," *Studia Patristica* 31 (1997): 445–51 (Leuven: Peeters, 1997).

the work of a sequel to the present essay, but it is to an extent prefigured in the differences between the exclusive orthodoxy of the end-point of the Nicaea myth and the equally exclusive divinely sanctioned heterodoxy of the endpoint of the Yavneh myth. Barnes sharply phrases the new narrative of Nicaea: "In the end, Nicaea 325 became orthodoxy only when its potential cost to real distinctions was contained at Constantinople 381."[94] Of Yavneh we could say (marking at once both the similarity and the difference from Nicaea): The myth of a universal, inclusive creation of a non-sectarian Judaism only became orthodoxy when its potential cost to the blurring of the boundaries of rabbinic Judaism was contained—also late in the fourth century, if not later than that.[95] By the time the Babylonian Talmud retales this story, the Rabbis have won the struggle for hegemony, the heresiological strifes of the past and of Palestine are over, the "parting of the ways" has taken place, the lines are clearly drawn between Jewish identity and Christian identity, Jewish practice and Christian practice, and it is plausible at least to speak at this point of a single Christianity and a single Judaism—at least for a time. It is at this moment (this perhaps fourth-, perhaps fifth-century and particularly Babylonian moment) that Cohen's Yavneh, his "grand coalition," comes into being. In this sense, as Rosemary Ruether put it a quarter of a century ago, "The fourth century is the first century for Christianity and Judaism."[96]

University of California, Berkeley

---

[94] Barnes, "Fourth Century as Trinitarian Canon," 62.

[95] The reasons and conditions for this containment remain to be explored elsewhere.

[96] Rosemary Radford Ruether, "Judaism and Christianity: Two Fourth-Century Religions," *Sciences religieuses/Studies in Religion* 2 (1972): 1–10.

"Turn it and turn it again": Culture and Talmud Interpretation

MICHAEL CHERNICK

The "Ethics of the Fathers" (Pirkei Avot), a section of the "constitution" of early rabbinic Judaism called the Mishnah, states, "Turn it [the Torah] and turn it again, for everything is in it."[1] Torah in the rabbinic world meant not only the Pentateuch or even the whole Bible, but the entire rabbinic tradition; and the highly diverse formative rabbinic world spoke its deepest faith when it taught that repeated visits to the tradition would reveal everything one needed to know. This faith was predicated on the Rabbis' own recognition that the tradition they were creating was multi-vocal, argumentative, intellectually restless, and concerned with all aspects of life. Returning to that tradition over and over meant hearing its voice and adding one's own; thus each deeply pondered "turn again" led to new insights and contributions to the ever growing body of the rabbinic Torah.[2] In this way the Mishnah grew into its greatest flowering, the Babylonian and Palestinian Talmuds.

The Babylonian Talmud, the most influential document of the rabbinic tradition, reached its completion, depending on whether one is a traditionalist or an academic, either ca. 525 CE or as late as the mid-eighth century, in what Jews called Babylonia and what we call Iraq and Iran. It is longer than its predecessor, the Palestinian Talmud, whose formation ended in the mid-fifth century in what the Romans called Palestine and the Jews called "the Land of Israel." It is, therefore, more accurate to speak of the Talmuds than of the Talmud. Both are compendia of *halakhah* and *aggadah*, legal dicta and lore. The legal dicta are usually formulated as unresolved disputes between sages, and the lore is described accurately as having no legal force.[3] Both genres cover virtually every

---

[1] Mishnah, Tractate Avot 5:22. *Mishnah*, ed. Chanoch Albeck (Jerusalem and Tel Aviv: Mossa Bialik/D'vir, 1957).

[2] "Just as a plant is fruitful and multiplies, so the words of the Torah are fruitful and multiply" (Yalkut Shimeoni, Ecclesiastes, Vilna edition, #589). All translations or paraphrases of rabbinic and other Hebrew and Aramaic sources are my own.

[3] Regarding the indeterminacy of talmudic discussions, including legal ones, see Rabbi Adin Steinsaltz, *The Talmud: The Steinsaltz Edition: Reference Guide* (New York: Random House, 1989), 2–3. Regarding aggadah's non-normative status see

imaginable aspect of life: adults' and children's education, acquisition of property, zoning rules, sexual mores and marriage law, dietary taboos, observance of holy times, and agricultural practices. This does not begin to exhaust the list, but it is a useful start toward understanding the Talmuds' range of interests.

Eventually the Talmud became the constitution of rabbinic Jewry and a commanding voice in Jewish communal life world-wide until the late eighteenth century. It was held to be authoritative not because it was divine, but because "it was agreed upon by all of Israel."[4] Therefore, vastly different Jewish communities expected the Talmud's dicta to be applied in places and times very distant from Sassanian Persia where it was born. To do so, it had to respond to the specific religious, cultural, social, economic, and political needs of varied Jewish communities unknown to the Talmud's creators. Clearly, a book alone could not respond to these needs; only its human interpreters and interlocutors could. The more the Talmud was interpreted, the more it became human; and in its human form it absorbed new information from its surroundings and returned new insights to its adherents. The darker side of this story is how some Talmudists turned into books and became absorbed only in themselves.

In this essay I will focus on aggadah, talmudic lore. This genre encompasses many sub-genres: ethical aphorisms, theological and theosophical thought, angelologies and demonologies, ancient science (much of which we would call superstition), parables, miracle tales, "history," and stories about biblical and rabbinic figures. A story about an important rabbinic personality, Rabbi Shim'on, son of Yohai, henceforth Rashbi (acronym for Rabbi Shim'on bar Yohai), will serve as my example of this genre of talmudic literature. Rabbi Shim'on bar Yohai's story appears in both Talmuds, giving us the opportunity to see how the Babylonian Talmud

---

ibid., 8; *Enzyklopedia Talmudit*, ed. Rabbis Meir Bar-Ilan and Shelomoh Yosef Zevin (Jerusalem: Enzyklopedia Talmudit, 1955), 1:60. The *Enzyklopedia* defines "aggadah" as "Matters of dogma, wisdom and ethics, stories and parables that do not include normative material."

[4] Maimonides makes this claim for the Talmud's authority in the Introduction to his legal code, *Mishneh Torah* 3a. The spread of the Babylonian Talmud to the various communities has a complex history, and certainly "the Jewish people" did not accept its authority at a single "vote." Rather, it moved from the Middle East to North Africa and then to Europe. By the tenth century all major Jewish communities had it. A century later its dominance as a "constitution" for rabbinic Jews was universal. Maimonides's view provides a useful working myth for his ideal of an ideologically undifferentiated and unified Jewish people whose constitution is the Talmud.

rereads the earlier formulation. I will then trace the revision and reinterpretation of this story from the talmudic period, ca. 525 CE, until the last decade of our century. By turning this talmudic story and turning it again I intend to study the symbiotic relationship between a text, the communities that studied it, and the cultures in which they lived.

Palestinian Origin of the Rashbi Story

As mentioned above, the Talmuds are, roughly speaking, commentaries on the Mishnah, a work of Jewish law and lore completed around 220 CE. The Palestinian Talmud's story of Rashbi appears as a gloss on a Mishnaic passage that cites one of his views.[5] In the ninth chapter of Shebi'it, a tractate that deals with the sabbatical fallow ordained in Exodus 23:11 and Leviticus 25:1–7, Rashbi holds that in the sabbatical year one may buy and use all spontaneously growing vegetables except cabbage. This is a very lenient view because the Torah prohibits any commercial transaction involving sabbatical-year produce. Rashbi excludes cabbage from his leniency because it is cultivated rather than wild, and Biblical law explicitly prohibits cultivation. The majority of sages represented in this Mishnah passage prohibit the purchase and subsequent use of all spontaneously growing vegetation. These rules function as the framework for the Rashbi story which I will present with explanatory comments in parentheses.

The story begins with Rashbi finding someone harvesting seventh-year produce in an amount that indicated he planned to sell it.

> He said to the harvester, "Is this not forbidden since these are the wild growing produce of the seventh year fallow?" The harvester replied, "Aren't you the one who permits it?" Rashbi retorted, "But don't my colleagues [who are the majority] prohibit it?" Rashbi applied to the harvester the verse, ... one who breaches a wall, a serpent shall bite him" [Ecclesiastes 10:8], and that is what happened to the harvester [he was bitten by a snake and died].

A second story now begins with Rashbi hiding, probably from the Roman forces during the Hadrianic war against Judaea (135–38 CE), in the cave of Ḥarubin de-Terumah until dryness cracked his skin.

After thirteen years he emerged to find out what was happening.

---

[5] Palestinian Talmud Shebi'it 9:1 (ed. prin. Venice: 1520). Reference is by Mishnah chapter and paragraph on which PT comments.

He sat at his cave's entrance where he saw a hunter trapping birds. When the hunter spread his net, Rashbi heard a heavenly voice calling, "Dimos,"[6] and the bird would escape. He reasoned, "A bird does not escape [its fate] without heaven's help, how much more so a human being" [so heaven must favor me since I have survived]. When he saw that things were quiet, he said to himself [thought], "Let me go down and visit the hot springs of Tiberias" [where his skin could be healed]. Then he said to himself, "I should do something to improve [the community, as an act of thanks for my escape from the ravages of the war and for my healing], as our forefathers did. [As it says of Jacob in Genesis 33:18,] 'and he camped before the city' [a pun on the Hebrew making "and he camped, *va-yihan*, before the city" mean "and he graced, *va-yahen*, the face of the city"]— they [the forefathers] made butcheries and sold the meat cheaply in the market-places.[7] He said, "I will purify Tiberias [which had been built on a graveyard, a source of ritual impurity]." He took lupines, cut them, and tossed them. Wherever there was a corpse, it flew up [due to the miraculous power of the lupines]. A certain Samaritan saw him and said to himself, "I will go and fool that old man of the Jews [Rashbi]." He took a corpse and buried it in a place which Rashbi had purified. Then he went to Rashbi and said, "Didn't you purify such-andsuch a place? I will go there and raise a corpse [thus you can never be certain that you actually purified Tiberias]." Through the agency of the holy spirit [a minor form of prophecy], Rashbi saw that the Samaritan had placed a corpse there. He said, "I command you who are above to go below,

---

[6] Two suggestions as to the meaning of this term have been put forward. Alexander Kohut in his edition of the classical rabbinic dictionary, *'Arukh Completum* (reprint of Vienna 1854; no publisher or date), 26, suggests that it is a Hebraism or Aramism of the Latin *demissio*, similar to *remissio*, meaning commutation of a sentence. Marcus Jastrow in his *Dictionary of Talmud Babli, Yerushalmi, Midrashic Literature and Targumim* (New York: Pardes, 1950), 1:300, suggests the term has its origin in the Greek *demos*, "populace." Since public games and festivals were times when Roman emperors or other significant Roman officials granted amnesties, the term became identified in Palestinian Jewish usage with amnesty.

[7] The material about the forefathers creating butcheries provides the example of how Jacob improved the city of his encampment. It interrupts the narrative's flow because biblical texts and their midrashic expositions circulate as a literary unit. This means that both the verse and its midrash will be present, even if one of them is irrelevant. See Chanoch Albeck, *Introduction to the Talmud, Bavli, and Yershalmi* (Tel Aviv: D'vir, 1969), 492–96, for a broader discussion, in Hebrew, of this phenomenon.

and you who are below to come above!" And so it was [that the Samaritan who was above ground was buried, and the corpse he planted rose]. As he passed before the tower [in Tiberias] he heard a scribe say [in a mocking way], "Rashbi [thinks he] purified Tiberias?" Rashbi replied, "[Punishment] should come upon me if I have not heard a tradition that Tiberias would eventually be purified. And still you don't believe?" [I.e., Rashbi had a tradition of the sages that Tiberias could and would be purified, nevertheless this scribe mocked his efforts.] [At that] the scribe turned into a pile of bones.

The initial Rashbi story relates directly to the Mishnah passage. Rashbi, as opposed to the harvester of seventh year fallow produce, defers to his colleagues, the majority of the sages. The harvester dies for his violation of the sages' words and for his unseemly attempt to force Rashbi to countenance unlawful behavior by confronting him with his own permissive ruling. The next story, however, is not related to the Mishnah text, but it continues the first story's theme in two ways. It maintains Rashbi as the central character and maintains the motif of people dying for making light of a sage's acts or words. The entire narrative clearly contains two separate units, one related directly to the Mishnah pericope, and the other a variation on the theme. Such associational connections are typical phenomena in both Talmuds.[8] The point is didactic: "Do not make light of things a sage says or does." Repetition strengthens the warning.

Beneath this story's surface are the historical conditions under which the Palestinian rabbinate functioned. These were not always the same. Rome, the dominant power in Palestine from 63 BCE until the rise of Islamic rule, gave the Palestinian Jewish community differing degrees of autonomy depending on whether Palestinian Jewry was quiet, in a state of revolt, or in the aftermath of a conflict. Usually after uprisings against Rome Jewish autonomy was strictly limited until the Roman authorities were satisfied that peace had been restored. The periods following the destruction of the Temple (70 CE) and the Bar Kokhba revolt, sometimes called the Hadrianic persecutions (135–38 CE), were such historical moments. Even when some autonomy was restored, it tended to be restricted to jurisdiction over ritual observances and minor civil cases which, if a Jew

---

[8] Rabbi Adin Steinsaltz, *Reference Guide*, 7. Abraham Weiss, *Studies in the Literature of the Amoraim* (New York: Horeb Yeshivah University, 1962), 59–64 (in Hebrew).

wished, could be argued before the Roman authorities in defiance of rabbinic dicta. Moreover, rabbinic Judaism was not the only contender for Palestinian Jewry's loyalties. Jewish Christianity, gnosticism, and other Jewish sectarian movements vied with rabbinic Judaism for dominance. If rabbinic Judaism wished to hold on to its adherents and gain others, it had to use all the tactics at its disposal. Some of these tactics were quite noble and included the wide dissemination of learning and the establishment of significant student circles and schools. Others included political action like co-optation of popular institutions and various degrees of accommodation with the Roman colonial government. But in the battle for supremacy, propaganda of the sort found in the Palestinian Rashbi story played a crucial role. With neither stable political power nor unchallenged hegemony over Palestinian Jewry's religious life, the claim that the rabbinic Sages' teachings had divine backing complete with sanctions and rewards was a persuasive argument for accepting rabbinic authority. The story of Rashbi demonstrated the supernatural powers that God bestowed upon the best rabbis; its hearers could take the story's warning to heart or take their chances.

One might wonder why the Palestinian Talmud's redactors would include this cautionary tale for the masses in their own elite literature. One reason would be the Palestinian Talmud's function as reference source for rabbis. One had to know this story before one could make use of it. However, I would suggest that the story's hagiographic elements also proved useful for the socialization of the rabbinic class itself. Rabbinic coteries could use the Rashbi story to remind highly individualistic colleagues or students that fealty to the group was an important virtue. The story also offered both teachers and students the hope that if they became as learned and pious as Rashbi, they would be empowered as he was. Consequently, Rashbi's story became a rabbinic tradition worth preserving for those in the rabbinic elite as well as for those whom that elite wished to influence.[9]

---

[9] The Palestinian Talmud's Rashbi story makes its appearance in other works, mostly in collections of aggadic *midrashim*, i.e., aggadic embellishments of biblical verses. The story takes on different shades of meaning in these works depending on the verse to which it is connected. For example, if the Rashbi story is connected to Ecclesiastes 10:8, its cautionary element will predominate, while the story's gratitude theme will tend to recede. Both elements of the story will be maintained because the talmudic story circulates as a literary unit, but the verse functions almost editorially. This is an important feature of talmudic and midrashic literature that allows a single story to serve many different didactic purposes.

The Babylonian Revision

The Rashbi story appears in the Babylonian Talmud in the tractate that deals primarily with the Sabbath on folio pages 33b–34a.[10] It is considerably longer and more detailed than the Palestinian version. In order to make the story more accessible I will divide it into small units. Again, short explanatory comments will appear in parentheses within the story. Observations about the Babylonian Talmud's presentation as compared with its Palestinian counterpart will follow each unit.

The story begins *in medias res* with little focus on Rashbi. The Talmud queries, "Why is Rabbi Yehudah [bar Ilai] called 'the chief spokesman [of the Jewish people]' in all places?" The question refers to an earlier passage that referred to Rabbi Yehudah using that title. The response constitutes an introduction to the Rashbi story found only in the Babylonian Talmud.

Three rabbis sit together holding a conversation that sounds like a symposium about the Roman occupation. A fourth party, Yehudah, the son of converts, sits nearby. Rabbi Yehudah bar Ilai praises Rome as a nation that brought good agoras, bathhouses, and bridges to Palestine. His colleague, Rabbi Yose, says nothing in response. Rashbi responds acidly, "Whatever they have done, they have done for their own benefit. They made agoras to install harlots therein. The bathhouses exist only for them to pleasure themselves. And the bridges are for the purpose of collecting imposts from us." Yehudah, the son of converts, spreads their conversation about. Ultimately the Roman authorities get wind of it and decree that Rabbi Yehudah would be honored and become his people's "chief spokesman." Rabbi Yose is exiled to Sepphoris, and Rashbi is condemned to death.

The unit just summarized is a new element found only in the Babylonian Talmud. It provides an introduction which gives a more personal and powerful motive for Rashbi's flight than the one in the Palestinian Talmud. Earlier it was "the [Hadrianic] persecutions" that were directed against all Jews. Here, Roman anger is specifically directed against Rashbi, and for good reason.

As a result of the decree, Rashbi and his son flee to a house of study.

---

[10] The standard edition of the Babylonian Talmud is the Vilna edition, published by the Romm family between 1880 and 1886. All subsequent printings have been based on this edition. Its pagination serves as the standard form of page reference for the Babylonian Talmud.

Each day Rashbi's wife provides her husband and son with bread and water. When the Romans are on the verge of discovering them, Rashbi says to his son, "Women are weak [literally, "light minded"]. Perhaps they will torture her [your mother] and she will reveal us."

They flee again and hide in a cave and a miracle occurs: a carob tree and a spring are created for them. Once they settle in the cave, they establish a routine. They disrobe, sit [buried] up to their necks in sand [for modesty's sake], and study [Torah] all day. At the [three daily] times of prayer, they dress and pray. After their prayers, they take their clothing off again in order to preserve it. This routine continues for twelve years.

After the twelve years, Elijah, the prophet, comes to the cave's entrance and says, "Who shall inform Rashbi that the emperor has died and his decree has been annulled?" On hearing this, Rashbi and his son exit the cave. They see people plowing and sowing, and they say, "These people put aside life eternal and engage in these ephemeral pursuits?!" Everywhere they look burns up. A heavenly voice upbraids them: "Have you exited [the cave] to destroy My world? Return to your cave!"

They return and live in the cave for twelve more months. After that period they conclude, "Even the punishment of the wicked in Gehenna lasts only twelve months." Once they recognize the error of their ways, a heavenly voice commands, "Leave your cave!" Rabbi El'azar, Rashbi's son, still destroys what he gazes at, but Rashbi repairs the destruction. Finally, he says to his son, "My son, you and I are sufficient for the world [as regards total dedication to Torah study]."[11]

On that sabbath's eve they see an old man running at twilight carrying two bunches of myrtle. They ask him what the myrtle is for, and the old man tells them, "For honoring the sabbath." When they ask why he needs two bunches when one would suffice, the old man replies, "One corresponds to [the sabbath commandment in Exodus 20:7 that says,] 'Remember [the sabbath day],' and the other to [the sabbath commandment in Deuteronomy 5:11 that

---

[11] Rashi, the eleventh-century Talmudic exegete par excellence, explains this difficult phrase to mean, "As regards (full time) students of Torah, you and I are sufficient for the entire world" (Rashi, BT Shabbat 33b, s.v. *dai*). His Talmud Commentary is printed in the Vilna edition of the Babylonian Talmud, which has become the standard edition.

says,] 'Observe [the sabbath day].'" At which Rashbi says to his son, "See how precious the commandments are to Israel!" And both father and son's minds are put at ease.

Rabbi Pinḥas ben Ya'ir, Rashbi's son-in-law, hears about his father-in-law's return and goes out to meet him. He brings him to a bathhouse, and he massages him. He sees that Rashbi's skin is filled with cuts, and he begins to weep. One of his tears falls onto Rashbi's skin, and it causes Rashbi to cry out. Pinḥas ben Ya'ir says, "Woe is me that I see you in such a state." Rashbi replies, "Happy are you that you see me in such as state. For had you not seen me in this state, you would not have found this much learning in me."[12] For at the outset [prior to his sojourns in the cave], Rashbi would pose a problem, and Rabbi Pinḥas ben Ya'ir would respond with twelve solutions. But in the end, Rabbi Pinḥas ben Ya'ir would pose a problem, and Rashbi would furnish twenty-four solutions.

Up to this point in the Babylonian Talmud retelling of the Rashbi story the only similarities to the Palestinian version are the flight to a cave and an oblique reference in the Babylonian Talmud to a carob diet. In the Palestinian version, carobs were supplemented with dates. The Babylonian Talmud stands alone in the following details: 1) an initial flight to a rabbinic house of study and the presence of Rashbi's wife; 2) the miracles in the cave; 3) details of Rashbi's and his son's mode of living in the cave; 4) details about the exit from the cave and the destruction caused by Rashbi and his son; 5) a second sojourn in the cave and exit from it; 6) the sabbath's eve encounter with the old man; 7) Pinḥas ben Ya'ir's ministrations to his father-in-law and the latter's growth in Torah learning due to his sojourn in the cave. The continuation, however, shows that the Babylonian Talmud's redactors had some Palestinian version of the Rashbi story available to them.

Rashbi says, "Since a miracle has occurred for me, let me go and improve something [for the community]." As it is written [Genesis 33:18], "And Jacob returned whole [or: to Shalem]."

(Rav said, "[This means] whole in body, wealth, and Torah learning.")

---

[12] My translation of Rashbi's reply to his son-in-law is based on Ch. N. Bialik and Yehoshua H. Ravnitzky, *The Book of Legends*, trans. William G. Braude (New York: Schocken Books, 1992), 250.

"And he encamped before the city."

(Rav said [based on a pun on the Hebrew, *vayihan*, "he encamped," being read as *vayahen*, "he graced or beautified the face of the city"], "Jacob organized a money system for them." Samuel said, "He established market-places [agoras] for them." Rabbi Yoḥanan said, "He established bathhouses for them.")[13]

He asks, "Is there something [in this unspecified locale] that needs repair?" The townspeople say to him, "There is an area where there is a suspicion of ritual impurity [i.e., a suspected graveyard], and it distresses those of priestly status because they are forced to circumvent it."[14] So Rashbi requests anyone who could remember a time when the problematic area had been presumed ritually clean to come forward. An old man, later identified as a sage, comes forward and testifies that Rabban Yohanan ben Zaqqai had cut lupines there for the priestly gifts (which had to be maintained in a state of ritual purity).[15] On the basis of this report Rashbi enters the suspect area and re-enacts Rabbi Yohanan ben Zaqqai's behavior. But he goes beyond that. He declares the firm ground in the area completely pure, but he marks off all the soft ground where a grave might have been dug, so that the priests can avoid it.

The old man says (derisively), "Ben Yohai has declared a graveyard pure." Rashbi replies,

> If you had not been with us and had not voted with us on this matter, what you have said would be fine. But now that you were with us and voted with us, people will say, "Even harlots make one another up [to attract their customers], so much more should scholars [help each other out]!"

Rashbi stares at the old man and he dies. Rashbi then goes out to the market-place and sees Yehudah, the son of converts. He exclaims, "Is this one still in the world?" He stares at him and turns him into a pile of bones.

At this point the Babylonian Talmud parallels the Palestinian versions

---

[13] See note 7 above.

[14] Those who are *kohanim*, priestly descendants of Aaron, are forbidden to defile themselves by direct or indirect contact with a human corpse. See Lev. 21:1–3.

[15] Priestly gifts, *terumah* in Hebrew, were donations of produce made by non-priestly Israelites for the maintenance of the priesthood. The gift could be as little as 1/60 of one's purchased or raised produce or as much as 1/40. It had to be preserved in a state of ritual purity in order for the priests to use it. One who was ritually contaminated would convey ritual impurity to the produce.

in the following ways: 1) Rashbi resolves to benefit a place in gratitude. Unlike the Palestinian tradition which represents Rashbi as grateful for the recovery of his health, the Babylonian Talmud represents Rashbi as thankful for the miracles performed for him and for his rescue from the Romans; 2) he does his beneficent work in imitation of Jacob; 3) the Babylonian Talmud appends midrashic interpretations to the Genesis 33:18 citation, as the oldest Palestinian sources do. In later Palestinian formulations the interpretations are incorporated into Rashbi's resolution; 4) the benefit Rashbi decides to bequeath to the city, always Tiberias in the Palestinian story, but unnamed in the Babylonian Talmud, is purification of a suspected graveyard; 5) this act is criticized derisively by a scribe in the Palestinian versions, and an old man who is part of the rabbinic elite in the Babylonian Talmud; 6) Rashbi stares at the story's malefactors thereby causing their death.

Still, the Babylonian presentation differs significantly from the Palestinian Talmud in its description of the purification process and in the way the story concludes. In the Palestinian story, Rashbi handles the purification by himself in miraculous fashion. In the Babylonian Talmud an old man, who is a sage, reports the suspected graveyard's former state of purity, and Rashbi decides the issue in a non-miraculous, typically rabbinic legal fashion. While Rashbi kills his critics in both the Babylonian and Palestinian stories, in the Babylonian Talmud he kills the old man because the latter withdrew his support from a fellow scholar. The death of Yehudah, the son of converts, is not part of the Palestinian story at all; he appears here to receive his punishment for causing Rashbi's tribulations. Both versions of the story, however, include Rashbi's execution of two parties.[16]

What prompted the Babylonian Talmud to rewrite and, thereby, reinterpret the Palestinian original? The answer lies in some rabbinic sages' idolization of Torah study.[17] For example, a talmudic report about Rabbi Akiba (ca. 120) says he held the opinion that the study of the Torah

---

[16] This explains why the Babylonian Talmud story's ending, unlike that of the Palestinian Talmud, is primarily a story about rabbis using or withholding their rabbinic knowledge or influence. The Babylonian Talmud's Rashbi tale is not about frightening the Jewish masses into support of rabbis and their views. It is about how rabbinic usefulness and responsiveness to Jewish communal needs promote the rabbinic class's continued existence, and how the converse contributes to its demise.

[17] Ephraim Urbach, *The Sages: Their Concepts and Beliefs* (Jerusalem: Magnes Press, 1975), 606; 608–9; 611–13.

outweighed actual practice of its commandments.[18] His students, Rabbi Meir and Rashbi, both suggested that one should study Torah to the exclusion of all other occupations.[19] Later statements of this ideology like "Torah study outweighs honoring parents," or "Torah study outweighs saving lives,"[20] become even more extreme. While the talmudic tradition includes the record of strong opposition to these views, they always threatened to dominate the rabbinic movement.

In the early generations of talmudic teachers called *amoraim* (ca. 250) a legal basis for extreme behavior surfaced. An unchallenged mishnaic ruling attributed to Rabbi Eliezer (ca. 90 CE) declared that students may leave for thirty days of annual study without asking their wives' permission.[21] Rabbi Ada bar Ahava, citing his teacher, Rav, asserted that the Mishnah's attribution of this rule to a single sage meant that the majority disagreed and permitted students to leave their wives for two or three years without permission. By the fourth amoraic generation a major rabbinic figure, Rava (ca. 340), reported that this was what students did, and his statement seems to indicate that their behavior determined normative Jewish law.[22]

Furthermore, the rabbinic class amassed privileges that others were denied. Members of this class had their lawsuits heard before others' cases, were freed from tax obligations and municipal duties, were served before others in the markets, and could sell their wares exempt from taxes in order to gain higher profits and market their merchandise more swiftly.[23]

---

[18] BT Kiddushin 40b.

[19] Mishnah, Tractate Avot 4:8 and Midrash Tannaim, Deuteronomy 11:14.

[20] BT Megillah 17b.

[21] Mishnah, Tractate Ketubot, 5:6. Tractate Ketubot deals with the contractual aspects of marriage in Jewish law. One of the husband's obligations is to provide his wife with sexual intimacy at her discretion. Therefore, under normal circumstances, a wife would have to approve her husband's absence. If a woman knowingly married someone whose profession demanded his regular absence, that absence was an understood condition of the marital contract. A student's "profession" might call him away for special thirty-day study sessions.

[22] This is the plain meaning of Rava's statement in BT Ketubot 62b. Rashi, however, interprets Rava differently in order to make his report of student behavior flow smoothly into a cautionary tale added by a later editor (Rashi ad loc., s.v. *benafshaiho*). The story is presented as if it was a case proving Rava's point. Because it demonstrates that students who forsake their wives do so at the risk of their lives, it subverts the original meaning of Rava's remark. Similarly, the Rashbi story overturns Rashbi's position on Torah study's supremacy over all other activities.

[23] See BT Nedarim 62a–b; Baba Batra 22a; and Baba Mezi'a 65a for the Talmudic sources of these privileges.

These advantages existed ostensibly to honor the sages and their students, but they also gave the rabbinic elite more time for what it had determined was its essential task: study.

It is not surprising that the rabbinic class became progressively more distanced from the "common" people they were originally supposed to teach and serve. Nor is it surprising that their subversion (perversion?) of Jewish values like normal family life and practical observance of the Torah's commandments estranged them from their fellow Jews. Finally, the privileges this class accrued might have been acceptable if there was a reciprocal return to the community that supported them; but it appears that the rabbinic class identified more with its own Torah study than with those who needed the Torah's guidance. All these sources of friction doubtlessly led to envy, anger, and hatred directed at those who had chosen the path of "Torah study only."

Babylonian Jewry in the late amoraic period did not have contending Judaisms from which to choose. The Sassanid Persian government granted autonomy to the Jewish community, and the rabbinic community played the political game skillfully enough to ensure that Jewish communal officials were either rabbis or parties closely aligned with them. Thus, Babylonian Jewry's law was the Torah according to rabbinic interpretation, and that arrangement had the full backing of the Persian government. If, however, the rabbinic class alienated the Jewish community it was supposed to lead, then its usefulness ended for both the Persian government and the Jews. This story and others like it were cautionary and hortatory tales warning that if Torah study did not contribute to real life, it would kill its students and the Jewish community with them.[24] And who could better embody the reform the rabbinic class had to undertake than a rabbinic hero like Rashbi who moderated his wellknown views on the absolute primacy of Torah study and proceeded to help the community?

The moment must have been critical for the rabbinic movement and its continued success, and failure to reorient rabbinic attitudes in a more humane direction might have meant the end of the rabbinic enterprise. It appears that insightful rabbinic storytellers were important participants in the reformation and renewal of rabbinic Judaism. Their form of "public relations" carried out both as critique and defense of rabbinic Judaism

---

[24] BT Yoma 82b cites the following midrashic comment: Rabbi Joshua ben Levi said, "This is the Torah that Moses placed (*sam*) before the children of Israel" (Deut. 4:44)—If a person is meritorious, the Torah becomes an elixir of life (*sam hayyim*). If not, it becomes poison (*sam mavet*).

proved successful in their time. That success made it possible for rabbinic Judaism to become what most Jews and non-Jews considered "normative" Judaism for centuries after. From that Judaism, all modern Judaisms descend.

Medieval Commentaries

Medieval commentary on the Babylonian Talmud began in Iraq in what is called the Gaonic period, around 750–1010. It reached its first peak in the eleventh century when Rabbi Solomon bar Isaac of Troyes (1040–1106), better known by the acronym Rashi, composed a line-by-line talmudic commentary. In order to fully appreciate Rashi's work, we must recognize that he received an intensive rabbinic education in Mainz (Mayence), the seat of the foremost rabbinic academy of his time. But he did not settle in Mainz. Rather, he returned to Troyes, a major trade center in the Champagne. Beryl Smalley describes the world Rashi was part of:

> The Jews of northern France in the twelfth century lived on generally friendly terms with their Christian neighbors. They were neither shut into ghettoes nor restricted to shopkeeping and money-lending, but scattered among the towns and villages in small communities, engaging sometimes in such "country" pursuits as vine-growing and horse-coping. The works of the north French rabbis show us typically French, prosperous middle class people, who keep a rich table, set prudent limits to their families ... lead respectable lives and practice their religion, are not intolerant and seldom saintly.[25]

The responses to questions of Jewish civil law addressed to Rashi and his predecessors show this description to be accurate. It is clear from those responsa that Jews and Christians—sometimes clergymen—formed business partnerships, were involved in joint investment ventures, and shared the tasks of wine and flour production as employers or employees. These images run contrary to prevailing Jewish "lachrymose" histories of the medieval period, which is assumed to have been one long era of degradation and pogroms. Yet, the period of the sixth through thirteenth centuries is one in which Jews live freely in towns and cities and intermar-

---

[25] Beryl Smalley, *The Study of the Bible in the Middle Ages* (Oxford: Oxford University Press, 1941), 149–50.

riages and voluntary conversions from one faith to another occur.[26]

In light of this, one of Rashi's comments on the Rashbi story becomes more understandable.[27] While most of his comments are philological, one is dedicated to the behavior of Yehudah, the converts' son. Rashi seems to be interested in the question of whether or not Yehudah betrayed the rabbis by reporting their various attitudes about the Roman presence in Palestine to the Roman colonial authorities. Rashi negates this possibility and exonerates Yehudah: Yehudah passed on their conversation to other students, perhaps as important teachings, or to his parents, without intending it to go further; eventually the sages' opinions reached Roman ears.

Traditionally, the student of Rashi's commentary is asked to ponder what prompted Rashi's interpretation. No doubt the Talmud's passive formulation, "[A]nd their [the rabbis'] words were heard by the Romans," influenced Rashi's view that no one actively betrayed the rabbis. But I believe that Rashi may also have wanted to parry the propensity of some Jewish readers to count Yehudah's non-Jewish ancestry against him, and in that way to influence those readers' attitudes towards contemporary converts to Judaism as well. As we have seen, converts were not uncommon in Rashi's world, and Rashi may have wished to impress upon his readers that the converts in their midst were, like Yehudah, often deeply attached to contemporary sages and loyal to the Jewish community. Sometimes, however, converts blundered because they had not yet fully assimilated Jewish culture and practice. That being the case, Jews were obliged by talmudic law to refrain from embarrassing these recent arrivals to Judaism about their past adherence to convictions and behaviors abhorrent to Jews,[28] and to treat them with trust, respect, acceptance, and support for their commitment.[29] Jews who behaved thus helped these

---

[26] Louis Rabinowitz, *The Social Life of the Jews of Northern France,* 2nd ed. (New York: Hermon Press, 1972), 103–9. Concerns about intermarriage between Christians and Jews were expressed in the canons of Elvira (313), Meaux, and Paris (845 and 846). As late as the thirteenth century, despite the increased segregation of Jews from Christians, rabbinic responsa and reports show that Jews willingly married non-Jews. Rabbi Moses of Coucy, a thirteenth-century Tosafist who moved to Spain, states that intermarriage was rife there.

[27] Rashi, BT Shabbat 33a, s.v. *siper divrehem.*

[28] Mishnah, Tractate Baba Mezi'a, 4:10.

[29] Rabinowitz, *Social Life,* 107–9. The last case discussed by Rabinowitz is reported in a responsum of Rabbi Joel bar Isaac of Bonn (eleventh century). Rabbi Joel describes a convert whose burning desire to study the Pentateuch led him to use a Latin translation by monks. Rabbi Joel upbraided him for using the monks' translation, and the convert promised to desist, even though the Rabbis of Speyers had given him such books to copy. This is certainly indicative of his will to follow

converts to integrate themselves into the Jewish community and thereby "remain under the wings of God's presence."

§ § §

Rashi's grandchildren and those who followed their method of talmudic analysis and commentary generated the final peak of medieval talmudic commentary. They were called in Hebrew *ba'alei hatosafot*, the "masters of additional commentary," or the Tosafists, and their school of interpretation began in the twelfth century in France and Germany and waned by the early fifteenth. Rashi had dealt with the Talmud as an entity made up of individual units of discussion (*sugyot*), and he provided each unit with a line-by-line commentary. The Tosafists distinguished themselves from Rashi by viewing the entire Talmud as a unit. They assumed that the Talmud was a well-edited and redacted work and, as such, should be consistent.[30] But the Tosafists recognized that there were inconsistencies between *sugyot*, often found in different talmudic tractates, and they sought to resolve them. Resolution of contradictions, improvements on Rashi's commentary, and textual criticism of the Talmud became the chief tosafistic activities.

Ephraim Urbach, whose study of the Tosafists, *Ba'alei ha-Tosafot*, is a classic, recognizes that Jews and Christians worked together not only in economic endeavors, but in intellectual ones as well.[31] In the realm of biblical textual criticism and interpretation this is well known, though it is the contribution of the Jews to that scholarship that tends to be emphasized.[32] But Jews did more than unilaterally contribute to medieval Christian biblical scholarship. They participated in a process of cultural cross-fertilization that was inevitable in an intellectual environment which engaged Jewish and Christian participants. Talmudists, who were mainly concerned with law, appear to have become familiar with the work of Christian glossators who were creating commentaries to the *Corpus iuris*.[33]

---

loyally what his teachers decided was proper. Rabbi Joel also speaks of the convert as "someone seeking to learn 'the Book' and the holy tongue [Hebrew]." The convert also raised the question of whether the Wurzburg community had acted properly when it prohibited him from acting as a prayer leader. Rabbi Joel opined that according to Jewish law the Wurzburg community was completely in the wrong. The convert's last question indicates exactly why Rashi may have had to commend converts.

[30] The traditional view about the Talmud's redaction was that it was essentially the work of two sixth-century rabbis, Rabbi Ashi and Ravina.

[31] Ephraim E. Urbach, *Ba'alei ha-Tosafot* (Jerusalem: Mossad Bialik, 1955), 27.

[32] Ibid., 27; Beryl Smalley, *Study of the Bible*, chapters 3 and 4.

[33] Urbach, *Ba'alei ha-Tosafot*, 27.

Glossation of Justinian's Code was begun in Bologna at the end of the eleventh century, by Guarnerius, and continued until the death of Accursius, glossator par excellence, in 1263. As the work of glossation progressed, collections of glosses (*apparati*) covering full sections of the *Corpus iuris* were organized. Accursius assembled these collections into a single work, the *Glossa ordinaria*, which displaced all other gloss collections. This did not occur in the case of the Tosafists, and we do not have a single "authoritative" collection of *Tosafot* even today. Otherwise, the contents of the *Tosafot* and those of the *Glossa ordinaria* glosses are quite similar: "The content is almost exclusively juristic; interpretation and harmonization (*solutiones contrarietatum*) of the text (*litera*), and illustrations of it."[34] Furthermore the glossators' and Tosafists' "golden ages" overlap.

Because the Tosafists, like the glossators, focused on law (halakhah), their comments on the aggadic Rashbi story are limited. Rabbi Jacob bar Meir Tam (1100–1171), one of the greatest Tosafists, directs his attention solely to Yehudah, the converts' son. He notes that there are some manuscripts which omit the honorific "Rabbi" before Yehudah's name, and he declares this omission incorrect. To prove his point, Rabbi Tam notes that in another talmudic context Rashbi himself calls Rabbi Yehudah, son of proselytes, "a man of stature," and orders his son, El'azar, to go to him and another rabbi for a blessing.[35] Such a man would not simply be called by his first name. This analysis leads Rabbi Tam to "emend" the Rashbi story's ending. The text should say that the impudent old scholar who appears at the story's end received the ignominious punishment of being turned into a pile of bones. Regarding Rabbi Yehudah, the converts' son, a rabbi respected by Rashbi, the text should say he simply died (lit., "his soul rested"), a natural, though untimely, death.

Rabbi Tam does not cite any actual manuscript tradition to substantiate his emendation, nor is there any indication that one existed.[36] This is because his interpretation is not so much a true emendation as a tosafistic harmonization of what appears, at least to Rabbi Tam, as an impossible inconsistency. Because Rabbi Tam possesses a magisterial grasp of the Talmud, he knows that the Rashbi story is the only place where a

---

[34] Hermann Kantrowitz, " Note on the Development of the Gloss to the Justinian and Canon Law," in Smalley, *Study of the Bible*, 37.

[35] BT, Tractate Mo'ed Katan 9a.

[36] The closest thing we have to a critical edition of the Talmud is a work called *Dikdukei Soferim* created by Raphael N. N. Rabbinovicz toward the end of the nineteenth century. There is no indication of an alternate manuscript tradition for the end of the Rashbi story in that work.

person named simply Yehudah, the converts' son, is mentioned, and then only in some manuscripts. This convinces him to dismiss those manuscript traditions as erroneous which, in turn, forces him to deal with the positive relationship between Rashbi and Rabbi Yehudah, the converts' son, as described in other stories about them.

Rabbi Tam's approach to the Rashbi story emerges from a totally different understanding of the formative Palestinian and Babylonian sources. The early medieval commentators did not regard the talmudic "sage stories" as fiction. Rather, for them the stories represented authentic biographical data about major Jewish teachers. That data, however, was problematic. Contradictions of factual detail, setting, action, or the characters' expressed attitudes toward persons or issues abound in manuscript variants, in different stories about the same characters, or between differing versions of a single story. Harmonization, a major tool of the non-Jewish glossators in dealing with conflicting rulings in the *Corpus iuris*, became a standard tosafistic method for dealing with any contradiction in the Talmud's legal or legendary material. Indeed, harmonization was considered so important to the Talmud's integrity and authority that even textual emendation based on reasonable conjecture was acceptable to the Tosafists.[37] In some respects, resolving conflicts in stories about the sages was more significant for the Tosafists than resolving conflicts between legal passages. Legal issues were matters of opinion; stories about sages were, for them, matters of fact.

§ § §

Rashbi plays a central role in the Jewish mystical tradition called *Kabbalah*. He is credited with revealing *Sefer ha-Zohar*, "The Book of Splendor,"[38] the principal text of Jewish mysticism, to Rabbi Moses de León, a late-thirteenth-century Castilian Jew. De León is generally recognized as the Zohar's author, and opinions about him vary considerably.[39] The Zohar's

---

[37] In his major work, *Sefer ha-Yashar*, Rabbi Tam objected strenuously to actual emendation of manuscripts, but he had no difficulty accepting proposed emendations if they were placed in talmudic commentaries. Emendation on the basis of reason and common sense is one type of emendation he discusses in *Sefer ha-Yashar*. See *Sefer ha-Yashar*, ed. Schlesinger (Jerusalem: no publisher named, 1959), 9.

[38] *Sefer ha-Zohar* is referred to in English academic works as "the Zohar," a translation of *ha-Zohar*. I follow that usage.

[39] Gershom G. Scholem, *Major Trends in Jewish Mysticism* (New York: Schocken Books, 1961, rprt. 1965), 190–204. Scholem's review of opinions about de León shows that some consider him a giant of mystical thought and spiritual enlightenment, while others deem him a very successful charlatan.

history begins in Hispanic mystical circles, centered in Castile and Gerona, from which de León drew many of his ideas.⁴⁰

De León revised the Rashbi story for his own purposes. In particular, he changed the meaning of Rashbi's sojourn in the cave.

One Zoharic presentation of Rashbi repeats aspects of the cave scene from the Babylonian Talmud's Rashbi story, but with a new preamble. The cast of characters has changed; for example, Rabbi Rehumai, a fictitious character created by de León, enters the picture.⁴¹ Rabbi Pinhas in the Zohar's version is not Rashbi's son-in-law, but rather his father-in-law. In order to provide a sense of the literary texture of the Zoharic Rashbi story, I will translate the passage.

> Rabbi Pinhas frequently spent time with Rabbi Rehumai on the coast of the Sea of Ginnosar. Rabbi Rehumai was a prominent and elderly man who had become blind. He said to Rabbi Pinhas, "Surely you have heard that our colleague Yohai [=Rashbi] has a gem. When one looks into the gem a light bright as the sun issues forth and illuminates the entire world. That light shines from heaven to earth and the world brightens until the Ancient of Days [an Aramaic synonym for God] sits properly on his throne. The light is completely contained in your home. From the light that is contained in your home a fine, small light issues and illuminates the world. You are fortunate. Go forth, my son, go forth after that gem that illuminates the world for the present hour is propitious."
>
> Rabbi Pinhas heeded Rabbi Rehumai's counsel and boarded a ship with two other men. He saw two birds flying above the sea, and he called to them requesting that they direct him to Rashbi. After awaiting some response, he commanded them again, but the birds disappeared into the sea. When Pinhas disembarked, the birds reappeared. One of them had an inscription in its mouth saying that Rashbi had left his cave with Rabbi El'azar, his son. When Rabbi Pinhas saw that Rashbi's body was covered with cracks, he

---

⁴⁰ F. Lachover and Isaiah Tishbi, *The Wisdom of the Zohar*, 2nd ed. (Jerusalem: Mossad Bialik, 1957), 1:92 (in Hebrew).

⁴¹ There are several rabbis in the Talmud named Rehumi or Rehumai, but they are all *amoraim*, sages who flourished from 220–500 CE. Rashbi is a *tanna*, a sage of the mishnaic period, who was active between 135–70 CE. No sage named Rehumi or Rehumai appears in tannaitic literature. For general information about the tannaitic and amoraic periods, see Rabbi Adin Steinsaltz, *The Talmud: The Steinsaltz Edition: Reference Guide*, 30. For information on sages named Rehumi or Rehumai, see Chanoch Albeck, *Introduction to the Talmud*, 310, 379, and 450.

wept and said, "Woe is me that I see you thus." Rashbi replied, "I am fortunate that you see me thus. For if I were not in this condition, I would not possess the knowledge I now have," and he began to expound the Torah's commandments.[42]

The story's "mystical" literary traits result from its use of grandiloquent dialogues, esoteric allusions, and narrative non sequiturs that appear to hide something from all but the initiated. The essence of this passage is that spiritual illumination dwells in Pinhas's house, meaning within his family, in the person of his son-in-law, Rashbi. Rashbi's "gem" is a form of concentrated mystical contemplation that leads to clear theosophical illumination and a proper understanding of God's relation to the world. Rashbi can teach that form of contemplation. The "fine, small light," is Rabbi El'azar, Rashbi's son and Pinhas's grandson.

Rabbi Pinhas finds his son-in-law and grandson, weeps as he did in the Babylonian Talmud version of this legend and receives the same response from Rashbi as is recorded there. Here, however, Rashbi is not escorted to a bath house for a good massage as he was in the Babylonian Talmud's version. Only his response that his poor physical condition and his learning are linked appears in the Zohar. Rashbi's response seems to indicate that his physical decay has made him spiritually free and enlightened. Having been initiated through his experience in the cave, Rashbi begins to expound upon the mystical contents of the Torah's commandments.

The social responsibility that Rashbi shows in the Babylonian Talmud version is nowhere to be found in the Zohar. He has become the teacher of a small circle of mystical seekers, and that is what makes him great as far as de León is concerned. Furthermore, the harsh characteristics of the talmudic Rashbi disappear in the Zohar's portrayal of him. Clearly, de León felt that a mystic of Rashbi's stature is better presented as a humble saint willing to endure physical deprivation for the sake of illumination than as a caustic critic of his society.

Another Zoharic passage refers to Rashbi's cave experience without going into great detail:

> It is taught: Rabbi Yose said, "From the day that Rabbi Shim'on [Rashbi] left the cave, mysteries were not concealed from the colleagues. They contemplated exalted secrets among themselves. [By

---

[42] *Sefer ha-Zohar*, Introduction, 11a–b (Jerusalem: Ma'oz Meir, 1955).

virtue of their discussions of these mysteries] they have been revealed to them [as clearly] as if they had been given at Sinai. After he died, '... the fountains of the depths and the windows of heaven were closed' [Genesis 8:2]. The colleagues discussed the mysteries, but they did not comprehend them."[43]

Again, this reference to a section of the talmudic Rashbi story implies that the cave experience was responsible for Rashbi's becoming the most notable mystic and mystical teacher of all time.

As we compare the talmudic and Zoharic Rashbi legends, we note first that the talmudic stories of Rashbi's cave experience do not portray him as someone who chooses asceticism. He deteriorates physically because he is forced to live in a cave (Palestinian Talmud) or because his intense desire to study the Torah there requires him to cover his nakedness with sand (Babylonian Talmud). Secondly, in the Babylonian Talmud's story Rashbi emerges from the cave a more capable scholar and aware person. In the Zohar, however, Rashbi emerges from his cave mystically enlightened by virtue of the deprivation he has experienced. Thus, Rashbi has been transformed from one of the greatest Jewish jurists into one of the greatest Jewish mystical teachers. Notably, the Roman authorities play no role in the Zohar's version. This is due to two factors. First, the Zohar is very distant from the historical framework and memory of the original talmudic stories. In that respect the Roman occupation government simply doesn't mean anything to de León. Second, I would propose that the Roman persecutors do not belong in the Zohar's Rashbi story because the Zohar wishes to portray Rashbi's action as self-imposed: he purposely went into seclusion in order to cling to God more intensely.[44]

Moses de León's *Sefer ha-Zohar* created a "library" which became the basis of all subsequent Jewish mystical thought.[45] That, however, is only one aspect of its impact. The other is the reconstruction of earlier Jewish myths and legends, the creation of new ones, and the rejuvenation of Jewish practice by renovation of its symbolic meaning.[46] In this respect, Jewish mysticism is part of an ongoing process within Judaism to protect

---

[43] *Sefer ha-Zohar*, 1:217a.

[44] "Clinging to God," in Hebrew *devekut*, is a central tenet of Zoharic teaching and ethics. See Scholem, *Major Trends in Jewish Mysticism*, 233–34.

[45] Lachover and Tishbi, *The Wisdom of the Zohar*, 1:40 and 44; Scholem, ibid., 244–86 and 325–50.

[46] Gershom G. Scholem, *On the Kabbalah and its Symbolism* (New York: Schocken Books, 1969; 5th printing, 1974), 96–117 and chapter 4.

itself from the reduction of its religious obligations to formal observance without spiritual content. While Maimonidean rationalism and the Tosafists' concentration on law may have satisfied the intellectual and spiritual needs of some of the Jewish elite, a yearning for a more intimate relationship with God was desired by others. This yearning generated the creation of the Zohar and its reception. Clearly, Moses de León, was a writer of great imagination and, to a certain extent, daring. He did in the late thirteenth century what nineteenth- and twentieth-century Hebrew writers would do in a more secular age, namely, resurrect the Jewish past in a completely new form. De León's radical rewriting of traditional *aggadot* went considerably beyond the more conservative rabbinic conventions of his time, and we ought to view de León's claim that Rashbi revealed the Zohar to him as an attempt to protect himself from his colleagues' censure as well as a means of increasing the Zohar's authority. We should recognize that the Zohar signals that some sectors of Jewry were beginning their emergence from what I would call the "Jewish Middle Ages." That process would take a long time and many labyrinthine turns, but the Zohar is both a marker of that process and a catalyst for further developments.

Having made this point, I would define the "Jewish Middle Ages" as the period in which rabbinic Judaism was the official culture of Jewry. Implicitly this means that Jews would, generally speaking, behave and think in certain ways. Talmudic law with its application to the realities of Jewish communal and personal life would be the publicly acknowledged standard of behavior during the Jewish Middle Ages. In that respect, the Jewish Middle Ages ended in some Eastern European and Middle Eastern locales only with the Second World War or the founding of the State of Israel. Intellectually and theologically, rabbinic views of history were central to "Jewish medieval" ideas. Thus, dispersion and suffering were regarded by Jews as just punishment for Israel's sins or as necessary preparatory afflictions that would lead to redemption. Either way, the Jewish people would have to suffer until their sins were expiated or until the Messiah came.

The Jewish mysticism that emerged from the Zohar would change both Jewish religious behavior and thought. In the case of observance, new rites and liturgies would develop.[47] In the realm of thought the belief

---

[47] Ibid., 135–46. Among these rites were more elaborate Sabbath meals, especially the last meal before the Sabbath's end, in which yearning for redemption was a central element of new table songs created for the event. Committed mystics also viewed the world around them as microcosmic revelations of the interactions within

that Jews could affect their own fate by mystical theurgic practices would change the Jewish people's sense of its own power, though initially with catastrophic and tragic communal consequences.[48] Nevertheless, the notion of any possibility of self-determination (ironically with God's help, of course) was a sea-change in Jewish self-understanding. Ultimately it would be a demythologized and secular political form of this self-understanding that led to Zionism and the establishment of the third Jewish commonwealth after almost two millennia of diaspora life; but the dream of self-redemption began with the popularization of mysticism that the Zohar inaugurated.

Early Modern Rashbi

Rashi and the Tosafists atomized the talmudic story by glossing it, and later talmudic commentators would do the same, though with different emphases. One of the most famous is Rabbi Judah Loew bar Bezalel of Prague (1512? or 1526?–1609). He is mostly associated with Prague where he served as the head of a yeshiva called *Die Klaus* (1573–84); but he also was *Landesrabbiner* (chief rabbi) of Moravia twice in his lifetime (1553–73; 1584–88), and the rabbi of Posen for a time as well. He died in Prague where, towards the end of his life, he held the office of chief rabbi.

I have listed Loew's rabbinic positions because the locales he served tell

---

the Godhead and felt empowered to help the best of those processes along. For example, the left side of one's body was considered analogous to God's attribute of strict justice; the right side was analogous to God's grace. An act like putting one's right shoe on first strengthened the power of God's grace; putting the left shoe on second, then tying it before the right shoe, bound in the force of God's strict justice. The mystic also used *kavvanot*, liturgical statements of mystical intention, to accomplish theurgic ends, when he or she performed a commandment. Further, the set canon of Jewish prayer ultimately changed to include mystical prayers, and in one case a full service called *kabbalat shabbat*, the welcoming of the Sabbath, was added into the traditional Ashkenazic and Sephardic prayerbooks.

[48] Scholem, *Major Trends in Jewish Mysticism*, 286–324. Scholem describes the mystical roots of several false messianic movements which wreaked communal and emotional havoc on major Jewish communities. The best-known pseudo-messiah of the seventeenth and eighteenth centuries is Sabbatai Zevi (1626–76), a remarkable Turkish Jew who convinced Jews worldwide that he was the messiah. His career ended in his conversion to Islam in Turkey in 1666. Jacob Leibovic (d. 1791), called Jacob Frank by the remnant of Sabbatai Zevi's Turkish followers, claimed he was the reincarnation of Zevi. His attempts to win over large sectors of the Jewish community were met with strong communal opposition. In the end, he and his few followers converted to Christianity. When political circumstances allowed, Frank continued to proclaim himself messiah even after his conversion. His daughter, Eve, continued proclaiming him the savior until 1817.

us a great deal about the two cultures he lived in: the culture of rabbinic Judaism and the culture of Prague. Prague began to be a major trade center in the thirteenth century, and by the fifteenth century it was the second largest city in Europe. Inevitably the wealth centered in Prague made it possible for it to be a Renaissance city. It was also a bastion of early church reformation in the form of the Hussite movement, and the seat of Czech nationalism. These cultural currents flowed from Prague to the rest of Bohemia and Moravia, and Judah Loew could not have avoided their impact, even if he had wished to.

Loew is best known for the legend that grew around him: the story of the Golem.[49] His real significance, however, is in the originality of his thought. Characterized by a synthesis of talmudic, kabbalistic, and classical philosophic knowledge with Renaissance secular learning and sensibilities, Loew's many commentaries on aggadah are unique.[50] A taste of this synthesis appears in Loew's comments on aspects of the Rashbi legend found in his *Hiddushei Aggadot*, or novellae on the Talmud's aggadah.[51]

Loew comments on the Babylonian Talmud's description of Rashbi's second exit from the cave. In that instance Rabbi El'azar, Rashbi's son, destroys whatever he looks at, just as he did when the two emerged the first time. This time, however, Rashbi heals whatever his son damages. Loew comments, "This is because mercy is a quality found among those who are mature more than among youths who possess [a stronger sense of] strict justice." Loew seems to know well the natural tendency of youth

---

[49] A *golem* is, according to kabbalistic belief and popular Jewish legend, a human-like form made out of the basic elements of creation, earth and water, and brought to life either by incantations or by insertion of the Tetragrammaton or other names of God into the form. The popular story of Loew's *golem* was that he was created to protect the Jewish community from its enemies and from blood libels.

[50] Loew's secular knowledge is evident from his works, and he was quite aware of the problems that Renaissance advances in the natural sciences caused for the talmudic tradition. Loew confronted those issues very directly in the sixth chapter of his defense of the Talmud's wisdom, *Be'er ha-Golah*, showing himself to be learned in the natural sciences and adept at religious thought. Loew had a living connection to the Renaissance culture of Prague through his relationship with the Danish astronomer, Tycho Brahe, who had been invited by Emperor Rudolph II to Prague to carry on his research there. Brahe compiled the greatest amount of astronomical information available prior to the invention of the telescope. Loew's and Brahe's shared interest in astronomy and mathematics was probably the catalyst for their friendship. In 1592 Loew met with Rudolph II, and some suggest that it was Brahe who arranged the audience. The meeting itself is testimony to Loew's prominence and involvement in his society.

[51] Rabbi Judah Loew bar Bezalel, *Sefer Hiddushei Aggadot Maharal Mi-Prague Zatzal* (London: L. Honig & Sons, 1960).

towards an idealism and perfectionism that older people have left behind in favor of a stable and useful realism. He also recognizes that the adult's position need not be either cynical or resigned, but may be one of compassionate understanding of what is possible and appropriate in a world that is good but imperfect. Thus, Loew begins to capture psychological undercurrents in the Rashbi story and a sense of the inner change Rashbi has undergone. This is a new approach in talmudic commentary. For the first time, we see attention paid to the inner life and motives of characters: a significant step toward a modern literary approach because it grants selfhood and distinct personality to the dramatis personae. Here, the impact of capitalism and humanism are quite clear: the individual has emerged as an independently significant entity, not merely a part of a class or estate. Loew, a strong individualist in his own right, interprets Rashbi and his son accordingly.[52]

Prague's influence on Loew is also evident in his comments on an excursus within the Rashbi story. Loew uses the talmudic material to analyze what makes a city excellent. He concludes that it is the city's ability to provide fully for its citizens' social and physical needs and desires that is the benchmark of its greatness. The city in Loew's comments is symbolic of the state. In Loew's case the symbol matched the reality: what happened in Prague shaped what happened throughout Bohemia and Moravia.

In the Babylonian Talmud Rashbi emulates Jacob's actions. Having escaped the dangers posed by his father-in-law, Laban, Jacob returns whole and, according to the midrashic rendering of Genesis 33:18, he decides to benefit the city before which he encamped. Three rabbis argue what he did. One says he created a monetary system. Another claims that

---

[52] Loew's individualism is evident in his literary style and expression which are unprecedented in either the literature of talmudic commentary or Jewish philosophical works. Even now there is unresolved academic debate as to whether he was primarily an adherent of philosophical or kabbalistic thinking. A contributing factor to this debate is Loew's assigning new meanings that express his personal views to older philosophical terms. Further, Loew argued for a reformation of Jewish education that would be consonant with the learner's capabilities from one stage of life to another. His suggestions flew in the face of his contemporaries' practice of teaching children the Talmud before they reached the stage where they could possibly understand its intricacies. Loew's curriculum, modeled on the Mishnah's (Tractate Avot 5:21), took the student gradually from the easiest subjects to the most difficult according to their age and level of development. Similarly, Loew's conception of how to decide questions of Jewish law was almost idiosyncratic compared to that of most of his colleagues: seek answers directly from the Talmud using "normative" halakhic codes sparingly; *Netivot ha-'Olam, Netiv ha-Torah*, ch. 15 (London: L. Honig & Sons, 1961).

Jacob created market-places. Yet another states that he provided the city with bathhouses. In the Babylonian Talmud these were three discrete opinions, but Loew interprets these views in cumulative fashion: Jacob provided all three benefits to the city, each of which represents aspects of a well-ordered society. A monetary system exemplifies social contract or *ius civilis*, because people have agreed on a symbol of value.

Market-places provide nourishment, clothing, and luxuries. But markets are not natural institutions, though they serve universal human needs that Roman legal classification called *ius naturale*. Certain aspects of the market-place are determined by social contract: hours, prices, etc. Thus, market-places symbolize those societal institutions that stand midway between social contract (*ius civilis*) and natural law (*ius naturale*). Jacob helped the city organize establishments based on nearly socially contractual custom.

Lastly, bathhouses are, for Loew, a matter of natural law. It is universal human nature, and the nature of all living creatures, to protect their bodies and to want to feel comfortable. Bathing achieves these objectives; hence, bathhouses represent societal institutions that emerge from the strictly natural needs or desires of human beings. Thus, Jacob helped the city become a well-ordered society. Rashbi, in imitation of Jacob, vows to restore proper (Jewish) order to a city as a celebration of his miraculous escape from the perils of Roman persecution.

Loew's point is larger than an essay on classical law's categorization of institutions. Jacob symbolizes the kind of Renaissance civic leadership that had changed medieval cities from communes into significant political and economic entities. In Loew's portrayal, Jacob is a biblical Cosimo de Medici: a self-made man, somewhat of an outsider because he was not a nobleman or directly involved in city politics, yet determinative of the culture of "the city before which he encamped." Loew's claim is that Jewry, symbolized by Jacob, had always had a salutary influence on emerging societies, and wherever Jews were welcomed they contributed positively to their hosts' economic and cultural success. His essay exhorts his community to continue to fulfill the biblical promise that Jacob's seed would be a source of blessing (Genesis 28:14) and "a light to the nations" (Isaiah 42:6).

Modern Approaches to the Rashbi Story

The French Revolution swept away not only the last vestiges of French medieval societal organization and its ideology but the local forms of medieval Jewish communal structure as well. Jews were given citizenship in 1791, though the full rights that went with this grant were withheld until

Napoleon's reign. Nevertheless, this period ushers in what is known in modern Jewish sources as the Emancipation. The new France, however, exacted a price for its benefaction. As a quid pro quo the Jewish community was expected to relinquish its sense of separate religio-national identity along with its traditional autonomy.[53] As Jewry accepted these terms, the relationship with what had previously been a foreign culture underwent radical transformation.

The fragile beginnings of an intellectual movement called Jewish Enlightenment began even before the Emancipation.[54] Jewish thinkers intuited what the implications of European liberalism would be for the Jewish community, and they began to prepare and press for realization of those implications. They also knew that Jewry would have to change in order to accommodate its new reality. Therefore they began to carry out a two-pronged program which they believed would revolutionize Jewish life. On one hand they sought to reform and "Westernize" traditional Jewish behavior, language, and cultural interests. On the other they endeavored to preserve a distinct Jewish identity. This was consonant with their understanding that Jewish Enlightenment meant a break with past suffering, degradation, and cultural deprivation, but not a break with Judaism. Difficult, confusing, and problematic as it is at times, this program continues in many ways to inform contemporary Jewish life.

Part of the program of the Enlightenment included the academic study of Judaism and the Jewish past. This was meant to buttress Jewish pride and self-esteem as Jews entered a world which simultaneously welcomed and reviled them. Not surprisingly, the earliest forays into the field turned out to be as much apologetic (in every sense of the word) as academic. Nevertheless they laid the groundwork for what would become the academically credible study of Judaism and Jewry by both Jews and Christians. As Jewish modernity continued along its path, German and French Jewry created what became known as *die Wissenschaft des Judentums* and *les études juives* respectively. History took a pre-eminent place within Jewish studies because it claimed to preserve specific Jewish memory while demonstrating that Jewish life had changed from era to era. Therefore, Jewish history

---

[53] In 1806, the Assembly of Jewish Notables, a group of French Jews convened by Napoleon, declared "The Jews are no longer a nation." This position, contrary to traditional Jewish self-understanding, had not been fully espoused despite France's grant of citizenship. The Assembly forfeited the traditional sense of *umah*, Jewish nationhood, and limited Jewish identity to a religious conviction.

[54] The Jewish Enlightenment movement is considered to begin with Moses Mendelssohn (1729–86).

could serve to show that it was possible to remain faithful to and proud of one's Jewish past while enjoying the benefits of the emancipated present.

The first significant modern Jewish historian, Heinrich Graetz (1817–91), provides us with a good example of how Rashbi's "biography" served Enlightenment and Emancipation objectives:

> Simon ben Jochai of Galilee was as striking but not so manysided a personage ... and he was falsely reported to be a worker of miracles—a mystic and a Cabbalist.... In opposition to his father, Jochai, who stood in favor with the Roman authorities, the son was a decided enemy of Rome, and was not much liked by them. For uttering a truthful censure on the Roman Governor, he was sentenced to death, and could save himself only by flight, and upon this fact legend has seized in order to surround Shim'on with wonders and miracles. Amongst the various legal decisions, sayings and remarks which have been preserved of him there is no trace of a mystical tendency.[55]

Notice Graetz's selectivity and emphases. As an enlightened German Jew, Graetz was culturally also a German rationalist. Therefore, in Graetz's "historical" retelling of the Rashbi story, miracles are omitted and there is a firm denial that Rashbi was a miracle worker or mystic. Graetz also depicts Rashbi as a brave man who uttered "a truthful censure on the Roman governor." In that way Rashbi could embody the liberal view that free speech was a value for which one might even sacrifice one's life. Finally, it is hard not to notice that Graetz shifts Rashbi's censure of Rome, a part of the original Babylonian Talmud version, to a censure of "a Roman governor." This may be part of an apologia regarding Jewish loyalty to legitimate governments, which was an issue constantly raised by anti-Semites in order to impede Jewish progress toward full acceptance in society. Graetz's rewriting of the Rashbi tale might imply that Jews are loyal to the state but, like all good citizens, critical of unfair officials and their illegitimate practices.

I have analyzed Graetz and his agenda because he is a seminal figure in Jewish historiography. He laid the methodological foundations and standards followed by subsequent Jewish historians, who approached talmudic aggadah much as he did. Given talmudic stories' didacticism, it becomes difficult to know whether the talmudic sages had any interest in historiography when they wrote.[56] Further, the mixture of "reasonable" and "fan-

---

[55] Heinrich Graetz, *History of the Jews* (Philadelphia: Jewish Publication Society, 1894), 440–41.

[56] Yosef Hayyim Yerushalmi, *Zakhor: Jewish Memory and Jewish History* (Phila-

tastic" elements in most talmudic stories tends to contaminate them as historical records and makes it impossible to know whether they include even a kernel of historical truth. Nevertheless, into the mid-twentieth century Jewish historians still used the Talmuds' Rashbi stories as essentially accurate historical statements about him and his era.[57] It is only recently that an approach that recognizes aggadah as a literary art form has persuaded historians that talmudic lore is usable historical material only when external witnesses support its historical content.

§ § §

The civil rights movement of the 1960s and 1970s in the United States raised American consciousness about African-American ethnicity, history, and culture and their contributions to American society. It was not long after that Black studies programs became part of the curricula of American universities and soon became a source of knowledge and pride for the African-American community and a source of information to others about a marginalized ethnic group. Other ethnic minorities in America began to realize that their story, including the part about their contributions to American life and culture, had not been told, at least not fully. Leaders of those minorities recognized that the cost in pride, preservation of important aspects of their group's culture, and sympathetic understanding on the part of others was similar to that paid by the African-American community. Inspired by the success of Black studies programs, Jewish individuals and groups began to provide funds to colleges and universities willing to open Jewish studies programs. Many Jewish students also re-evaluated the meaning of their Jewishness by virtue of their connection to the civil rights movement. Further, Israel's victory in the 1967 Six Day War became a major source of pride and questioning because it reversed the sense of many young Jews that Jewishness meant a victim identity.[58] Young Amer-

---

delphia: Jewish Publication Society, 1982), 18–22, especially 18 n19. For an alternative view see Amos Funkenstein, *Perceptions of Jewish History* (Berkeley and Los Angeles: University of California Press, 1993), 10; 15–20.

[57] Similar use of the Rashbi story has been made by noted Israeli historians and American Jewish historians. See Gedaliah Alon, *The Jews in their Land in the Talmudic Age* (Cambridge: Harvard University Press, 1989), 546; M. Avi-Yonah, *The Jews Under Roman and Byzantine Rule* (Jerusalem: Magnes Press, Hebrew Univerity, 1984), 15; Salo W. Baron, *A Social and Religious History of the Jews* (New York: Columbia University Press, 1952–83). In Baron's index, Baron describes the Rashbi story as a legend (2:485, s.v. Simon bar Yohai). Nevertheless, Baron speaks of Rashbi as a zealot, a portrayal that depends on the Babylonian Talmud's version of the Rashbi story (2:96 and especially 2:265).

[58] It is not coincidental that the Association for Jewish Studies, the professional

ican Jews who flocked to Israel in that period often remained there. Those who returned to the United States came back with a desire to know more about Judaism and Jewish identity. Jewish studies now had more than institutional infrastructures; it had students. Today hundreds of academic institutions house Jewish studies programs of distinction. The more Jewish studies have become a commonplace in the American academy, the more they have adopted the contemporary academy's tendency toward an interdisciplinary approach to subjects. I will, therefore, conclude this comparative study with my own reading of the Rashbi story using a contemporary method of literary analysis. The major aim of this analysis is to show how the story's literary form and content support its teachings: how art supports talmudic didacticism.[59]

§ § §

At the beginning of the story, three rabbis discuss Roman contributions to the Land of Israel. Rashbi alone dismisses all Rome's works as evil: agoras are for prostitution; bathhouses are for selfish pleasure; bridges and good roads are for taking imposts from the Jewish population. A hanger-on is present: Yehudah, son of proselytes. His name indicates strong Jewishness, but his immediate ancestry signals recent connection to a non-Jewish ethos and culture. Symbolically, he represents an internally divided personality. He listens to the rabbis' conversation and spreads its contents around until it reaches Roman ears. Consequently, Rashbi is sentenced to death for his disloyalty to Rome. Thus far Rashbi's "crime" appears to be completely political.

Rashbi flees with his son to a *bet midrash* (rabbinic House of Study),

---

and intellectual organization for Jewish Studies, was organized in 1968.

[59] This approach differs from the traditional approach to the Talmudic story which deals with the story's surface, either as "fact" or "lesson." The traditional approach does not raise the question of how the Talmudic story communicates its point of view as a literary piece. A specifically Israeli literary-analytical approach to the talmudic story developed in the 1980s in the circle of scholars who studied with Yonah Frankel, professor of rabbinic literature at Hebrew University. The best source for Frankel's approach is his *'Iyyunim ba-'Olamo ha-Ruhani shel Sippur ha-Aggadah (Studies in the Spiritual World of the Aggadic Story)* (Tel Aviv: Hakibbutz Hameuchad, 1981). In the United States, Daniel Boyarin's *Carnal Israel* (Berkeley and Los Angeles: University of California Press, 1993), Steven Fraade's *From Tradition to Commentary* (Albany: SUNY Press, 1991), and David Stern's *Midrash and Theory* (Evanston: Northwestern University Press, 1996) are examples of the recent important contributions to academic literary analysis of aggadic midrash and talmudic aggadah. All of these are interdisciplinary works combining rabbinics and literary analysis or criticism.

quite likely assuming that their spiritual pursuits will protect them from all physical harm.[60] Though Rashbi's flight to a place where one would naturally expect to find a rabbi might strike some readers as clever—who would look for him in the most obvious place?— it might also strike other readers as incredibly foolish since it is likely the Romans would look for a rabbi in his natural habitat. The story will soon determine whether Rashbi is a truly wise man or not.

Rashbi's wife supplies her husband and son with physical sustenance while they study Torah in the *bet midrash*. She is the one who makes those pursuits possible and she puts herself at risk as she transports their needs from home to study-house, yet the best her husband can say of her is, "Women are light-minded. Put to torture she will give us away." Rashbi's judgment of this woman, who has shown considerable courage on behalf of her husband and son, is clearly unwarranted. Her son does not come to her defense either; he is his father's child, not his mother's. In short, here are two men who do not appreciate anything related to physicality. Agoras, bathhouses, good roads, and food all symbolize the "merely" physical which is fit for selfish and hedonistic Romans but not for Jews. As a further sign of the insignificance of the physical in Rashbi's view, Rashbi's wife, who has kept her husband and son alive physically, is nameless in the story. Further, she is accused of being untrustworthy because she is "light-minded," as are all women, who spend their lives in housework instead of Torah study,[61] and so she will betray her own flesh and blood in order to protect herself physically.

The next scene starts with Rashbi and son recognizing the physical danger they are in and fleeing to a cave. Suddenly, the physical matters, but as we shall see the protagonists are not fully conscious of that fact beyond the Roman threat of violence. They enter their cave and a miracle occurs: a carob tree and a spring are created for their sustenance. God has replaced the bread and water previously delivered by Rashbi's wife with similar provisions. Yet God's interest in their physical life goes without comment at this point, indicating that Rashbi and his son do not see the value physicality has in God's eyes. Now we are treated to a description of Rashbi's and his son's life in the cave that is so provocative that it must

---

[60] BT, Tractate Sotah 21a suggests that the merit of Torah study shields and saves a person from harm. While the historical Rashbi antedates this notion, the legendary Rashbi does not.

[61] According to talmudic law, women are exempt from Torah study (BT Kiddushin 29b). Women who did become rabbinic scholars were the exception to the rule.

catch one's attention. The two men undress and bury themselves up to their necks in sand in order to study Torah. When the thrice-daily prayer times occur, they dress and pray.[62] Then they undress themselves again in order to preserve their clothes. The prayer they recite, the *'Amidah*, contains praise, requests, and thanks, but out of its nineteen benedictions, thirteen are for temporal personal or communal benefits. Consequently, the *'Amidah* is a spiritual act that asks God to provide us with both spiritual and physical needs. It requires physical gestures and clothing: intermeshing the spiritual and physical makes up the thematic setting here.

Looking at the total picture of the cave, we find that it provides complete nutrition through the newly-created carob tree and spring. In it reside two naked men covered with sand. The womb imagery is unavoidable, and we should expect that if adults are forced back into a womb, they will eventually be reborn. There is also another aggadah in the Babylonian Talmud that describes conditions of gestation in terms that are reminiscent of the conditions in Rashbi's cave.[63] It teaches that every Jewish fetus spends its nine months *in utero*, fully provided for physically, studying Torah day and night in nakedness covered by the caul, much like Rashbi and his son. Unfortunately, as we shall see, our "odd couple" does not recognize the cave as a womb that will thrust them forth with new insights about the world, but rather they mistake it for a garden of Eden

---

[62] Jewish law requires the covering of nakedness in order for one to study Torah verbally (BT Shabbat 150a). Prayer also requires a clothed state, but in addition there must be separate coverings for the torso (heart) and the lower body (genitals; Tosefta Berakhot 2:14). The term for prayer used in the Rashbi story is *zelota*, a technical term reserved for the *'Amidah*, "the standing prayer." This prayer requires an upright stance punctuated with genuflections at the prayer's beginning and end (Tosefta Berakhot 1:8), unlike the *Shema'*, a creedal statement proclaiming God's absolute uniqueness and unity, which could be said in any position (Mishnah, Tractate Berakhot 1:3). The *'Amidah* was in existence at least two generations before the historical Rashbi (135–70 CE) since Rabban Gamliel (80–110 CE) and his colleagues already discuss its recitation (Mishnah, Tractate Berakhot 4:3). The rules governing the *'Amidah* that I have mentioned are found without attribution in tannaitic literature and, therefore, may pre-date, post-date, or be coeval with Rashbi. The rule regarding nudity and Torah study is, however, attributed to Rabbi Yohanan, who lived almost four generations after Rashbi. This does not preclude the possibility of the rule being in existence much earlier, but we must remind ourselves that the Babylonian Talmud Rashbi story is a sixth- or seventh-century legend about him. Retrojections should be expected; they are the storyteller's way of making early characters fit into his audience's contemporary experience.

[63] BT, Tractate Niddah 30b.

where no physical needs require their attention.⁶⁴ Thus they remain ungrateful for the carob and spring provided by God, the cave provided by nature, and the clothing provided by human labor. Further, a philological analysis suggests that the carob and spring have a subversive function. Carob is called *haruv* in Hebrew, a word related to the Hebrew for sword (*herev*) and destruction (*hurban*), probably because of its sword-like shape. The Hebrew and Aramaic words for spring are *'ayin* or *'eina*, respectively, which also means eye, in both languages. These sources of physical maintenance presage the destruction of Rashbi and son's inadequate "spiritual" worldview by opening their eyes to a new reality.

After Rashbi and his son have dwelt in the cave for twelve years, Elijah the Prophet arrives at the cave but does not enter. In a noticeable circumlocution he asks, "Who will inform the son of Yohai that the Caesar is dead and his edict annulled?" Elijah the Prophet is God's messenger in Jewish lore. He makes regular appearances to particularly saintly people. Here, however, he refuses to speak directly to Rashbi, and he even refuses to recognize him as a rabbi, but addresses him only as "the son of Yohai." Not even the warmth of a first name finds its way into Elijah's speech. Moreover, Elijah addresses Rashbi in the language of the unlearned, Aramaic. If anything should inform Rashbi and son about what God thinks of them, it is Elijah's cool and distant approach. Clearly they are not in favor.

Good Talmudists that they are, Rashbi and son deduce from Elijah's statement that they may leave their cave. Outside, they see farmers plowing and sowing. Rashbi proclaims, "They leave behind eternal life [Torah study] for the life of the transient moment [physical labor]?!" Having rendered this judgment on the physical work that sustains human life, Rashbi and his son destroy with a poisonous gaze whatever they look at. A heavenly voice addresses them: "Have you come forth to destroy My world? Return to your cave." Properly chastened, they return to their cave, now knowing that it is not meant to be their garden of Eden.

After another year in the cave that has been changed from Edenic paradise to hell, Rashbi says, "Even the punishment of the wicked in Gehenna is limited to twelve months." Finally, Rashbi understands that he is being punished; he recognizes himself as a destructive person. His statement, however, also reveals his desire to be forgiven and set free. The cave as womb was not useful. It merely allowed these two adults to remain

---

⁶⁴ I am indebted to Ari Elon for this insight. See his *'Alma Di* (Tel Aviv: Shedemot, 1990), 99.

infantile and ignorant. The cave as hell encouraged them to leave its confines, and when one is freed from hell, one is on the way to heaven. As it turns out, heaven is on earth.

Now a heavenly voice addresses Rashbi and El'azar directly and in Hebrew, ordering them to leave the cave. They do so, but El'azar is still filled with the zeal and perfectionism associated with youth. His glance destroys, but whatever he harms, his father heals. Rashbi mollifies his son by telling him that the world's needs for ideal spiritual examples are met by having the two of them in the world. No one else is required to be so devoted, nor are physicality and pleasure the opposites of spirituality and godliness. Rashbi has recognized that God returned him to the cave in order that the physical world S/he had created and called "very good" (Genesis 1:31) should be saved. Evidently, that world must be valuable. However, a full integration of the physical and spiritual has not yet been achieved: El'azar still destroys the physical, and Rashbi appeases him with an elitist statement about spirituality.

On the eve of their first Sabbath out of the cave, Rashbi and El'azar see an old man running at twilight with two bundles of myrtle. They ask him why he has the myrtle bundles, and he replies, "In honor of the Sabbath." Pressing him as to why he needs two bundles, he replies, "One to represent the commandment to observe the Sabbath [Deuteronomy 5:11] and the other to represent the commandment to remember the Sabbath [Exodus 20:7]." Rashbi says to his son, "See how precious the commandments are to Israel," and finally both father and son are calm.

Twilight is the liminal moment on Sabbath eve when the spiritual world of Sabbath rest and the physical world of the workdays touch each other. The image of the old man running also adds to the sense that mature spiritual wisdom can combine with physical vigor. The myrtles are leafy plants which produce a beautiful fragrance when their leaves are crushed. Fragrance of course is physical and sensual, but it is also ethereal to such a degree that Jewish law ponders whether fragrance is substantial.[65] Thus, the myrtle also symbolizes the inhering of the ethereal and spiritual in the physical. Repeatedly in this section of the Rashbi story the mundane or physical and spiritual unite. By the end of this scene, Rashbi and his son are calm. Finally they have recognized that the ultimate message of the Torah is to seek wholeness rather than fragmentation of the self.

Rabbi Pinhas ben Ya'ir, Rashbi's son-in-law, hears that his father-in-

---

[65] BT, Tractate Pesahim 76b and Tractate Avodah Zarah 66b.

law has returned and goes out to meet him. Seeing his terrible physical condition, he takes him to a bathhouse and "repairs" him.[66] During the treatment, Pinḥas begins to weep and his tears fall on Rashbi's wounds. The pain causes Rashbi to cry out. At this Pinḥas exclaims, "Woe is me that I see you thus." But Rashbi replies that Pinḥas should be happy to see him in his present condition because, were he not in such a state, he would not have his present degree of wisdom. There follows a description of how prior to the cave experience Rashbi would propound a question related to the Law, and Pinḥas would supply twelve answers. After the cave sojourn, however, Pinḥas would propound a question and Rashbi would supply twenty-four answers.

The story begins to come full circle now. Rashbi's actual healing in its fullest sense begins in a bathhouse, probably a Roman one.[67] There his son-in-law tends to his physical wounds, and when Rashbi recognizes through his pain that physicality is basic to human nature, he tells his son-in-law that awareness of his physical being has made him wiser. Knowing this makes Rashbi a sharper Torah scholar than thirteen years of isolated "spirituality."

The number twelve has played a conspicuous role in the Babylonian Talmud's Rashbi legend. Literary analysis cannot miss such an oft-repeated trope. Twelve years in a male Jew's life places him at the edge of adulthood, but he is still a minor who is not considered fully responsible to observe God's commandments. In a system that awards rights and privileges to those who are most highly obliged to the commandments, being twelve years old is being a second class citizen. Note that only after their thirteenth year in the cave do Rashbi and his son mature and change. Rashbi shows he has reached mature Torah knowledge when he can produce twenty-four replies to Pinḥas ben Ya'ir's questions. Notice that Pinḥas, the son-in-law, was the masterful respondent to his father-in-law's questions before Rashbi's cave experiences. In a sense, Pinḥas was in the position his older father-in-law should have occupied, but Rashbi's lack of worldly sensibility left him poorer in Torah scholarship. Now, in his experienced state, Rashbi's doubly increased knowledge places him in a proper relationship with his son-in-law first and with the larger world next.[68]

---

[66] This translation accords with Rashi's commentary on BT Shabbat 33b, s.v. *arikh*.

[67] The term used to describe the bathhouse is *be bania*. *Bania* is derived from the Latin *balnea, balineae*, bath or bathing. The implication is that Pinḥas ben Ya'ir brought Rashbi to a Roman bath, one of the things Rashbi railed against.

[68] Elon, *'Alma Di*, 102–3, unnumbered note.

Rashbi's new understanding of his connection to earthly life leads him to seek an opportunity to benefit his community. Notably, he views this action as an act of gratitude to God, a sign that he understands that action in the world can serve spiritual purposes. In this he seeks to emulate Jacob, who celebrated his escape from Laban by benefitting the city where he encamped. In the Babylonian Talmud's excursus three rabbis tell us what Jacob did. One says he created a money system; another opines that Jacob created agoras; and the last holds that he organized bathhouses. These rabbis' views undermine Rashbi's initial objections to the benefits the Romans have brought to Israel. Indeed, they co-opt all these Roman institutions by claiming they were invented by Israel's progenitor, Jacob.

Rashbi learns that there is a field in the city that might be a cemetery. This situation has created difficulties for *kohanim* (sing., *kohen*, members of the priestly caste), who are forbidden any contact with the dead, and therefore cannot walk across the field. The story uses the laws of the priesthood in emblematic fashion: distancing the *kohanim* from death signifies that Judaism's concern is with life. Rashbi turns to the work of protecting the priests' spiritual purity by easing their physical access from one side of the city to the other. In order to do this, he must overcome the present halakhic difficulty by re-establishing a presumption of purity for the field, and his Torah learning tells him that the best way to do this is to find a witness to the field's purity. Torah learning is now applied to real life problems, and human beings are called in to resolve a Torah-defined issue.

Again an old man appears on the scene and declares that Rabbi Yohanan ben Zaqqai harvested lupines for priestly use in the area in question. This is doubly useful testimony because Rabbi Yohanan himself was a priest who needed to maintain his ritual purity. Furthermore, the food he gathered had to remain pure if *kohanim* were to use it. Rashbi copies Rabbi Yohanan ben Zaqqai's actions, but nevertheless checks the field. Wherever the earth is soft, indicating the possibility of a grave beneath the surface, he marks the area off. Thus he creates a path that benefits the community both spiritually and physically. He, like the Romans he earlier reviled, has become a builder of a bridge from one side of the town to the other.

One would imagine that all's well that ends well, but the old man—always a pivotal figure—returns. Despite his own testimony, he goes about town declaring that Rashbi has purified the "graveyard," something the Law does not sanction. Rashbi takes him to task with what I consider to be one of the best lines in aggadic literature:

If you had not been with us, or even if you had been with us but not voted with us [about the purity of the suspected area], you would be speaking well. Now that you were with us and voted with us, people will say, "Prostitutes pretty each other up [to entice their clients], shouldn't sages certainly do the same for one another?"

The old man in this scene is no less an alter ego than the old man in the Sabbath's eve scene. There the old man was probably a rabbi since he spoke to Rashbi in Hebrew. Because Rashbi was not an integrated rabbinic personality until the end of that scene, he could not recognize this symbol of a unified personality as a rabbinic sage. Now having reconciled Torah and worldliness, spirituality and physicality, Rashbi knows a rabbi when he sees one, and the old man in this scene is clearly a rabbi, like Rashbi himself. Here the old man's role is to test Rashbi's resolve to remain true to his newly integrated view of life. This test is necessary because Rashbi himself did not simply rely on the old man's testimony about the field's purity, which should have ended the matter. Rather, after he cut food for priestly use, he tested its ground. The old man therefore plays tempter in order to see whether Rashbi will succumb to his former rarified and unreasonable "spirituality" or stand his ground as a well-integrated human being and Jewish sage. Rashbi now stares at the image of his old self, and instead of destroying the world, puts that self to rest, or so he thinks.

Shortly after, however, he meets Yehudah, the proselytes' son, another symbol of the riven personality. Looking at yet another reflection of his former self, he is amazed that his tendency to fragmentation reveals itself over and over. Astounded by the persistence of the problem, he asks, "Are you still in the world?" In one final and violent act of thrusting away the temptation to be a divided self, he uses his "look that can kill" for the last time on Yehudah, the symbol of his own former non-integrated Jewish soul, and turns him into a pile of bones.

As a complete literary unit, the story is about a process of reversal. At the story's outset Rashbi finds no redeeming value in the Romans' agoras, bathhouses, and bridges. By its end, he has used a bathhouse to begin his physical healing, built a "bridge" for *kohanim* through a city, and used the imagery of prostitutes—whose presence in agoras is the essence of his complaint about those marketplaces—to rebuke a fellow scholar. The storyteller, too, rebukes his fellow scholars and students: Reverse the path of elitist "spirituality" that you have chosen, or find your honored position and influence in the Babylonian Jewish community suffering a reversal from which neither you nor it will recover.

§ § §

In my "unpacking" of the Rashbi story I have used an eclectic mix of literary critical methods: philology, semiotics, psychological analysis, elements of deconstructionism, and feminist criticism. These are some of the tools of contemporary practical literary criticism that have developed in our culture and inform our way of reading ancient and modern texts. I, like those who preceded me, am a child of my time, and I read the Talmud inevitably influenced by the cultures of the academy and larger society in which I participate. In this view of the Talmudist's work I part company with those who hold that evolutions in talmudic perspective and interpretation developed in hermetically sealed Jewish milieus and must continue to develop in that fashion if they are to be authentic. As we have seen, that has rarely, if ever, been the case. Time and again social and cultural factors surrounding different Jewish communities influenced Jewish scholars' and leaders' ways of constructing and reading the Talmud's law and lore. Their greatest achievement was not insularity, a quality for which they are praised endlessly in revisionist histories created by those who believe that Jewish continuity in our time depends on distance or withdrawal from contemporary society. Rather, the genius of these scholars and leaders was similar to that of the reconstructed Rashbi: they learned how to make use of the social, intellectual, and cultural developments emerging from their surroundings as a prism through which to view their own tradition and culture, and they shared the insights that emerged from their varied Jewish worlds with the "city" in which they lived. Their readings of the talmudic tradition have shown our generation how they "turned" that tradition again and again. It is our "turn" now.

Hebrew Union College, New York City

Jewish Women Martyrs:
Changing Models of Representation

SUSAN EINBINDER

During the twelfth and thirteenth centuries, Jewish writers composed a variety of literary works about the persecution of Jewish communities in northern France and the Rhineland. These sources portray the single-minded willingness of Jewish men, women and children to offer their lives *beqiddush haShem*, "in Sanctification of God's Name."[1] The simplest sources are lists of names, preserved for recitation on commemorative anniversaries; dozens of these have survived the Middle Ages.[2] Three prose chronicles describe the persecutions of 1096, and one additional chronicle spans later twelfth-century persecutions.[3] Liturgical

---

An earlier version of this paper was presented at Tel Aviv University on April 12, 1999, as part of a conference on "The Representation of Women in the Middle Ages," organized by Professor Simcha Goldin. My thanks to Professors David Sperling of the Hebrew Union College (New York) and William C. Jordan of Princeton University for their comments on that paper, and to Professor Sheila Delany for the helpful editorial suggestions that have gone into this revision.

[1] A discussion of the relationship between early Jewish martyrological traditions (preserved in rabbinic descriptions of the second-century Hadrianic persecutions, the books of Maccabees and Josephus) and the later medieval phenomenon, is beyond the purview of this paper. Medieval European Jews received some of these traditions, probably via southern Italy, and revered them. However, the sudden re-emergence of martyrological writing following the crusader assaults of 1096 cannot be explained in terms of continuity with these traditions, and the discontinuous nature of Hebrew martyrological writing is more striking than its continuity. For a recent summary of the scholarship on the origins of medieval Hebrew martyrological traditions, see Jeremy Cohen, "The Hebrew Crusade Chronicles in Their Cultural Context," in *Juden und Christen zur Zeit der Kreuzzüge*, ed. Alfred Haverkampf (Sigmaringen: Jan Thorbecke, 1999), 17–34, especially notes 2–3 with reference to the work of Soloveitchik, Yuval, Grossman, Marcus and Abulafia.

[2] S. Salfeld, *Das Martyrologium des Nurnberger Memorbuches* (Berlin: Leonhard Simion, 1898).

[3] The chronicles of 1096 are by Solomon bar Samson, Eliezer bar Natan and the socalled "Mainz anonymous" author. All three were published by A. Neubauer and M. Stern, *Hebräische Berichte über die Judenverfolgungen während der Kreuzzüge* (Berlin: Quellen zur Geschichte der Juden in Deutschland, 1892), and again by A. Habermann, *Sefer Gezerot Ashkenaz veTsarefat* (Jerusalem: Tarshish Books, 1945). See also Robert Chazan's *European Jewry and the First Crusade* (Los Angeles: University of California Press, 1987), which contains an English translation. Ephraim of

poems called *piyyutim* (*piyyut* in the singular) comprise by far the largest source.[4] Numerous martyrological laments survive, many of them originally intended for use in the penitential liturgies that appear during this period. The portrayal of idealized characters, including women and children, is typical of the martyrological literature, which contains many scenes of pathos that bring female and children characters to the fore. Nonetheless, each genre has its own specific aims, reflected in differing styles of representation. In this paper, I will examine one particular convention of the Jewish martyrological literature, the representation of women martyrs.

Crusader armies passing through the Rhine valley in early 1096, en route to the Holy Land, brought terror to Jewish communities that had flourished there since the ninth century. Both Jewish and Christian sources describe the crusaders' reasoning in identical terms: if Christian armies were risking their lives to battle the "infidel" nations that refused to acknowledge the Christian God, then how much more deserving of their wrath were the Jews, who had killed and crucified him![5] Many Jews met the crusader attacks willing to accept death, either passively at the hands of crusaders, in active resistance, or in mass suicide. The three Hebrew chronicles written within fifty years of these assaults also depict many courageous Jewish women who kill themselves and their families rather than fall into crusader hands. A fourth prose chronicle, from the later half of the twelfth century, Ephraim of Bonn's *Sefer Zekhirah*, portrays women very differently. The *Sefer Zekhirah* describes only two female martyrs,

---

Bonn's chronicle, the *Sefer Zekhirah* (*Book of Remembrance*) was included in Habermann's anthology, 115–37, and later published separately with several laments in a critical edition, also by Habermann, *Sefer Zekhirah, Seliḥot veQinot* (Jerusalem: Bialik Institute, 1970).

[4] The word *piyyut* derives from the same Greek root that gives us the word "poetry," i.e., *poiesis*, to make or create. The earliest known Hebrew piyyutim survive from Palestine of the Byzantine period. The medieval martyrological piyyutim fall into two general liturgical categories, laments (*qinot*) and penitential hymns (*seliḥot*); approximately forty examples were included by Habermann in his anthology *Sefer Gezerot Ashkenaz veTsarefat*. Other Hebrew editions of note are Hayim (Jefim) Schirmann's "Laments on the Persecutions in Eretz Israel, Africa, Spain, Germany and France," in *Qobetz 'al yad* n.s. 3 (1939): 25–74, and S. Berliner, *Sefer Dema 'ot*, 4 vols. (Berlin: Eshkol, 1923–26). Many martyrological piyyutim remain scattered in individual *diwans* (collected works by a single author), some published in the late nineteenth or early twentieth centuries; some are undoubtedly still unpublished, in liturgical manuscripts or codices.

[5] See Robert Chazan, *European Jewry*, 65–66.

whose deaths by live burial are relatively passive martyrdoms. Other female characters, Jewish and Christian, are negatively or ambivalently portrayed.

It is difficult to draw any solid conclusions about the representation of women from four relatively short chronicles. However, the martyrological piyyutim produced throughout the twelfth and thirteenth centuries amplify our pool of texts considerably. Examined carefully, they exhibit signs of change consistent with those in the chronicles. Both genres document a move away from the striking presence of women in the 1096 chronicles and towards the suppression of a model of active martyrdom for women. The thirteenth-century poetry continues the trend initiated in twelfth-century prose and verse, stressing a passive female ideal and reflecting a growing concern with female sexual purity.

This literary shift accompanies historical changes both outside and within the Jewish communities. By the end of the twelfth century, spontaneous mob (generally crusader) violence against Jewish communities gave way to anti-Jewish legislative, ecclesiastical, and social policies. When these policies resulted in acts of violence, that violence was usually orchestrated and judicial. Conversion, not death, was its ideal outcome. Harassment and humiliation, mass arrests and crippling fines, expulsion and intimidation, were all aspects of a larger policy aimed at weakening the Jews physically, economically, and psychologically. To some extent, these policies succeeded, for there is evidence that Jewish men and women did convert, under varying degrees of duress. Neither Jewish nor Christian sources warrant the conclusion that Jewish women were more vulnerable to conversionary efforts than men; nor does the historical evidence support the view that anti-female violence was a deliberate or normative aspect of anti-Jewish policies. Indeed, one recent study has suggested that the segment of the Jewish community most vulnerable to conversionary efforts was adolescent males.[6] Yet the claims both of vulnerability and of targeted violence are implicit in the *literary* treatment of Jewish women. Moreover,

---

[6] William C. Jordan, "Adolescence and Conversion in the Middle Ages: A Research Agenda," originally presented at Notre Dame University in October 1996 at the conference *In the Shadow of the Millennium* and forthcoming in the published version of the conference proceedings. The paper deals with the question of voluntary conversion. Jordan notes, "Although scholars have identified a number of Jewish female converts to Christianity in the Middle Ages, males appear to have constituted the vast majority of voluntary and individual converts ... the demographic profile was far more varied, of course, for forced and mass converts." I thank Professor Jordan for generously making a copy of his paper, which I heard in 1996, available prior to publication.

Jewish legal literature constructs a link between women's consent to rape and their conversion. The martyrological literature echoes these legal attitudes by describing women both as passive and as victims of sexual violence. Over the period of our investigation, the authors of Jewish martyrological literature are also less likely to acknowledge Jewish women's ongoing commercial activities. The resultant focus on "women as [a] site of dishonor" reinforces traditional male institutions and identity, as David Nirenberg has argued in another context.[7] The changing female model also reflects a deterioration in women's legal status, at least in domestic rights related to marriage and divorce.

Let me look first at the prose texts, then at a selection of piyyutim.

I

In 1986, Ivan Marcus published a modest survey of the activities of medieval Jewish women, illustrating their immersion in family life and business, especially moneylending, as well as their prominence in martyrological literature. Marcus described the women martyrs in Jewish accounts of the First Crusade as women of "strong personalities" who resisted the crusaders by slaughtering their children and themselves. In the literary depiction of women as well as men performing acts of ritual slaughter, he saw an "egalitarian portrayal" that suggested a new understanding of women's role in "the mandate of family martyrdom."[8]

The cultic equality of women and their autonomy are only two characteristics of the female martyrs in the 1096 texts. Collectivity is another, for generally the women act in groups. Stories that do feature a lone woman reinforce her ties to spouse and family, now expressed in death: note Sarit the betrothed, whose "marriage" is consummated by sword, and Rachel the mother killing her children. Sometimes a lone female character may be killed protecting family assets, as with Mistress Rivka in Cologne or Mistress Mina of Worms.[9] These bold women are often the spiritual and

---

[7] David Nirenberg, *Communities of Violence: Persecution of Minorities in the Middle Ages* (Princeton: Princeton University Press, 1996), 151. Nirenberg is describing incidents of miscegenation among Christians, Muslims, and Jews in Spain, with a particular focus on the role of prostitutes as cultural "border guards" between confessional groups.

[8] Ivan Marcus, "Mothers, Martyrs and Moneymakers: Some Jewish Women in Medieval Europe," *Conservative Judaism* 3.3 (Spring 1986): 34–45, at 38.

[9] See the narrative of Solomon bar Samson, in Habermann, *Sefer Gezerot*, 47, 34, 44, and 97 respectively.

economic mainstays of their families. Frequently, they taunt the crusaders while goading their men to rally and resist. Of all three First Crusade chronicles, Eliezer bar Natan's adoption of this model is the most restrained. Eliezer's chronicle includes Jewish women who kill themselves and their children, but they appear relatively infrequently, and they do not talk. More typical is Solomon bar Samson's narrative. There, when the "pure and saintly women" of Mainz witness the desecration of the community's Torah scrolls, they call out to their husbands, "Look, look, the enemies are tearing the sacred Torah!" and inspire them to repel the attack. During the ensuing battle,

> The righteous women hurled stones through the windows onto their enemies and the enemies stoned them in return until their flesh and faces were shredded. They [the women] were reviling and rebuking the crusaders in the name of the defiled and impure hanged one, the son of whoredom: "In whom do you trust but a stinking corpse!"[10]

It is no surprise, given this behavior, that the Christian attackers in Trier blame the Jewish women for the vigorous resistance of the community, saying "this is because of the women who incite their husbands and strengthen them to rebel against the hanged one."[11]

The *Sefer Zekhirah* marks a dramatic shift in Hebrew martyrological prose conventions for the portrayal of women. The Raban's nephew, Ephraim of Bonn, composed this chronicle in two parts, one relating persecutions from the second Crusade period (1147–49) and a sequel devoted to incidents ranging from 1171 to 1196. Robert Chazan has dated the first portion of the work to the 1170s and the second to the end of the century.[12]

The *Sefer Zekhirah* displays little interest in female martyrs, even where their historical presence is documented, as in Blois (1171) and York (1190). In fact, Ephraim describes only one female martyr in each half of

---

[10] Solomon bar Samson, in Habermann, ibid., 33–34. All translations in this article are my own, unless otherwise indicated. The derogatory reference to Jesus as the "hanged one" is common in the polemical literature, and reflects medieval Jews' belief that Christianity worshipped a dead god, moreover one who had been killed ignobly.

[11] Ibid., 55.

[12] Robert Chazan, "Ephraim ben Jacob's Compilation of Twelfth Century Persecutions," *Jewish Quarterly Review* 84.4 (April 1994): 397–416.

the work. The first, Gotheila of Aspenbruck, drowns herself rather than accept baptism.[13] The second, an unnamed mother in the town of Neuss, is buried alive.[14] The live burials (by water or earth) are passive forms of death compared to the violent deaths inflicted by crusaders and provoked by the women of 1096. Ephraim elevates a passive ideal in other tales, too, such as the young woman in Wurzburg who plays dead while beaten, and a dead Jewish girl from Speyer whose corpse is defiled. The active female suicides, homicides, and infanticides that dominate the portraits of the 1096 texts are absent. Ephraim's female characters are isolated from other women and rarely speak. Moreover, women who do speak cause trouble, such as the Christian woman in the Cologne market who accuses the Jews of coin-clipping, or the Austrian crusader's wife who complains when a wealthy Jew seizes her husband for theft.[15]

By extension, powerful women are problematic in this text. Both Pucellina of Blois and the Countess of Brie, one a Jew and one a Christian, endanger a Jewish community and are powerless to prevent its annihilation. Ephraim edits and adapts the fuller description of Pucellina found in his major source, a letter from the Jewish community of Orléans written immediately following the execution. Read carefully, the Orléans letter implies strongly that Pucellina was a moneylender with powerful enemies.[16] Yet Ephraim deliberately suppresses references to Pucellina's commercial activities and suggests her influence derives from an amorous liaison with Count Thibaut of Blois. In so doing, he patterns her story on the biblical character of Esther, the Jewish wife of the Persian king who risks her life to save her people from death. Unlike Esther, Pucellina is unable to save her people. In the same year (1171), the Countess of Brie permitted the execution of a Christian who had slain a Jew. When the Christian turned out to be a vassal of the French king, the king responded by burning a number of Jewish community notables, including men of learning, wealth and status.[17]

Remarkably, none of the Jewish women in the *Sefer Zekhirah* is

---

[13] Ephraim of Bonn, *Sefer Zekhirah*, *Selihot veQinot* 121–23, ed. Habermann (1970), 22.

[14] Ibid., 40–41 (lines 514–45).

[15] Ibid., 37 (lines 436–41) and 42 (544–45).

[16] For a full discussion of this story, and the representation of Pucellina in the various sources, see my "Pucellina of Blois: Romantic Myths and Narrative Conventions," *Jewish History* 12.1 (1998): 29–46.

[17] Ephraim, *Sefer Zekhirah* 415–28, 36.

depicted as married. Mina of Speyer and Gotheila of Aspenbruck are not linked to families; the Wurzburg girl is described only as the sister of a yeshiva student; and the dead daughter of Rabbi Isaac is unmarried, as are the three daughters and the unnamed fourth girl in Neuss. Pucellina of Blois and the Neuss mother are both widows. Ephraim's deviation from the nuclear-family model represented in the 1096 texts is puzzling, although he continues the restrained narrative precedent of his uncle.[18]

Ephraim was a gifted writer of prose who exploited contemporary narrative techniques as well as traditional Jewish sources in creating his female characters. His Pucellina of Blois is a romantic heroine, the victim of a bitter love triangle. Favored by Count Thibaut V, she is detested by the Countess Alix (in reality the second daughter of Eleanor of Aquitaine), who ensures she has no access to him once the Jews are arrested for ransom. This is hardly the portrait of Pucellina that emerges in the documentary letter from Orléans, in which Pucellina's highhandedness seems to derive more from her financial than her romantic connections. Significantly, Ephraim prefers a romance characterization. Indeed, the real Pucellina's arrogance may even be behind the catastrophic refusal of the imprisoned Jews to offer more than a trivial pledge towards their own ransom. In contrast, Ephraim describes a valiant heroine urging her fellow prisoners not to despair.[19] Two memorial rosters list the widow Pucellina and her two daughters at the head of the female victims in Blois, yet she is dropped so precipitously from Ephraim's prose account that her death receives no mention at all.[20]

The story of the Wurzburg sister also exploits a romance narrative plot. The 1147 attack on the Wurzburg Jews followed a murder libel: a corpse found in the river began to "make [miraculous] signs" and the Jews were blamed for its death.[21] Seeking vengeance for this alleged murder,

---

[18] Compare Kenneth Stow, "The Jewish Family in the Rhineland: Form and Function," *American Historical Review* 92 (1987): 1085–1110, and summarized in his book, *Alienated Minority: The Jews of Medieval Latin Europe* (Cambridge: Harvard University Press, 1992), 196–210. Ephraim's text does not accord with Stow's perception of an increasing emphasis in the martyrological texts on small, nuclear families.

[19] See my "Pucellina of Blois." The portrayal of imprisoned female martyrs as more defiant than those not confined also characterizes Christian tales. See Brigitte Cazelles, *The Lady as Saint: A Collection of French Hagiographic Romances of the Twelfth Century* (Philadelphia: University of Pennsylvania, 1991), 44.

[20] See Salfeld, *Martyrologium*, 16–17.

[21] Ephraim, *Sefer Zekhirah* 128, 23.

crusaders attacked the Jewish community, killing Rabbi Isaac ben Rabbenu Eliakim and twenty-one of his students. Another student, Simon bar Isaac, was gravely wounded. His sister was dragged into a church to be baptized:

> They brought his sister into their house of pollution, where she sanctified the Name and spit on the abomination, and they struck her with their fists and with stones ... but she didn't die. She fell prostrate there among them and made herself appear as if she were dead. They wounded her with their hands and struck her, dealing her burn upon burn to see if she was dead or not. They laid her on a marble slab from Ramerupt, but she did not awaken nor stir nor flutter a hand or foot. In this way she deceived them until nighttime, when a Christian laundry woman came and carried her to her house and hid her and saved her.[22]

Ephraim emphasizes the sister's fate as a parody of retributive justice. The Christians who mistake the dead corpse in the river for a "live" saint now invert their error by assuming that the living girl is dead. (Similarly, their belief in a "dead" god is a foolish error to be contrasted with the Jews' belief in a "living" one.) The description of the prostrate girl evokes the terminology of ritual slaughter, where the "fluttering" or wriggling of the sacrificial animal can spoil a sacrifice. "Keviyah taḥat keviyah" ("burn upon burn") is a grim reminder of the prescriptions of Exodus 21:24–25: "Eye for eye, tooth for tooth, hand for hand, foot for foot, burn for burn, wound for wound, stripe for stripe." The Christians seek retribution for their drowned saint; the Jews await their own revenge to come.

In the 1096 narrative of Solomon bar Samson, another young woman, from Triers, had played dead before her captors. Escaping the crusaders, she met her aunt the next morning, when the two women cast themselves off a bridge to drown.[23] The story does not resemble Ephaim's narrative, which emphasizes the Wurzburg girl's death-like passivity. However, the motif of the live woman who appears to be dead, often a stratagem to join her beloved, is an old one. The Greek myth of Persephone contains its essential elements, an older woman (Demeter) also escorting the young woman back from the world of the dead. But Chrétien de Troyes used this narrative, too, in his verse romance *Cligès* (second half of the twelfth

---

[22] Ibid., 23 (134–43). The "abomination" is probably a crucifix.
[23] Solomon bar Samson, in Habermann, *Sefer Gezerot*, 56.

century), where the young queen Fenice, planning to elope with Cligès, drinks a potion supplied by her nurse that simulates death. When Fenice is laid out in her mausoleum, three skeptical doctors attempt to revive her, first with prayer and flattery, then by force. In a parody of martyrdom, they beat and torture her in a vain attempt to evoke some response. Finally, the old nurse rescues and heals her mistress, and the lovers escape.[24]

Whether Ephraim knew Chrétien's story is uncertain. At the least, he was able to manipulate a plot remarkably similar to one also enlisted by the leading romance writer of his time. Both narratives include the faked death of the heroine, her simulated burial, and the rescue by an older woman who restores the girl to the world of the living. Years later, and substituting a friar for the nurse, Shakespeare would rely on the same trope to tell the story of Romeo and Juliet. (Romeo and Juliet, of course, commit suicide before they escape.) Both Chrétien's romance and the Hebrew author use martyrological imagery to construct a passive feminine ideal. In fact, neither Fenice nor the Wurzburg girl is a martyr in the fullest sense, for neither dies of her ordeal. Both experience a near-death: Fenice from the doctors' beating, the Wurzburg girl from the crusaders' blows. Furthermore, the placement of the Wurzburg girl in the church and then in the laundry woman's home describe her exposure to the cultic and domestic spaces of Christian life. Both are dangerous and potentially contaminating; moreover, they mirror the sacred spaces of Jewish martyrological geography, those which define synagogue (or metaphorically, the Temple) and the family.

The *Sefer Zekhirah* marks a real change in the use of female characters in martyrological prose. They no longer actively defy the Christian enemy, but are idealized for their passive responses to violence. They are not attacked at home but on the geographical fringes of the Jewish world or in the markets and courts beyond it. Thus they become liminal figures whose activity in the Christian world is dangerous ritually and physically. Women who venture outside the limits of the Jewish community bring danger to themselves and to their communities. The poetry, to which I now turn, reflects and extends this trend.

---

[24] Chrétien de Troyes, *Cligès*, in *Arthurian Romances*, trans. W. W. Comfort (London and New York: Everyman's Library 1976), 168–70.

II

Many martyrological piyyutim do not mention women at all, or else restrict descriptions of women to a formulaic verse or two. However, even these brief references rely on tropes and allusions that suggest the authors' desire to emphasize a certain model of behavior. The literary challenge was great. Unlike Hebrew prose, which was new and hence free to explore new techniques and models of representation, Hebrew liturgical verse largely adhered to traditional and long-established forms.[25] Using complex forms of rhyme and acrostic, the medieval Hebrew poets *(paytanim)* constructed highly allusive verse forms that relied on biblical and rabbinic language. From the first medieval attempts to write medieval martyrological verse, that is, following the violence of 1096, the poets struggled with a lack of biblical precedent for describing the range of female behavior they wished to represent. Traditional religious literature simply did not provide a reservoir of sources or topoi for illustrating the daring actions of the martyr women. Indeed, the biblical corpus rarely bothered to describe the deaths of women at all. As the twelfth-century exegete Joseph Bekhor Shor of Orléans acknowledged in his commentary to Genesis 23:1, "it is not the custom to write about women's deaths, even righteous ones, except in the context of a [larger] narrative."[26] Jewish writers resolved this problem in two ways, either by resort to post-biblical language and allusions, or by resort to a few biblical stories that might jar in their medieval settings, but at least offered prooftexts for descriptions of women.

In the 1096 piyyutim, as in the prose, women are described amidst a

---

[25] The Hebrew First Crusade chronicles mark the emergence of Hebrew narrative prose in Christian Europe. Two prior instances are from southern Italy, the pseudo-chronicle known as the *Megillat Ahimaatz* and the "translation" of Josephus known as the *Yosippon*. Unlike the case of the vernacular literatures, however, Hebrew narrative prose did not dominate literary production of the twelfth and thirteenth centuries. See my general introduction in my chapter on the Blois martyrs in Thomas Head, ed., *Medieval Hagiography: A Sourcebook* (forthcoming, Garland, 1999). The debate on the significance and function of medieval Hebrew prose continues; see Jeremy Cohen, "The Hebrew Crusade Chronicles," and the bibliography cited on 18 n3.

[26] Joseph Bekhor Shor of Orléans, *Bekhor Shor: Perushei haTorah*, ed. Yehoshafat Nebo (Jerusalem: Mosad harav Kook 1994), 39. The biblical passage describes the death of Sarah, in Bekhor Shor's reading because this information is necessary for the narrative's description of Abraham's purchase of land for her burial. Bekhor Shor is not simply commenting on a convention of modesty, I think, but also on the unavailability of descriptive models.

flurry of activity. They do not talk, although they sometimes weep and mourn. But like the women of the prose chronicles, they appear with other women or in families; they hurry, and they actively slaughter their daughters and sons. Usually, they are mothers or brides. In a poem by Abraham of Mainz, for instance,

> The mother ties her son so that he will not defile the sacrifice by
> fluttering;
> And the father finishes by saying the blessing on the slaughter.
> Tender women strangle their sons;
> Pure virgins shriek in protest.
> Brides are parted with kisses from their bridegrooms,
> And cling and press to slaughter.[27]

Or, from a piyyut by David bar Meshullam, where the women are sanctioned to make sacrificial offerings as if they were priests in the Temple cult:

> Priestly servants authorized women [to act] like men.
> They make sacrifices and offerings, [perform acts of] slaughter,
> sprinkling and
> Receiving blood.[28]

In general, the 1096 poets rely on a set of shared language, topoi, and allusions, many of which are not biblical but refer to rabbinic usages and texts.[29] For instance, the description of the women hastening to slaughter their children or to be slaughtered themselves, a martyrological topos, is not associated with any biblical story. True, Abraham tells Sarah to "hurry up, prepare three measures of meal, knead it and make cakes" for their angelic visitors (Genesis 18:6), but otherwise there is no biblical indication that speed is a feminine virtue. Yet speed remains a favorite attribute of the female martyr at least through the thirteenth century, suggesting male approval for female industry and efficiency. Since many medieval Ashken-

---

[27] Abraham of Mainz, "Adabrah be-tsar ruhi" ("I speak in bitterness of spirit") 16–18, in Schirmann, *Laments*, 29–31; also in Habermann, *Sefer Gezerot*, 62.

[28] David bar Meshullam, "Elohim al domi ledami" ("God, do not be silent before my blood") 41–42, ibid., 62.

[29] For instance, both the piyyutim and the prose often refer to women as *rahmaniyot* (compassionate, or merciful ones) or *tsadqaniyot* (righteous ones), rabbinic expressions. See, for instance, their use in Mishnah, Tractate Hullin 12:1 or Tractate Kinnim 2:1.

azic women managed both businesses and households, one can understand why.

The image of martyrdom as a wedding, and of the martyrs as brides and grooms hurrying to their nuptials, is another nonbiblical topos that flourishes in the piyyutim. It is an image found in Christian literature, too, where many a virgin martyr refuses a mortal husband to join her heavenly spouse in the world to come. Other poems refer to women as keeners, *meqonenot*, drawing on the biblical description of Jeremiah 9:16–19 but likely reflecting a medieval reality as well. Among the Jews of Islamic lands, professional female keeners remained common until the modern period; in medieval Christian society, female keeners also played an important role in public mourning rituals, and it is reasonable to assume the Jewish authors were referring to a parallel activity in Jewish mourning behavior.[30]

When the 1096 poems do use biblical texts to describe female martyrs, their associations can be startling. The result illustrates the absolute linguistic void confronted by the poets who struggled to describe the unprecedented behavior of these women, and the uneasiness, perhaps ambivalence, their courage aroused.[31] The poem by David bar Meshullam cited above for instance, includes a motif not seen in prose treatments of women. The 1096 prose consistently emphasized an egalitarian sense of communal martyrdom, referring frequently to decisions made by entire communities *belev ehad*, with a single mind. So, too, the deliberate inclusion of a vast range of individual types, from converts and simple men and women to the most learned and wealthy Jews, drew a picture of collective unity in which all Jews preferred death to apostasy. This polemical insistence extended even to the prose narratives' representation of Jewish corpses, the texts often describing the mingled blood of men and women, young and old, husbands and wives, teachers and students, parents and children. In the poetry, however, a description of violence specifically against women emerges. Its sexualized rhetoric is startling:

---

[30] See the striking illustrations of a Christian woman keener in Patrick Geary's *Phantoms of Remembrance: Memory and Oblivion at the End of the First Millennium* (Princeton: Princeton University Press, 1994), 55–60.

[31] Certainly the image of men slaughtering their children is as shocking as that of women slaughterers. However, the poets could describe the men's acts in the language of the biblical cult, metaphorically evoking the biblical priests making sacrificial offerings. As we have seen, this topos did occasionally describe women as well, but it was surely less "natural," and for the most part died out with the First Crusade texts.

> May all see what happened to the trusting women!
> Stretched out naked in the heat of the day
> The most beautiful of women with their bellies split and ripped open
> Sending forth the afterbirth from between their legs.[32]

David's image of the bloody afterbirth, quoted above, comes from Deuteronomy 28:7, where it refers to the "delicately bred woman" who in starvation will eat her own afterbirth (or infant) and hoard it from her husband and other children. In the medieval poem, this allusion follows David's description of the *tsadqaniyot* (righteous women) who raid their own nests for their "tender darlings" (*'olelei tipuḥim*), an allusion to the starving women reduced to cannibalizing their children in Lamentations 2:20. As we shall see, both sets of references—from Deuteronomy and Lamentations—come to dominate later descriptions of women martyrs. Moreover, the Lamentations verse would have also been familiar as the opening line of a lament by the Byzantine paytan, the Kallir, recited annually on the fast day commemorated on the Jewish calendar date of the ninth of Av.[33]

Strikingly, the piyyutim link the violation of Jewish women to that of Jewish sacred texts. Both are torn from their homes by strange men, stripped, "torn" open and left lying exposed on the ground. Two typical

---

[32] David bar Meshullam, "Elohim al domi ledami" 49–52.

[33] Usually commemorated in August, the fast marks the destruction of the First and Second Temples and a number of subsequent tragedies. The liturgy for the day includes the recitation of Lamentations and a variety of liturgical laments. The Kallir, whose dates of activity are uncertain but often placed in the sixth century, was a major composer of liturgical poetry. His piyyutim were widely known in Byzantine Italy, whence they travelled (with the Jews themselves) to the medieval Rhine communities. The Kallir's poetry was particularly revered among the Jews of Ashkenaz. The lament "Im tokhalnah nashim piryan" ("When women eat their offspring") is included in *The Authorised Kinot for the Ninth of Av*, tr. Abraham Rosenfeld (London: C. Labworth & Co., 1965 and Israel 1970), 120–21. The tremendous popularity of the Kallir's poetry in medieval Ashkenaz was also reflected in the composition of numerous commentaries on his verses, many of which are unfortunately still scattered in manuscript and microfilm sources. In the *'Arugot haBosem* of Rabbi Abraham bar 'Azriel (thirteenth century), we find a tantalizing confirmation that a study of the commentaries on this particular poem might prove fruitful. For the Kallir's verse, "im tishakavnah beyn shefatayim, benot melakhim meshubahim" ("When the daughters of noble kings were laid among the rubbish heaps"), Rabbi Abraham explains, "they were taken sexually by the nations [i.e., Christians] when they went walking outside the limits [of their territory] in Exile," see *'Arugot haBosem*, ed. E. Urbach (Jerusalem: Meqitzei-Nirdamim, 1963), 3:281–82.

descriptions of the desecration of texts, from the chronicles of Eliezer bar Natan and Solomon bar Samson, respectively, illustrate this topos. Eliezer describes the crusaders in Worms, who "took the sacred Torah and trampled it in the mud and tore it, desecrated it and shamed it, while they mocked and laughed."[34] Solomon bar Samson provides a similar but fuller description of the desecration of sacred scrolls in Cologne. Notice that "Torah" in Hebrew is a feminine noun:

> Then they destroyed the synagogue and took out the Torah scrolls and desecrated them and trampled upon them outside. On the day [we celebrate] the giving of the Torah, which shook the world and its foundations until they split, now insolent men, evil-doers, have torn her and burned her and trod on her, and vandals have come upon her and defiled her.[35]

This association depends, of course, on a pre-existing connection between the sanctity of Jewish texts and that of women. Such an association can be traced back to the rabbinic literature.[36] In the medieval period, too, rabbinic authority endorsed this connection through a web of regulations articulating and defining the limits of family and institutional relationships. The boundaries of these relatioships defined the limits of (male) community.[37]

What happens to these conventions in the next generation of poems? The ideal female martyr still hastens quickly to her death, encouraging her female companions. In depictions of mob attacks, she is still ripped open

---

[34] Eliezer bar Natan, in Habermann, *Sefer Gezerot*, 73.

[35] Solomon bar Samson, in Habermann, *Sefer Gezerot*, 44. The holiday on which the giving of the Torah is celebrated is, of course, Shavuot.

[36] See, for instance, Daniel Boyarin, *Carnal Israel: Reading Sex in Talmudic Culture* (Berkeley and Los Angeles: University of California Press, 1993), 65–66 and 188.

[37] Again, see Nirenberg, *Communities of Violence*, 155, where the prostitute also illuminates this bounded network of relationships and community. If the prostitute symbolically represented "a community of men united to each other by a common sexual bond," this was conversely true of the symbolic valence of permissible women and sacred texts, possession of which (in marriage or in knowledge) defined the religious community. Nirenberg cites L. Roper's observation that "masculinity, virility and membership of the polity were intimately connected;" see L. Roper, "Discipline and Respectability: Prostitution and the Reformation in Augsburg," *History Workshop* 19 (1985): 4. In the homosocial world of the Jewish academy, the sexualized symbolism of learning underscores the degree to which male relationships defined the bounds of community.

and exposed in the streets. En route to the pyre, she rejoices as if at her wedding, and, as a wife or mother, she has pity on her children but refuses to save them. For the most part, however, she no longer kills them herself. More typically,

> For making their offerings, the priest
> > Bound children and their mothers
> > > And burned their flesh in the fire.[38]

Or

> Children stretched forth their necks from their mothers' breasts
> And fathers said the blessing for a sacrifice and immediately
> > slaughtered them.[39]

Only one later twelfth-century poem among the several dozen I surveyed describes women sacrificing their children, and that is Ephraim of Bonn's lament for the martyrs of Blois.[40] In the thirteenth century, too, this motif is largely suppressed until the Rindfleisch massacres at the century's end, when it reappears in several piyyutim.[41] The cultic equality of the female martyr has thus disappeared, in favor of attributes portraying passivity and vulnerability to defilement.

Overall, the dramatic heroism of Jewish women no longer parades triumphantly through texts of martyrdom. In the second-generation texts, two images dominate female representation, that of living women joyfully

---

[38] Isaac bar Shalom, "Ein kamokha ba'ilmim" ("There is none like You among those who keep silent") 11, in Habermann, *Sefer Gezerot*, 113–14. The original verse is one tri-partite line.

[39] Menahem bar Jacob, "Aleleli li ki va'u" ("Woe is me for the time has come") 89–90, in Habermann, Sefer Gezerot, 147–51.

[40] Ephraim of Bonn, "Lemi oy lemi avoy" ("Who has sorrow, who has woe") 55–56: "And the mothers hurried and rushed their friends to be burned / and they sacrificed their children as voluntary offerings." The poem has been published many times, see, e.g., the appendix of poems following Habermann's edition of the Sefer Zekhirah, 91–96, or in the *Sefer Gezerot*, 133–36. For my own annotated translation see Head, ed., *Medieval Hagiography*.

[41] Moshe ben Elazar, "Mah qol hatson" ("What is the voice of the sheep") 173–76, in Habermann, Sefer Gezerot, 220–26. Menahem bar Jacob, "Eikhakha rahameikha" ("Where is Your mercy") 13–16, *Sefer Gezerot*, 239–40. A fourteenth-century manuscript anthology of laments used by Ashkenaz communities preserves a few others, see MS Vatican Hebrew 319, e.g., the lament by Kalonymous the Lesser (haQatan) beginning "Amarti she'u meni amarrer," fol. 26a–28a, where not only do the women kill their children but the children announce that they would rather "say the *Shema*" (i.e., die) than convert.

hurrying to be slaughtered, and that of dead women split open and defiled. Both images depend on motifs already present in the 1096 texts, but now they exclude other descriptions. Moreover, the jarring associations of the biblical verses make for uneasy reading. In Baruch of Mainz's poem for the martyrs of Blois (1171), the women still hurry to their deaths, but here they carry cakes, as if celebrating:

> The women bring cakes to the King of Heaven [so as] not to be ashamed;
> The sons gather wood and the fathers burn the fire.[42]

Here Baruch paraphrases Jeremiah 7:18, where the prophet describes the idolatrous practices of the Israelites, which extend to entire families:

> The children gather wood, the fathers kindle fire, and the women knead dough to make cakes for the Queen of Heaven, and they pour out drink offerings to other gods to provoke me to anger.[43]

Of course, Baruch may have been struggling to portray a scene of family intimacy for which his holy language did not adequately equip him. The traditional poetic style required him to seek associative phrases and verses from biblical and rabbinic texts. He may also have sought to allude to an Ashkenazic ritual for the induction of young boys into school on Shavuot, a ceremony involving the consumption of cakes.[44] The Blois martyrdom took place close to Shavuot, and Shavuot imagery characterizes a number of the commemorative verses. Yet even so, it is hard to imagine that the biblical text would not have echoed in the medieval listener's ear, introducing a dissonant chord to the poignant domestic tableau.[45]

---

[42] Baruch of Mainz, "Esh okhlah esh" ("Fire consuming fire") 35–36, in A. Habermann, "The piyyutim of Baruch bar Samuel of Mainz," *Yedi'ot haMakhon leHeqer haShirah ha'Ivrit* 6 (1945), 132–39.

[43] Jeremiah 7:18, quoted from the Revised Standard Version of the Bible.

[44] This ceremony has recently been analyzed by Ivan Marcus, in Rituals of Childhood: Jewish Acculturation in Medieval Europe (New Haven: Yale University Press, 1996); see especially 64–65. The cake verses reappear in a Rindfleisch lament by Joshua bar Menahem, "El Melekh ne'eman" ("O Lord, Faithful King") 23–24, in *Sefer Gezerot*, 213–19.

[45] One of the most intriguing facets of piyyut style is how it demands that the reader/listener hear both the poetic verse and its (often multiple) layers of association at once in order to be understood. For an illustration of how such associative reading was essential to constructing the "sense" of the medieval poem, see my "The Troyes Laments: Hebrew Martyrology in Hebrew and Old French," forthcoming in *Viator* 30.

Similarly, the constant evocation of the cannibalistic women of Deuteronomy 28:57 and Lamentations 2:20 in later martyrological descriptions of slaughtered women disrupts the attempt to evoke the readers' pity and wrath. No longer are Jewish women girded "kaanashim" ("like men") for heroic battle, but their vulnerability to defilement is described with disturbing ambivalence. Metonymically, the violated woman expresses the violation and permeability of the community; she becomes a marker of communal purity. Three piyyutim for the approximately one hundred-eighty martyrs of Frankfurt (1241), for example, describe the mass destruction of the community.[46] The slaughtered men and boys are piled in heaps, trampled in the dirt and left unburied to be eaten by animals. The women are with them, but unlike the men, they are naked, "their genitals exposed," trampled, aborting (in one case twins), the blood of the slain mothers mingled with the blood of their born and unborn children. The descriptive reduction of the women to their reproductive and sexual characteristics is striking in contrast to the descriptions of the men, defiled mainly by unburial.

Jewish legal discussions, preserved in the form of responsa, shed some light on the obsessive focus on women's purity suggested in the piyyutim. For instance, the survivors of the mob attack in Frankfurt in 1241 were twenty-four men and women who agreed to undergo baptism. Most later reverted to Judaism. One young girl among them protested the betrothal of her former fiancé to a second girl in Wurzburg. One of the rabbis asked to rule on this question, Rabbi Isaac Or Zaru'a, articulates clearly the Jewish male fear of the defilement of Jewish women.[47] Thus he reopens an old theoretical debate concerning the fate of a Jewish woman who accepted baptism (or rape) as an alternative to death. The legal literature established a link between a woman's hypothetical willingness to consent to both sorts of defilement in order to save her life. (The link is symbolic as well as tautological, since both rape and baptism involve the contaminating pollution of fluids.)

---

[46] Rabbi Judah b. Moshe haCohen, "Ve-et'onen va'aqonen" ("I shall mourn and lament"), in Simon Bernfeld, ed., *Sefer Dema'ot*, vol. 3 (Berlin: 1926), 332–33; anonymous poem beginning "Esa' bekhi unehi" ("I shall raise weeping and moaning"), in Bernfeld, vol. 1 (1923), 299–301, and Rabbi Samuel bar Abraham haLevi, "Eyn lanu elohim zulatekha" ("We have no God beside You"), in Bernfeld, 1:301–5.

[47] It should be said that the Or Zaru'a held a minority position in this case. However, because he was so well known and of such stature, his decision may have been the decisive one.

A long legal discussion on the status of captive women preceded the medieval period, which the medieval rabbis had to address and adapt. The Mishnah (completed in the early third century) had long ago established that all women taken hostage in situations where they might be killed must be presumed to have been raped, because the woman will "consent" to rape to try and save her.[48] Nonetheless only the wife of a *kohen* (of the lineage of the biblical priesthood) is forbidden to return to her husband afterwards. Other women can return to their marriages, and indeed, the implication is that the priest's former wife can be remarried to a non-priest. In other words, rape invalidates the cultic status of a woman, but not her personal status. This distinction held throughout the Talmudic period and into the early Middle Ages. However, beginning with Rabbi Solomon bar Isaac ("Rashi"), the famed twelfth-century exegete whose academy flourished in Troyes, the medieval rabbis prohibited the return of *all* Jewish captive women to their husbands. Rabbenu Tam, Rashi's formidable grandson and the leading legal authority of his generation, continues to strengthen this position. Thus, by the mid-twelfth century, there was a growing tendency among the northern French and Ashkenazic authorities to assume that women taken captive would be sexually assaulted, and that they should be forbidden to their former husbands. The blanket presumption of rape is a theoretical construct and not a measure of actual or threatened violence against women. It must be stressed that it is therefore impossible to draw any conclusions about the real frequency of sexual violence against women from the responsa literature. Significantly, women's verbal testimony concerning their experience is invalidated as untrustworthy. In the case of the young girl from Frankfurt, Rabbi Or Zaru'a dismissed not only her own testimony but that of her sister, who was apparently held captive with her. In his final decision, he forbids the Frankfurt girl to her original fiancé and upholds the boy's second marriage.[49]

---

[48] See Mishnah Ketubot, chapter 2.

[49] For a generous sample of responsa in Hebrew illustrating the new distrust of women's ability to resist Christian pressures, physical and religious, see Jacob Blidstein, "The personal status of captive and apostate women according to the halakhah in the Middle Ages," *Shenaton hamishpat ha 'ivri* 3–4 (1976–77): 35–116. For a discussion of the Frankfurt case, see 86–97. Rabbi Isaac Or Zaru'a's opinion is found in his collected responsa, ed. L. Goldman (Brooklyn: 1959; facsimile of Zhitomir 1862 and Jerusalem 1887–90), part 1, no. 747. Blidstein also discusses the suppression of women's testimony in cases of supposed rape by Christians. For an analogous case in which a woman's verbal testimony is invalidated in a case of domestic violence, see Jonathan Cohen, "Some Aspects of the History of Restitution

The association between Jewish women's assumed weak resistance to sexual and to religious assault is not expressed directly in the poetic literature, because the women depicted in the poetic literature have died rather than submit to the foe. Nonetheless, ambivalence undergirds the *descriptions* of these women, too, descriptions that frequently evoke cannibalism and betrayal. Moreover, the uneasy focus on the sexual humiliation and violation of the female dead finds a counterpart in the anxiety and distrust characterizing the legal discussion of female survivors. A rare instance of a vernacular martyrological lament confirms the link made in the legal literature between the potential for sexual and religious betrayal. Jacob ben Judah's Old French lament for the thirteen martyrs of Troyes burned in 1288 includes a description of two women, the pregnant wife of Isaac Chatelain and the Chatelains' young daughter-in-law. When the Dominican preachers extend the girl one last chance to save her life, their offer includes a new husband as well as a new god:

Un ekier riche te donro[n]s ke tenret mot chier
Tantot ele akemense encontre as a crachier
Je ne lere le Ge vif; portat me pores ecorchier!

We will give you a rich squire who will hold you dear.
She immediately began to spit on them:
"I will not renounce the Living God; therefore you can flay me!"[50]

The Chatelain bride is subjected to precisely the kind of psychological pressure that haunts the rabbis' imagination, and her religious faith is linked vividly to her preservation of sexual honor. (Incidentally, this is our second spitting woman, suggesting this, too, is a literary topos.) The vernacular poem is important for two reasons. One is that the use of the vernacular apparently freed the author from some of the typological and motival constraints that controlled the presentation of the martyrs in Hebrew. This becomes evident with a comparison of the vernacular poem to the Hebrew lament it ostensibly "translates." The Hebrew portrait of the young Chatelain bride mentions neither the preachers nor their offer, but merely says

---

in Jewish Law" (Ph.D. dissertation, University of Liverpool, 1998), and his discussion of a responsum of the Rashba, part 4, no. 113.

[50] The Old French lament was first published by A. Darmesteter in "Deux élégies du Vatican," *Romania* 3 (1874): 1–46 and "L'auto da fé de Troyes," *Revue des études juives* 2 (1881): 199–247. I have treated both poems and re-edited the texts with translation, in "The Troyes Laments: Hebrew Martyrology in Hebrew and Old French." The above excerpt is from stanza 7.

that the "nations spoke meaninglessness to the beautiful bride."[51] The vernacular poem, relying on its own (often romance) conventions, reveals some of the attitudes encoded in the Hebrew verse and more patently visible in the responsa's attempt to build a theoretical model of the psychology of Jewish women in captivity and how they will respond to pressure. The vernacular poem is important for another reason, too. Although few Jewish women would have understood Hebrew well enough to hear themselves depicted in the holy tongue, they would have surely understood the French version. Thus, Jacob ben Judah's lament demonstrates that even when repackaged for a mixed audience, the ideal female martyr retained the same essential traits that she exhibited in Hebrew—loyalty to her husband and family as her expression of loyalty to God.

Significantly, then, the dominant images of female martyrdom in twelfth- and thirteenth-century piyyutim rely on images of violence against women as a symbolic expression of threats to the defining limits of male community. These images find their counterpart in the anxiety about female survivors in the responsa literature. The new women martyrs are idealized for their obedience and their unquestioning willingness to be martyred, often in settings that ratify their marital and maternal loyalty. Their deaths are depicted in images of defilement that focus on the shameful exposure of dead female bodies and the blood that pours from slashed wombs and miscarriages. At the same time, by alluding to biblical stories of desperate women who sacrifice their families and even consume their children to save themselves, the poetry conveys an ambivalence towards the female martyr reflected in the responsa's critical treatment of the female survivor.

III

The disappearance of the strong, energetic, and independent female type from the martyrological literature, and her replacement by a more passive and ambivalent model, raise questions about social change. The moving elegy by Eleazer bar Judah (the "Rokeah") for his wife, Dolce, and two daughters, killed in a Third Crusade attack in 1197, celebrates Dolce's industry, intelligence and piety.[52] The Rokeah explicitly mentions that

---

[51] See Darmesteter, ibid., and Einbinder, ibid., for the Hebrew text.
[52] Eleazer bar Judah haRokeah, "Eshet ḥayil mi yimtzah," in Habermann, *Sefer*

his wife supported him and his family with her earnings. Thus, although idealized portraiture, the elegy describes no real change in the position of Jewish women as wage-earners since the First Crusade. The responsa literature confirms the extent to which northern European Jewish wives, mothers, daughters and widows helped maintain their households and communities. As William Jordan has shown in his studies of medieval Jewish women moneylenders, archival sources also confirm the active presence of Jewish women in economic life.[53]

Despite their commercial activity, however, women's status seems to have deteriorated on other fronts. Cheryl Tallan claims that the thirteenth century saw some erosion in the rights of Jewish widows, specifically of their ability to hold onto and control the use of dowry and inheritance properties.[54] Shlomo Riskin has traced a parallel trend in changing halakhic attitudes towards marital rights and divorce. He cites, for instance, Rabbenu Tam's decision to void the right of a woman to seek divorce on grounds of incompatibility, a right upheld from Talmudic times through the works of the Geonim, Rabbi Meir (the "Light of the Exile") and Maimonides.[55] And as we have seen, the evolution in the legal treatment of women captives and forced converts suggests a harshening in attitudes towards women which demands closer examination.

The same scholar-rabbis who wrote responsa and exegetical works often wrote the martyrological piyyutim. Indeed, the martyrological literature, prose and verse, must be seen as part of a larger effort to shape and control responses to persecution and the traumas it wrought. Even

---

Gezerot, 164–67. A partial English translation appears in T. Carmi, *The Penguin Book of Hebrew Verse* (New York: Penguin Books, 1981), 387–88.

[53] William C. Jordan, "Jews on Top: Women and the Availability of Consumption Loans in Northern France in the Mid-Thirteenth Century," Journal of *Jewish Studies* 29 (1978): 39–56; and *Women and Credit in PreIndustrial and Developing Societies* (Philadelphia: University of Pennsylvania, 1993).

[54] Cheryl Tallan, "The Position of the Medieval Jewish Widow as a Function of Family Structure," *Proceedings of the Tenth World Congress of Jewish Studies* 2 (1990): 91–98. Tallan argues that the deterioration of widows' rights is related to a shift towards a "more patrilinear pattern of family structure," a shift whose presence has also been argued by Stow, "Jewish Family" and *Alienated Minority*.

[55] Shlomo Riskin, *Women and Jewish Divorce: The Rebellious Wife, the Agunah and the Right of Women to Initiate Divorce in Jewish Law: A Halakhic Solution* (Hoboken, N.J.: Ktav, 1989), 91–111, and Irving A. Breitowitz, *Between Civil and Religious Law: The Plight of the Agunah in American Society* (Westwood, Conn.: Greenwood Press 1993), 47–52. I thank my colleague, Professor Jonathan Cohen of the Hebrew Union College in Cincinnati, for steering me to these sources.

more, I think it can be concluded that over the twelfth and thirteenth centuries, the rabbis responded to an increasingly desperate situation by adapting their martyrological tropes. As crusader attacks gave way to calculated secular and ecclesiastical policies of harassment and judicial violence, the rabbi-poets increasingly emphasized the sanctity of familial bonds and religious authority (not coincidentally their own). The evolving image of women in the martyrological texts increasingly ratifies their passivity, obedience and loyalty to family and God. At the same time, the defenseless and violated women and texts of the literature rally male community precisely around these two institutions.

What Jewish women thought of this picture of themselves is nearly impossible to ascertain. The words they speak in the chronicles and poetry are invented by their male authors, and the testimony of real women survivors, like the young girl from Frankfurt, was "not reliable."[56]

Obviously, real Jewish women, like men, must have exhibited a spectrum of responses when faced with the ultimatum of conversion or death. Some of them showed great courage: at least one responsum written in reaction to the Or Zaru'a's decision describes how the young Frankfurt girl not only turned down a Christian husband—"one of the richest and most important men of the city"—but repeatedly tried to flee her Christian home.[57] Yet the martyrological conventions for depicting women make such bold reactions increasingly hard to see. Whether the rabbi-authors could have made different literary choices, or what would have happened if they did, no one will ever know. But we can ask how the choices they made helped to shape the literature they did write, and then how the literature shaped real life, where the image of woman and her living counterpart sometimes must have met.

Hebrew Union College, Cincinnati

---

[56] Or Zaru'a, 213.
[57] Ibid.

Ontology, Alterity, and Ethics
in Kabbalistic Anthropology

ELLIOT R. WOLFSON

> *alles ist weniger, als*
> *es ist,*
> *alles ist mehr.*
> Celan

I

Kabbalah, which literally means "tradition," is the generic term used by pious practitioners and critical scholars to denote the various currents of esoteric lore and mystical praxis that have been cultivated by elite rabbinic circles from the High Middle Ages to the present. The kabbalah is not monolithic in nature; on the contrary, it can be described most appropriately as a collage of disparate doctrines and practices.[1]

For the purposes of this study, I will limit my analysis for the most part to the corpus of the *Zohar*, the major sourcebook of theosophic kabbalistic symbolism.[2] Apparently, the literary units that make up the fabric of zoharic literature were composed and began to circulate in the

---

The present study is a much-abbreviated version of the first chapter of a forthcoming book on the relationship of mysticism and ethics in the history of kabbalistic speculation and practice. The book is based on the three lectures I delivered as the Shoshana Shier Visiting Professor of Judaic Studies at the University of Toronto in the Spring of 1998. I express my gratitude to Sheila Delany whose meticulous editing of the original draft improved my essay in both form and content.

[1] Gershom Scholem suggested two typological trends in medieval kabbalah: theosophic and ecstatic. For a brief but incisive review of this typology, especially as articulated by Moshe Idel, see H. Tirosh-Rothschild, "Continuity and Revision in the Study of the Kabbalah," *AJS Review* 16 (1991): 174–76. A challenge to Scholem's typological distinction is developed in my *Abraham Abulafia, Kabbalist and Prophet: Hermeneutics, Theosophy, and Theurgy* (Los Angeles: Cherub Press, 2000).

[2] On the literary structure and authorship of the Zohar, see G. Scholem, *Major Trends in Jewish Mysticism* (New York: Schocken, 1956), 156–204; I. Tishby, *The Wisdom of the Zohar*, trans. D. Goldstein (Oxford: Oxford University Press, 1989), 1–126.

latter decades of the thirteenth century and the beginning of the fourteenth. It is probable that the different literary strata of the *Zohar*, composed in Hebrew and/or Aramaic, were the product of a fraternity of kabbalists who assembled in the region of Castile.³ Like other mystical fraternities within rabbinic societies of this period, the zoharic circle was elitist in its composition. The extant historical documents provide relatively sparse biographical information about the Spanish kabbalists who participated in this circle. Nevertheless, we may conclude that they were practicing rabbinic leaders or had been trained in the talmudic academies and were thus well versed in classical Jewish learning. We can assume, moreover, that these kabbalists availed themselves of the religious institutions that served the rest of their extended communities. In that respect, it is doubtful that the kabbalists were separated from the society at large even though there is good reason to assume that they belonged to a small fraternity made up exclusively of fellow practitioners. One must suppose that to some degree this circle functioned autonomously, laying claim to a secret knowledge that explained the essence of Judaism but that was not readily available to all Jews.

In this study, I shall consider to what extent the kabbalistic orientation, cultivated by this circle, fostered a sense of social consciousness and a call to moral action on behalf of the human community at large. In my judgment, the study of ethics in kabbalistic tradition must begin with a proper understanding of the ontological place accorded non-Jewish nations. In this regard, I am naturally indebted to a host of philosophers who have identified in one way or another the centrality of the status of the other in ethical discourse.⁴ Indeed, as one contemporary philosopher reminds us, the sense of the other entailed in the notion of obligation

---

³ For an extensive discussion of this hypothesis, see Y. Liebes, *Studies in the Zohar*, trans. A. Schwartz, S. Nakache, and P. Peli (Albany: SUNY Press, 1993), 85–138.

⁴ For example, see M. C. Taylor, *Altarity* (Chicago: University of Chicago Press, 1987); W. Farley, *Eros for the Other: Retaining Truth in a Pluralistic World* (University Park: Pennsylvania State University Press, 1996); E. Wyschogrod, *An Ethics of Remembering: History, Heterology, and the Nameless Others* (Chicago: University of Chicago Press, 1998); S. Glendinning, *On Being With Others: Heidegger, Derrida, Wittgenstein* (London and New York: Routledge, 1998). Perhaps no single philosopher has been more insistent on emphasizing the importance of the other to the ethical project than Emmanuel Levinas; cf. the essays collected in *Ethics as First Philosophy: The Significance of Emmanuel Levinas for Philosophy, Literature and Religion*, ed. A. T. Peperzak (New York and London: Routledge, 1995).

must "include not only other human beings but what is other than human—animals, e.g., or other living things generally, and even the earth itself."[5] My discussion, however, will focus on intersubjective alterity as expressed in the place accorded the non-Jew within the zoharic ontology. My emphasis on ontology reflects the way of thinking adopted by the kabbalists from the thirteenth century until the present, but it does not indicate my own personal preference or what I would consider an adequate approach to moral theory and praxis. In the pre-Kantian world in which traditional kabbalistic symbolism was formulated, there was no justification for separating ontology and axiology: For the kabbalists, value is grounded in the nature of being.

Scholars who have written about kabbalistic ethics have noted symbolic representations of Islam and Christianity, but have usually ignored the position of the non-Jewish other in the ontological scheme that informs kabbalistic theosophy and anthropology.[6] The point is epitomized in Yitzhak Baer's seminal study on Jews in Christian Spain.[7] Baer called his chapter on the thirteenth-century Catalonian and Castilian kabbalists "Mysticism and Social Reform." He argued that the kabbalists, particularly as presented in the later strata of the zoharic corpus, derived from an inferior social and economic class and that they vigorously attacked the courtier aristocracy, amongst them the rabbinic leaders. Thus the kabbalists, according to this perception, sought to improve the moral and religious life of the Jewish masses. Baer writes, "A marked affinity existed between the ideologies of the ascetics and mystics and the aims of the practical reformers bent upon achieving a higher standard of social morality."[8]

Without challenging the main thrust of Baer's historical analysis, I would question the appropriateness of his locution "ethical-social reform" to characterize the mystical speculations and practices of the kabbalists. Baer is surely correct in saying that the intent of some of the kabbalist

---

[5] J. D. Caputo, *Against Ethics: Contributions to a Poetics of Obligation with Constant Reference to Deconstruction* (Bloomington and Indianapolis: Indiana University Press, 1993), 5.

[6] See Tishby, *Wisdom of the Zohar*, 68–71; Liebes, *Studies in the Zohar*, 149–50, 154–61, 244 n92, and R. C. Kiener, "The Image of Islam in the *Zohar*," *Jerusalem Studies in Jewish Thought* 8 (1989): 43–65 (English section).

[7] Y. Baer, *A History of the Jews in Christian Spain*, trans. L. Schoffman, 2 vols. (Philadelphia: Jewish Publication Society of America, 1961), 1:243–305; see also idem, "The Historical Background of the Ra'aya' Meheimna'," *Zion* 5 (1940): 1–44 (in Hebrew).

[8] Baer, *History of the Jews*, 250.

moralists was to improve the pietistic standard of Jewish society by attacking the ethical deficiencies of the rabbinic leadership. Nonetheless, scholars have not properly examined the appropriateness of his terminology to depict the kabbalistic sources. Do the concerns with social morality expressed in kabbalistic writings refer to the Jewish people only or to humanity at large? Does the moral standard embraced by the kabbalists reflect a narrow exclusionary ethnocentrism or, instead, a broad universalism? Has the utilization of terms like "ethics" and "social reform" prevented scholars from appreciating a leitmotif of this material? From my perspective the suitability of such terms to the esoteric tradition depends on a careful exploration of the symbolic constructions of the other that informed the major kabbalistic texts. Before we adopt this terminology we must probe the ethnocentric and in some measure misanthropic assertions strewn throughout the literature, especially the anthropological presumption that humanity in its most ideal sense refers to Israel alone. Can a mystical tradition that ontologizes ethnic difference foster genuine social reform by promoting an ethical standard of behavior, as Baer proposed? Is it appropriate to speak, as some scholars have done, of a genre of literature composed of ethico-kabbalistic treatises? In what sense is the term "ethical" meaningful in this context?

I would like to contextualize the framing of the other in the theosophic symbolism of medieval kabbalah; such framing is an integral part of self-definition. First, let us acknowledge that the tendency to divide the world into we and they is instinctual, originating probably in the most elemental form of territorialism.[9] Even the most advanced aspects of human culture—cognitive apprehension and linguistic discourse—are predicated on the act of differentiation. It stands to reason, therefore, that one's self-understanding will be based in great measure on one's sense of social and cultural otherness.[10] From that vantage point it is no exaggeration to say that the attitude towards the other is a key factor in defining the identity of a given group.

In medieval kabbalistic sources, the construction of alterity occurs in a

---

[9] R. Redfield, *The Primitive World and Its Transformations* (Ithaca: Cornell University Press, 1953), 92.

[10] See J. Z. Smith, "What A Difference A Difference Makes," in *"To See Ourselves As Others See Us:" Christians, Jews, and "Others" in Late Antiquity*, ed. J. Neusner and E. S. Freirichs (Chico: Scholar's Press, 1985), 4–48; idem, "Differential Equations: On Constructing the 'Other'," *Thirteenth Annual University Lecture in Religion*, Arizona State University, March 5, 1992, Department of Religious Studies.

context of historical contingencies that fostered negative stereotypes of the other. We cannot stand in moral judgment of medieval kabbalists when our own attitude is shaped by the present social, political, and economic realities; to do so would be anachronistic. Nevertheless, we are obliged to investigate the symbolic rhetoric of kabbalistic material and its effect on later Jewish attitudes towards the other, particularly as this rhetoric pertains to the relationship between ethics and mysticism. Although I personally would not condone the use of kabbalistic material to justify either the right-wing political agenda in the state of Israel or the tacit denunciation of non-Jews by certain segments of the ultra-orthodox Jewish community elsewhere, as a scholar I would argue that these applications do not necessarily distort the sources (as some more liberal-minded Jews might claim). On the contrary, some recently published works written by individuals deeply influenced by the symbolism of traditional kabbalah depict Islam (under the guise of the biblical Ishmael) and Christianity (portrayed as Edom) in overtly negative, at times even demonic, terms; these works accurately reinscribe attitudes that arose in the medieval context. What is remarkable is that the rhetoric of hatred forged in the crucible of medieval animosity continues to be used in the service of a political agenda.[11] The task of responsible scholarship is to acknowledge the reverberations of kabbalistic ideas in contemporary Jewish culture even when we want to avoid ethical condemnation of a tradition shaped in a different time. In short, we need to navigate between the extremes of pious apologetics and moral dogmatism.

II

Before I turn to an analysis of passages from zoharic literature, I want to make a methodological observation. With respect to many of their most important themes kabbalistic texts exemplify a remarkable degree of homogeneity; surprisingly, changes in time and place hardly have any effect at all. This textual phenomenon can be explained in part by the fact

---

[11] A good example of my point is an anonymous eschatological work based on kabbalistic sources, 'El Qeṣ ha-Tiqqun, "Concerning the End of the Rectification," which was published in Israel in 1982. Another is Gilluy ha-'Or ha-Ganuz le-Yisra'el, "The Disclosure of the Light Hidden for Israel," a massive and rambling compilation of traditional kabbalistic symbolism composed by Judah Kalfon, a kabbalist who lives in Tel-Aviv.

that the conditions of production and consumption[12] of kabbalistic ideas and practices have been so severely limited through the ages, restricted as authors and audience were to men with rabbinic training, that there is little change with regard to the major themes that engaged their imagination. I would suggest that, had these conditions been more diverse, the range of attitudes reflected in the sources would have been wider. But the historical reality is that in the formative period of kabbalistic symbolism such variety in social context is absent. I sympathize with the contemporary tendency to seek multiple voices in the reading of texts, and I applaud the attempt to avoid a totalizing and reductive hermeneutic. However, in the case of traditional kabbalistic sources, I submit that the general invariability and redundancy are due to male exclusivity and social homogeneity fostered by the androcentrism of medieval rabbinic culture. Of course, kabbalistic texts yield a range of opinions on any number of theological, anthropological, and cosmological issues; but the point is that with respect to many major themes, like the one that I will discuss here, uniformity is far more striking than diversity.

What guiding principle informs zoharic symbolism regarding the nature of humanity, a concept that arguably lies at the foundation of any ethical orientation? In the various literary strata of the zoharic anthology, a consistent anthropological picture emerges: Israel is considered the "holy seed" (*zar'a' qadisha'*),[13] whereas the other nations of the world (with the possible exception of Islam according to some[14]) are said to derive from the demonic "other side" (*siṭra' aḥra'*), the realm of ten impure potencies on the left that correspond to the ten holy *sefirot*, or luminous emanations, on the right.[15] In some measure, the attitude expressed in zoharic litera-

---

[12] I am grateful to Sheila Delany for this locution.

[13] *Zohar* 2:6a, 78b, 124a, 125a; 3:152b, 237a. All translations are my own based on *Sefer ha-Zohar*, ed. R. Margaliot, 3 vols. (Jerusalem: Mosad ha-Rav Kook, 1984). Also see Baer, *History*, 246.

[14] Some passages associate Islam with the demonic potency (*Zohar* 1:103b, 110a, 118b; 2:17a, 124a; 3:124a, 246b, 282a; *Zohar Ḥadash*, ed. R. Margaliot [Jerusalem: Mossad ha-Rav Kook, 1978], 78d), whereas others locate it in a realm of being that is above the demonic (*Zohar* 2:86a). Because it practices circumcision, Islam is situated beneath the wings of the *Shekhinah*, i.e., in the lower part of the last of the divine emanations, which is also the place accorded to those who convert to Judaism (*Zohar* 1:13a–b). On the ambivalent attitude of the zoharic authors to Islam, see Kiener, "Image of Islam," 62–65; P. Giller, *The Enlightened Will Shine: Symbolization and Theurgy in the Later Strata of the Zohar* (Albany: SUNY Press, 1993), 51 and other relevant references cited on 146 n114.

[15] Scholem, *Major Trends*, 35–36, 235–39; idem, *Kabbalah* (Jerusalem: Keter,

ture, and confirmed in other kabbalistic sources, elaborates a position articulated in earlier rabbinic texts, which in turn echo ethnocentric tendencies evident in parts of the Hebrew Bible. In the words of one scholar, "the rabbinic image of the non-Jew is xenophobic in the extreme."[16] Empirically, the Rabbis may have had positive interactions with non-Jews, but their process of cultural self-identification was fostered by promulgating the stereotypical image of the non-Jew as an inferior and intrinsically wicked being.[17] Consider, for example, the blunt interpretive gloss on one of the three blessings that, according to Rabbi Judah, the Jewish male is required to utter each day (a formula that is still part of the traditional liturgy), "Blessed are you for not making me a Gentile:" "For the Gentiles do not amount to anything [*she-'ein ha-goyim kelum*] [as it is written] 'All the nations are nothing in relation to him' [Isaiah 40:17]."[18] So unworthy are the non-Jews that no specific reason for their unworthiness is given. In still other rabbinic texts, a more definitive contrast is drawn between the intrinsic purity of Israel and the impurity of the nations,[19] classified as worshippers of a foreign god, an orientation epitomized in the remark addressed by God to Israel:

> In this world I abhor all the idolaters for they are from the seed of impurity [*zeraʿ ṭumʾah*], but I chose you, for you are the seed of truth [*zeraʿ ʾemet*], as it says "I planted you with noble vines, entirely the seed of truth" [Jeremiah 2:21], and it is written "The Lord God chose you from among all other peoples on earth to be his treasured people" [Deuteronomy 14:2]. Even in the future I will choose only you, for you are the seed of holiness [*zeraʿ qedushah*], blessed by the Lord, as it says "They shall not toil to no purpose, they shall not

---

1974), 122–28; idem, *On the Mystical Shape of the Godhead: Basic Concepts in the Kabbalah*, trans. J. Neugroschel, ed. and rev. J. Chipman (New York: Schocken, 1991), 56–87; Tishby, *Wisdom of the Zohar*, 447–546.

[16] S. Stern, *Jewish Identity in Early Rabbinic Writings* (Leiden: E. J. Brill, 1994), 4. Other scholars have emphasized the universalizing tendencies in biblical and rabbinic sources. While this is not a completely distorted or falsified portrait of ancient Judaism, it is only partial. One can surely understand the lingering desire to combat an anti-Semitic stereotype of parochial Judaism and its negative attitude towards the Gentile, but the scholarly task requires a balanced assessment that takes into account the laudable and reprehensible elements of the past.

[17] Ibid., 5–6, 22–30.

[18] Palestinian Talmud, Berakhot 9:1, 12b.

[19] Stern, *Jewish Identity*, 31–32.

bear children in vain, for they shall be a seed blessed by the Lord" [Isaiah 65:23].[20]

In other rabbinic texts, Israel's holiness is related more specifically to the observance of ritual commandments (*miṣwot*).[21] In some passages, the distinctive potentiality for holiness is expressed as a homology between the community of Israel and the heavenly angels.[22] The Jewish people are an angelic race inasmuch as Jews have the capacity to realize their divine nature by becoming like angels in the liturgical service of God through prayer, study, and good deeds. In opposition to angelic Israel stand the inherently impure and idolatrous nations. Such extreme disavowal of the worth of non-Jews is not necessarily the normative, or even majority, rabbinic opinion; but it was articulated and preserved in the classical rabbinic literature and had an impact on subsequent generations.[23]

The demonization of non-Jewish nations in kabbalistic texts has much to do with the mythologoumenon preserved in rabbinic sources based on the sexual relationship of Eve and the serpent (identified with the angel Samael). An early formulation of this aggadic motif is found in the

---

[20] *Tanḥuma'*, Naso', 7.

[21] *Tanḥuma'*, Shelaḥ, 15; *Numbers Rabbah* 17:6; Stern, *Jewish Identity*, 32, 71–79.

[22] Babylonian Talmud, Qiddushin 70a; *Exodus Rabbah* 15:6; *Midrash Mishle*, ed. B. L. Visotzky (New York: Jewish Theological Seminary of America, 1990), 8:1, 57–58; *Pirqei Rabbi 'Eli'ezer* (Warsaw: 1852), chapter 22, 51a; Stern, *Jewish Identity*, 40–41. It is possible that the rabbinic depiction of Israel as angelic is based on the portrayal of the righteous as angels in earlier apocalyptic and sectarian literature. See J. H. Charlesworth, "The Portrayal of the Righteous as an Angel," in *Ideal Figures in Ancient Judaism*, ed. G. W. E. Nickelsburg and J. J. Collins (Chico: Scholars Press, 1980), 135–51; D. Dimant, "Men as Angels: The Self-Image of the Qumran Community," in *Religion and Politics in the Ancient Near East*, ed. Adele Berlin (Bethesda: University of Maryland Press, 1996), 93–103; W. F. Smelik, "On Mystical Transformation of the Righteous into Light in Judaism," *Journal for the Study of Judaism* 26 (1995): 122–44; D. L. Bock, *Blasphemy and Exaltation in Judaism and the Final Examination of Jesus* (Tübingen: J. C. B. Mohr, 1998), 113–83.

[23] The prayer *'Aleynu le-Shabbeaḥ*, which originates in the talmudic period and is still recited in many Jewish congregations on a daily basis and featured in the High Holiday liturgy, praises God "for not making us like the nations of the lands, for not placing us amongst the families of the earth, for not allocating our portion with them nor our fate in all of their masses." In the continuation of the prayer (according to the oldest textual witnesses still preserved in many prayer-books), the God of Jewish worship is contrasted with the false gods of the nations. What meaning can this prayer have when it is uttered in a synagogue in the end of the twentieth century, and how should it affect the ethical sensibility of the worshiper? On the background of this prayer, see M. D. Swartz, "*'Alay le-Shabbeaḥ*: A Liturgical Prayer in Ma'aseh Merkabah," *Jewish Quarterly Review* 77 (1987): 179–90.

Targum Pseudo-Jonathan to Genesis: "And Adam knew that his wife Eve was impregnated from Samael, the angel of the Lord."[24] Particularly important is the view attributed in some talmudic sources to Rabbi Yoḥanan: that the pollution with which the serpent inseminated Eve, when she and Adam disobeyed the divine command in the Garden of Eden, was removed from Israel when they stood at Sinai; but it was never extracted from the other nations.[25] I do not think we would be far off the mark in saying that the aggadic myth comes remarkably close to the conception of original sin enunciated in Christian tradition, for the claim it makes is that the ontological status of humanity was changed with the insemination of Eve by the serpent. The antidote to this seminal pollution is Torah, the efficacy of which will be fully realized only in the time of the messiah when the evil force in the world will be completely eradicated and non-Jews will be purified in the manner that Jews were purified at Sinai.[26]

The portrayal of the Jews vis-à-vis the other nations in kabbalistic literature is enhanced by the claim found in a number of rabbinic texts that the term 'adam, which denotes humanity in its fullest sense, applies only to Israel and not to the idolatrous nations. In the Babylonian Talmud, non-Jews are excluded from a number of halakhic rulings on the basis of this philological assertion, which is supported exegetically by a

---

[24] My translation is based on the version of the text established in *Targum Pseudo-Jonathan of the Pentateuch: Text and Concordance*, ed. E. G. Clarke with W. E. Aufrecht, J. C. Hurd, and F. Spitzer (Hoboken: Ktav, 1984), 5. In the continuation of the targumic text, this impregnation produces the birth of Cain, which parallels the birth of Abel from Adam's seed. In this particular textual accretion of the tradition, the insemination of Eve by Samael accounts for the birth of Cain rather than for humanity at large. On the midrashic theme of the demonic Cain, see D. M. Eichhorn, *Cain: Son of the Serpent*, 2nd ed. (Chappaqua: Rossel Books, 1985), and the interesting analysis of the image of the "monstrous Cain" in Western culture in R. J. Quinones, *The Changes of Cain: Violence and the Lost Brother in Cain and Abel Literature* (Princeton: Princeton University Press, 1991), 41–61. On the possibility that the aggadic depiction of Cain may have generated the Gnostic myth of the impure seed born from the union of the earthly female and the demiurge, see G. Stroumsa, *Another Seed: Studies in Gnostic Mythology* (Leiden: E. J. Brill, 1984), 45–49. The negative stereotype of Cain in the biblical narrative is discussed by R. M. Schwartz, *The Curse of Cain: The Violent Legacy of Monotheism* (Chicago: University of Chicago Press, 1997).

[25] Babylonian Talmud, Yevamot 103b; 'Avodah Zarah 22b.

[26] See E. E. Urbach, *The Sages: Their Concepts and Beliefs* (Jerusalem: Magnes Press, 1969), 148 (in Hebrew).

gloss on the verse, "For you, my flock, flock that I tend, are men" (Ezekiel 34:31): "You are called men, but the idolaters are not called men."[27] Underlying this philology is the anthropological presumption that Jews alone possess the human soul (*nefesh ha-'adam*) and thus are ontologically different from other nations.[28] The contrast between Israel and the nations is not simply a matter of difference in custom or belief, but an essential difference of their being. The ontological divergence is expressed in striking terms in the following statement attributed to Rabbi Bun:

> The blessed holy One said: "I have established prophets in Israel, for they are called men ['*adam*], as it says, 'for you are men' [Ezekiel 34:31], but I have not established prophets in idolatrous nations, for they are called beasts [*behemah*], as it says, 'and many beasts'" [Jonah 4:11].[29]

The viewpoint expressed here, although not consistently maintained in rabbinic literature, is that prophecy is unique to the Jews because they are fully human, whereas the other nations are comparable to beasts.[30]

The portrayal of Jews as human in contrast to the beastly character of non-Jews was greatly accentuated in medieval kabbalistic literature, and

---

[27] Babylonian Talmud, Yevamot 61a; Bava' Meṣi'a 114b; Keritut 6b; Sanhedrin 72b; Stern, *Jewish Identity*, 39–40. Other passages in the classical rabbinic corpus attest that the exclusive attribution of the term '*adam* to Israel was expanded beyond the specific issue of ritual purity. See *Exodus Rabbah* 4:1; *Leviticus Rabbah* 5:3; *Numbers Rabbah* 12:14; *Deuteronomy Rabbah* 1:2; *Esther Rabbah* 7:11; *Tanḥuma'*, Ki Tissa' 4; Wayaqhel 3; *Pesiqta' Rabbati* 10:4, 47:5; *Pesiqta' de-Rav Kahana'* 2:3. The exclusion of non-Jews from the category of human ('*adam*) was certainly not the only opinion expressed in rabbinic literature. The inconsistency of the Rabbis on this point was duly noted by M. Smith, "On the Shape of God and the Humanity of the Gentiles," in *Religions in Antiquity: Essays in Memory of E. R. Goodenough*, ed. J. Neusner (Leiden: E. J. Brill, 1968), 320–26.

[28] *Genesis Rabbah* 34:13, 325.

[29] *Ecclesiastes Rabbah* 3:22. On the portrayal of non-Jews as animals in rabbinic sources, see Stern, *Jewish Identity*, 33–39.

[30] An important exception to the dichotomy of the human nature of Israel versus the beastly character of the non-Jews is found in *Zohar* 3:147a wherein Israel itself is said to comprise both human ('*adam*) and beast (*behemah*), a point that is derived exegetically from "man and beast you deliver, O Lord" (Ps. 36:6). See also ibid., 125a (*Ra'aya' Meheimna'*), but in that context the beastly component of the community of Israel is the "mixed multitude," the '*erev rav*, that journeyed together with the Israelites in the desert on the way out of Egypt (Exod. 12:38). On the use of the symbol of the mixed multitude to denote the inherently flawed members of the Jewish community derived from Lilith, see Giller, *Enlightened Will Shine*, 49 and references given on 145 n97.

especially in the corpus of the *Zohar*.³¹ To cite one of the bolder formulations of this idea from the zoharic text:

> These [sefirotic] lights form an image below to establish the image of everything that is contained within Adam, for the inner form of all inner forms is called by this name, and from here [we know that] every form that is contained in this emanation is called "Adam," as it is written, "for you are men" [Ezekiel 34:31], you are called men but not the rest of the nations, for they are idolaters.... The spirit that emanates on the rest of the idolatrous nations, which derives from the side that is not holy, is not considered [to be in the category of] humanity [*'adam*]. *Zohar* 1:20b

Building upon the rabbinic exegesis of Ezekiel 34:31, the zoharic authors demonstrate that Israel alone of the nations is called *'adam*, which denotes that ontologically only the Jew is human in the fullest and most proper sense.³² The point is made poignantly in the following passage from the commentary on Ruth that is part of the *Midrash ha-Ne'elam* stratum of the *Zohar*:

> Rabbi began [his exposition] and said: "The primal Adam is the soul of the soul, and Eve is the soul. Cain and Abel: Abel is of the same type as Adam and Eve, which is called the holy spirit. Cain is the spirit of impurity of the left, which is called an admixture [*kil'ayim*], that is, an unnecessary combination, the other side, which is not of the type of Adam and Eve. Concerning this [it says] 'You shall not plow with an ox and an ass together' [Deuteronomy 22:10]. Thus you should not enter the holy covenant in the other dominion, [as it says] 'You shall not have the other god before me' [Exodus 20:3]. Adam is in the pattern of that which is above. The 'other god' is the ass and the she-ass, male and female. Accordingly, it is written

---

³¹ *Zohar* 1:28b; 2:25b (*Piqqudin*), 86a, 120a (*Ra'aya' Meheimna'*), 275b; 3:125a (*Ra'aya' Meheimna'*), 219a, 238b (*Ra'aya' Meheimna'*); *Zohar Hadash*, 37b, 78c–d. See, however, *Zohar* 3:173b, where *benei 'adam* (in Ps. 31:20) is interpreted as a reference to the worshipers of the stars and the constellations.

³² This philological usage is attested in other kabbalistic works contemporary with the composition of the zoharic corpus, including the Hebrew theosophic works of Moses de León. See, for instance, J. H. A. Wijnhoven, "*Sefer ha-Mishkal*: Text and Study" (Ph.D. dissertation, Brandeis University, 1964), 39–47; *Rabbi Moses de León's Sefer Sheqel ha-Qodesh*, ed. C. Mopsik (Los Angeles: Cherub Press, 1996), 14 (in Hebrew).

with regard to the one who enters the holy covenant into the other dominion, 'They have rebelled against the Lord, and thus they have begotten alien children' [Hosea 5:7]. There is no jealousy before the blessed holy One except for that which concerns the holy covenant. The blessed holy One created in man [*'inash*] YHWH, which is his holy name, the soul of the soul, and this is called *'adam*."

Zohar Ḥadash 78c

The radical ontological distinction between the Jews and the other nations is expressed typologically in terms of Cain, representing the left side of impurity, and Abel, being aligned with the right side of holiness. Cain was the offspring of the illicit union of holy and demonic (Eve and the serpent), whereas Abel is the progeny of the sanctioned coupling of the holy pair (Eve and Adam). The presumption here, borne out by many other passages (for example, *Zohar* 1:34b), is that the first Adam, the prototypical human, is the idealized Jew created in the image of God (*ṣelem 'elohim*). The male Jew is forbidden to engage in intercourse with a non-Jewish woman, for to do so would be to "enter the holy covenant into the alien domain," a sexual transgression equivalent to worshipping a false god.[33]

In contrast to the other nations, which are compared to the male and the female ass,[34] the soul of the Jew is the genuinely androgynous human

---

[33] In the zoharic polemic against other religions, principally Christianity, theological and sexual themes are intertwined: heretical belief is treated as form of illicit sexuality and illicit sexuality as a form of heretical belief. The common denominator is defilement of the holy covenant by effacing the boundary between sacred and profane. See E. R. Wolfson, "Re/membering the Covenant: Memory, Forgetfulness, and History in the *Zohar*," *Jewish History and Jewish Memory: Essays in Honor of Yosef Hayim Yerushalmi*, ed. E. Carlebach, D. S. Myers, and J. Efron (Hanover, N.H.: University Press of New England for Brandeis University Press, 1998), 214–46.

[34] Later on in this passage, *Zohar Ḥadash* 78c, the verse "Cursed is the one who lives with any beast" (Deut. 27:21), is interpreted as a reference to a Cuthite woman, which is the "body that is from the side of the other impure beast above." It seems that this is a cryptic allusion to a Christian woman. Compare the reference to the Cuthite man in *Zohar* 3:200a, who inquires of Rabbi Eleazar about the seemingly superior power of Balaam in comparison to Moses. I would suggest that in that case as well there is an encoded hint to a Christian, and the figure of Balaam stands typologically for Jesus. The use of the ass to symbolize non-Jews is based on rabbinic sources, which in turn expand on the imagery of Ezekiel 23:20. See Stern, *Jewish Identity*, 37–39. One wonders if implicit in some of the rabbinic texts there is a polemic against Christians who are depicted as a race of asses, an image that is especially related to the issue of sexual promiscuity. See A. Rousselle, *Porneia: On*

(signified by the term *'adam*), which is linked to the deity by way of numerology, an association that is best appreciated if one bears in mind that when the four letters of the name YHWH are written out in full (*ywd he' waw he'*) their numerical value is 45, the same as the numerical value of the word *'adam*, a theme widely attested in kabbalistic literature. The word *'adam*, therefore, applies most precisely to the Jew, a connotation that is conveyed as well in the Aramaic idiom frequently used in the zoharic corpus, bar nash, which contemporary scholars have misleadingly rendered in generic terms as a reference to human beings in an unqualified sense.[35] Dozens of textual examples can illustrate the point, but for my purpose it is sufficient to mention one that relates to the issue of the contrast between the essential impurity of the nations and the purity of Israel:

> Rabbi Eleazar and Rabbi Yeisa were sitting one night and they were engaged in [the study of] Torah. Rabbi Eleazar said: "Come and see: When the blessed holy One will resurrect the dead, all the souls that will be aroused before him will rise in images [*diyoqnin*], in the very image that they had in this world...." Rabbi Yeisa said: "We have seen that as long as the person exists in this spirit [of holiness] he is not defiled, but when his soul departs, he is defiled." [Rabbi Eleazar] said to him: "It is certainly this way, for it has been said that when the evil inclination takes the spirit of the person, it defiles him and his body is impure. With respect to the other idolatrous nations, they are impure when they are alive, for their souls are from the side of impurity, and when that impurity is removed from them, their bodies remain without any defilement at all. Therefore, he who is conjoined to a woman from the other idolatrous nations is impure, and the child born to him will receive upon himself the spirit of impurity." *Zohar* 1:131a–b

The Aramaic word that I have rendered as "person" is *bar nash*; my translation is dubious insofar as one might assume that the zoharic author is speaking about human beings in a generic sense. From the context, however, it is obvious that bar nash relates specifically to the Jews who are set in contrast to "the rest of the idolatrous nations," a coded reference in

---

Desire and the Body in Antiquity, trans. F. Pheasant (Cambridge: Harvard University Press, 1988), 117–18.

[35] In the fuller version of this study, I will discuss in detail the philological issues by analyzing some critical texts.

zoharic literature to Christians.[36] In a parallel to this zoharic passage, in *Sefer ha-Rimmon*, Moses de León, the thirteenth-century Spanish kabbalist who appears to have had the principal role in the composition and redaction of the main body of the *Zohar*, expresses himself in even bolder language, for he remarks without qualification:

> You know that all of the Gentiles [*goyim*] and all of their matters are in the category of the impure.... You must know and discern that the Gentiles come from the side of impurity, for the souls of the Gentiles derive from the side of impurity.... [S]ince their cause is impure their bodies will perish and their souls will burn; their root and their source is impure.[37]

Similarly, in another composition, *Mishkan ha-'Edut*, in the context of discussing the transgression of a Jewish man having intercourse with a non-Jewish woman, who is referred to (on the basis of Malachi 2:11) as the "daughter of an alien god," de León contrasts the holiness of Jews and the impurity of other nations:

> Know that the elements of the supernal gradations are divided into several aspects and functions, and in accordance with their secrets and their divisions all the families of the earth are divided below. Israel is amongst them as a unique and holy nation, which persists in its holiness and in the secret of the reality of the blessed holy One that disseminates in them in the secret of the holy forms that are given to them from the power of the river that comes forth without cessation.[38] And just as the branches and the leaves sepa-

---

[36] See D. Matt, *Zohar: The Book of Enlightenment* (New York: Paulist Press, 1983), 240; Liebes, *Studies in the Zohar*, 161, 234 n47, 244 n92; E. R. Wolfson, "Woman—The Feminine As Other in Theosophic Kabbalah: Some Philosophical Observations on the Divine Androgyne," in *The Other in Jewish Thought and History: Constructions of Jewish Culture and Identity*, ed. L. Silberstein and R. Cohn (New York: New York University Press, 1994), 189–90; idem, "Re/membering the Covenant," 217.

[37] *The Book of the Pomegranate: Moses de León's Sefer ha-Rimmon*, ed. E. R. Wolfson (Atlanta: Scholars Press, 1988), 211–12 (Hebrew section). The radical position whereby all of the non-Jewish nations are indiscriminately characterized as impure in relation to the holiness of the Jews is affirmed by other kabbalists from the period of the *Zohar* as well.

[38] In many passages in the *Zohar* and Hebrew theosophic works of de León, this is a standard way of referring to *Yesod*, the ninth of the ten *sefirot*, which corresponds to the phallic potency of God.

rate as the foxes hold on to them, so the souls of the nations separate from the place of their separation, from the secret of holiness, and the souls separate and fly out from the side of impurity, the side of the other god, in accordance with the impurity of the filth of the serpent, which is in the secret of the male and his female mate.[39]

The souls of the nations stem from the demonic power, but the soul of Israel comes from the mystery of the divine. Needless to say, the texts of the *Zohar* (and all subsequent kabbalistic works influenced by its terminology) will yield a radically different anthropological conception when it is understood that in the vast majority of cases terms such as *bar nash* and *benei nasha'* denote not humanity in general, but the Jewish people in particular. Indeed, inasmuch as *'adam* in the most exact sense denotes the divine image, and the latter is the supernal Israel, it follows that texts that depict the formation of *'adam* in the terrestrial world should be understood as referring to the embodied configuration of the Jewish soul,[40] a point that is often missed by scholars who apply the anthropocentric orientation of the *Zohar* (or related kabbalistic literature) to human beings in general.[41] From the perspective of the kabbalists, the symbol of primal Adam does not denote "Man" in an unqualified sense, but it refers rather to Israel, which is the ideal human, the Archanthropos, that bears the image of God. Consider, for example, the following passage:

> Rabbi Simeon said: "It is written, 'This is the book of the generations of man' [*zeh sefer toledot 'adam*] [Genesis 5:1]. Did he have a book? Rather it has been established[42] that the blessed holy One showed to primal Adam each generation and its interpreters. How did he show it to him? If you say that he saw by means of the holy spirit that in the future they would come to the world like one who sees through wisdom what will come about in the world, it is not

---

[39] MS Berlin, Staatsbibliothek Or. Quat. 833, fol. 26a. The fox image is based on Song of Songs 2:15.

[40] See, for instance, *Zohar* 1:134b, 104a–b, 186b; 2:75b, 166a–b, 178a; 3:48a, 147a; *Zohar Ḥadash*, 68d, 78c.

[41] See, for example, Scholem, *Major Trends*, 239–43; Tishby, *Wisdom of the Zohar*, 677–722; A. Altmann, "The Delphic Maxim in Medieval Islam and Judaism," in *Biblical and Other Studies*, ed. A. Altmann (Cambridge: Harvard University Press, 1963), 208–13; idem, "*Homo Imago Dei* in Jewish and Christian Theology," *The Journal of Religion* 48 (1968): 257–58.

[42] Babylonian Talmud, 'Avodah Zarah 5a; Sanhedrin 38b.

so; rather he saw everything with the eye, and that image that in the future will exist in the world he saw with the eye. What is the explanation? From the day the world was created all the souls that in the future would exist in people [*benei nasha'*] stood before the blessed holy One in that very image with which they would be in the world. In this manner, after all of the righteous ones depart from this world, all of the souls ascend, and the blessed holy One prepares for them a new image in the pattern of that world in which they will be garbed. Thus they all exist before him, and primal Adam saw them with the eye. You might say that after he has seen them they no longer exist in their reality. Come and see: All the words of the blessed holy One actually exist, and they stand before him until they descend into the world. In this manner, it is written 'but both with those who are standing here with us [this day before the Lord our God and with those who are not with us here this day]' [Deuteronomy 29:14]. It has been established[43] that all of the people [*benei nasha'*] that would in the future be in the world were found there [i.e., at Sinai]."   *Zohar* 1:90a–b

Prima facie, one might argue that the author of this passage, basing himself on an earlier rabbinic source, affirms that the souls of all humankind—here depicted as the image (*diyoqna'*, from the Greek *ikon*) of this corporeal world in which the individual is garbed in the manner that the righteous are garbed in the image of the divine realm when they depart from this world—existed before God from the time of the creation of the world and they were shown to Adam. It would seem, accordingly, that at least in this context the term *benei nasha'* does indeed signify humanity at large, which would justify my translation "people." At the end of the citation, however, it becomes evident that this is not the author's intent, for his reference to the appearance at the Sinaitic theophany of the images of all the people that would exist in the future can only denote the Jewish nation. The rabbinic texts upon which these words are based unequivocally assert that the souls of all future Jewish generations were standing at Sinai, but there is no mention of the souls of humanity at large.[44]

---

[43] *Exodus Rabbah* 28:6; Tanḥuma', Neṣavim, 3; Pirqei Rabbi 'Eli'ezer, chapter 41, 97b.

[44] There are rabbinic texts that emphasize the universal dimension of revelation. See, for example, *Mekhilta' de-Rabbi Yishma'el*, ed. H. S. Horovitz and I. A. Rabin (Jerusalem: Wahrmann, 1970), Yitro, chapter 1, 205, and parallels noted in n. 16 *ad*

Yet the matter is even more clear, for *bar nash* (and its semantic equivalents) in the most precise sense denotes, in most zoharic sources, not only Jews but the circumcised Jewish male. Let me cite as an illustration of this point the following warning to Jewish men not to engage in sexual intercourse with Gentile women:

> It has been established that the verse "Let us make Adam in our image and in our likeness" [Genesis 1:26] refers to the moment of intercourse [*ziwwuga'*], and thus [the words] "image" [*ṣelem*] and "likeness" [*demut*] refer to the union of the two [male and female]. I have found in the "Book of King Solomon" that in the moment of intercourse, the blessed holy One sends an image of a human countenance [*diyoqna' ke-parṣufa' de-varnash*], an impression engraved in the image [*reshima' ḥaqiqa' beṣolma'*], and it stands over that union. Had permission been given to the eye to see, the person [*bar nash*] would see over his head this image inscribed with the human countenance, for through this image a person is created.... With respect to Israel, who are holy, this image [*ṣelem*] is holy and from a holy place it exists within them. The image of those who worship the stars and constellations is from evil matters and from the side of impurity it exists within them. Thus a person should not mix his image with the image of an idolater because the one is holy and the other is impure. *Zohar* 3:104b (cf. 1:219b–220a)

In this passage, the expression *bar nash*, which I have equivocally rendered as "person," specifically denotes the Jewish male who should avoid having intercourse with a non-Jewish woman, for by so doing he would mix the holy and the impure images.[45] To cite a second example that drives the point home even more emphatically,

> Rabbi Hamnuna said, "'Do not let your mouth cause your flesh to sin' [Ecclesiastes 5:5], for a person [bar nash] should not let his mouth lead him to an evil thought, which will cause him to sin with respect to the holy flesh upon which is inscribed the holy covenant." *Zohar* 1:8a

Conversing about sexual matters can lead a Jewish man to an improper

---

locum. These sources, however, do not affirm that all of the nations, let alone all the future souls of these nations, were present at the Sinaitic epiphany.

[45] On the doctrine of the image (*ṣelem*) in zoharic kabbalah, see Tishby, *Wisdom of the Zohar*, 770–73; Scholem, *On the Mystical Shape*, 261–71.

thought, which in turn can cause him to sin with his penis, the flesh upon which the holy covenant of circumcision is inscribed. Inasmuch as this covenant is restricted to Jewish males, the expression *bar nash* in this passage can only refer to a Jewish man. In a similar vein, we read in another passage,

> "For the Lord God is sun and shield" [Psalms 84:12], "sun and shield" refers to the holy covenant: Just as the sun shines and illumines the world, so the holy covenant shines and illumines the body of the person [*gufa' de-var nash*], and just as the shield is to protect the person [*bar nash*], so too the holy covenant is a shield for the person.... He who lies with respect to the holy covenant that is sealed on his flesh is as if he lied with respect to the name of the blessed holy One; the one who lies with respect to the seal of the king lies with respect to the king.   *Zohar* 2:3b

These statements (and dozens more that could have been cited) make no sense unless we render *bar nash* as a reference to the Jewish man. The textual evidence is overwhelming on this point: The status of human being in its most precise sense refers to the circumcised male Jew. As De León writes, "When one receives the holy covenant that is sealed and inscribed on his flesh, then he is included in the category of a human being [*nikhlal bi-khelal 'adam*]."[46] The link between circumcision and the classification *'adam* underlies the zoharic assertion, *u-ma'an 'ihu de-qa'im be-raza' de-'adam ma'an de-natir 'ot qayyama' qadisha'*, which translates literally as "and who is the one who exists in the secret of Adam? The one who guards the sign of the holy covenant" (*Zohar* 2:214b). Only the Jewish man who avoids illicit sexual acts, and thereby protects the covenant incised on his flesh, maintains the status of human being.

To be sure, the zoharic authorship on many occasions (following the line established in classical rabbinic sources, which is based on the textual authority of Scripture) emphasizes that the complete human being entails the union of male and female.[47] The purpose of ritual observance is to raise the feminine aspect of the divine (*Shekhinah*) from a state of degradation and humiliation so that she may be reunited with her masculine consort in holy matrimony, a process that mimics and thereby anticipates

---

[46] Text in Wijnhoven, "*Sefer ha-Mishkal*," 131.

[47] The point has been discussed by many scholars too numerous to list here. For a succinct review of the relevant zoharic texts, see Tishby, *Wisdom of the Zohar*, 1355–79.

the redemption from exile. This conjugal repairing is advantageous to the male as well, for his own sense of completion is dependent on being unified with the female: neither is whole without the other. From this perspective one can speak of gender in zoharic symbolism as a correlative phenomenon: to converse meaningfully about gender we must posit the polarity of male and female. However, as I have noted elsewhere, the ontological structure that informs the concept of gender in the *Zohar* and other kabbalistic writings is that of the male androgyne, meaning that the female is perceived ontologically as a part of the male.[48] That is to say, the condition of separation, which is characteristic of the spiritual nature of exile by the kabbalists, necessitates the heterosexual bonding of male and female, a union that marks the redemption, the restoration of the female to the male and the consequent overcoming of gender dimorphism. For the purpose of this study, my main point is that this conception of gender implies that the ideal *anthropos* is the male Jew who contains within himself his feminine counterpart, just as the original Adam contained within himself his female other.

That the kabbalistic conception of the *anthropos* in its idealized form refers exclusively to the male is implicit in the recurrent aggadic idea that the community of Israel that left Egypt numbered 600,000 adult males.[49] According to the theosophic appropriation of this rabbinic motif, the Israelite nation in the mundane sphere corresponds to the sixth of the ten divine emanations, the central *sefirah* of *Tiferet*, which represents the balance between the left side of severity and the right side of grace. The contextualization of the 600,000 Israelite men in this aspect of the Godhead signifies the divine status of the Jewish males, the "holy sons" of God who are bound to the body of the king,[50] for they represent the totality

---

[48] Wolfson, "Woman—The Feminine As Other," 166–204; idem, *Circle in the Square: Studies in the Use of Gender in Kabbalistic Symbolism* (Albany: SUNY Press, 1995), 79–121; idem, "*Tiqqun ha-Shekhinah*: Redemption and the Overcoming of Gender Dimorphism in the Messianic Kabbalah of Moses Ḥayyim Luzzatto," *History of Religions* 36 (1997): 289–332; idem, "Eunuchs Who Keep the Sabbath: Becoming Male and the Ascetic Ideal in Thirteenth-Century Jewish Mysticism," in *Becoming Male in the Middle Ages*, ed. J. J. Cohen and B. Wheeler (New York: Garland, 1997), 151–85; idem, "Constructions of the Feminine in the Sabbatian Theology of Abraham Cardoso, with a Critical Edition of *Derush ha-Shekhinah*," *Kabbalah: A Journal for the Study of Jewish Mystical Texts* 3 (1998): 11–143.

[49] *Song of Songs Rabbah* 3:17, 6:23; *Numbers Rabbah* 11:3. In some sources, it is specified that the minimum age to be included in this census was twenty years old.

[50] *Zohar* 1:162a (*Sitrei Torah*), 216a, 223b; 2:86a.

of the community of Israel, which encompasses both men and women, just as the attribute of *Tif'eret* comprises left and right, severity and grace (*Zohar* 1:2b, 22a; 2:2b, 195a).

To state the matter in stark but not exaggerated terms: The anthropological perspective articulated in the *Zohar* is that the soul of Israel is most fully manifest in the circumcised male body and derives from divine potencies, whereas the soul of idolatrous nations derives from demonic forces. The contrast is cast exegetically in terms of the verse "God said, 'Let the earth bring forth every kind of living creature: cattle, creeping things, and wild beasts of every kind'" (Genesis 1:24): The "living creature," *nefesh ḥayyah*, refers to Israel, for they embody the soul that emanates from the supernal, holy creature, i.e., the *Shekhinah*, whereas the rest of the idolatrous nations are the "cattle, creeping things, and wild beasts of every kind," for they originate in the demonic foreskin (*Zohar* 1:47a). According to another passage, the souls of the nations are "dried wood upon which no light shines," and thus "they remain still and they do not shake for they have no Torah." By contrast, Jewish souls are compared to the burning light of a candle that flickers to every side, a sign of their vitality and dynamism (*Zohar* 3:219a). Thus the verse "the soul of man [*nishmat 'adam*] is the lamp of the Lord" (Proverbs 20:27) is applied solely to the Jews for they alone are called *'adam* (based on the rabbinic reading of Ezekiel 34:31). So noxious is the impurity of the non-Jew that in several passages the zoharic authorship insists that the Jew must avoid all contact with living non-Jews. There is an essential difference between the Jew and the non-Jew: The soul of the non-Jew is intrinsically impure since his soul derives from the demonic realm, and thus he can transmit this impurity only through his soul when he is alive; the Jew, by contrast, is intrinsically holy since his soul derives from the divine realm, and thus he transmits impurity only through the body after the soul separates from it at death.[51] According to another passage, which may represent a somewhat later interpolation into the zoharic text,[52] the children of Israel are commanded not to eat the thigh muscle (*gid ha-nasheh*) for it represents the demonic force, but the idolatrous nations can consume this part of the animal since their nature is innately demonic.[53]

---

[51] See *Zohar* 1:47a, 131a, 220a; 2:21b; 3:25b, 37a, 104b, 105b, 119a, 259b; *Zohar Ḥadash*, 78d; *Book of the Pomegranate*, 211–12.

[52] See A. Altmann, "On the Question of the Authorship of the Book *Ta'amey ha-Mitzwoth*," *Kiryat Sefer* 40 (1965): 275 (in Hebrew).

[53] *Zohar* 1:170b. Cf. *Tiqqunei Zohar* 56, 91a; J. Hecker, "Each Man Ate an

It might be objected that the zoharic portrayal of the idolatrous nations is simply an elaboration of a much earlier tradition, and without any immediate application. However, it is clear that the medieval authors radically altered the tradition in light of their own social and theological context.⁵⁴ For example, the following remark (attributed to Simeon ben Yoḥai) comes from an older work of rabbinic scriptural exegesis: "The blessed holy One said to Israel, 'I am God for all the inhabitants of the world, but I have not assigned my name except to you. I am not called the god of those who worship the stars and constellations, but the God of Israel.'"⁵⁵ Here, a universalist posture is presupposed insofar as the God of Israel is recognized as the God of all people; yet particularism immediately qualifies that universalism because the divine name is given only to Jews. Hence, the God of Israel (*'elohei yisra'el*) is sharply contrasted with the god of the idolaters. When the medieval zoharic circle appropriates this locution, it imposes a fundamental change. The issue of idolatry no longer refers to actual astral worship, as it did in the rabbinic statement, but now connotes a false theistic faith, which can only point to Christianity.⁵⁶ The true meaning of the worship of stars and constellations is suggested in the following passage:

> Thus the blessed holy One warned Israel to be holy, as it is written, "You shall be holy for I am holy" [Leviticus 11:44]. What is [the import of the word] "I"? This refers to the blessed holy One, the

---

Angel's Meal: Eating and Embodiment in the *Zohar*" (Ph.D. dissertation, New York University, 1996), 109–66.

⁵⁴ Liebes, *Studies in the Zohar*, 244 n92, offers several other examples of the zoharic transformation of classical rabbinic passages into a polemic with the Christianity contemporary to the time of the composition of the medieval kabbalistic anthology.

⁵⁵ *Exodus Rabbah* 29:4.

⁵⁶ Following the view of a number of medieval halakhic authorities, including Maimonides, the kabbalists of the zoharic circle maintained that Christianity is idolatry. See above, n. 37. Although Islam is treated as a demonic force in some passages in the *Zohar*, especially in the later strata of *Ra'aya' Meheimna'* and *Tiqqunei Zohar* (see discussion above, n. 14), for the most part this religion is not considered idolatrous, a position that is also affirmed by Maimonides. The theological ruling is reflective of the broader cultural symbiosis between Judaism and Islam in the early Middle Ages. For a succinct review of this recurrent attitude in the historiographic portrait of medieval Jewish society, see D. Berger, "Judaism and General Culture in Medieval and Early Modern Times," in *Judaism's Encounter With Other Cultures: Rejection or Integration*, ed. J. J. Schacter (Northvale: Jason Aronson Inc., 1997), 61–84.

holy heavenly kingship [*malkhut shamayim qadisha'*]. The other kingship [*malkhuta' 'aḥra'*] of the nations who worship the stars and constellations is called "the other" [*'aḥer*], as it is written, "You shall not bow down to the other god [*'el 'aḥer*], for the name of the Lord is the jealous one" [Exodus 34:14]. Come and see: The sovereignty of the "I" is in this world and in the world-to-come, and everything depends upon it. The sovereignty of the other, the side of impurity, the other side, is in this world, and it has nothing of the world-to-come. Therefore, he who cleaves to this "I" has a portion in this world and in the world-to-come, and he who cleaves to the other is destroyed in this world and he has no portion in the world-to-come, but he has a portion in the world of impurity on account of the other kingship of the nations who worship the stars and constellations.   *Zohar* 1:204b

Reversing a standard trope of medieval Christian polemic against the Jews that contrasted the otherworldly spirituality of Christianity with the thisworldly orientation of Judaism, the zoharic authorship instead associates Christianity with the power of impurity in this world. By contrast, Jews alone know the path of holiness that leads to eschatological reward. Far from being people only of the letter of the law, which was long associated with carnality in Christian attacks on Judaism, the zoharic text presents the Jews alone as having access to the spiritual realm—not at the expense of the physical world, but in conjunction with it. In terms of the more specific symbolic language employed in the aforecited text, the holiness of Judaism depends on cleaving to the aspect of God referred to as "I," i.e., the kingdom of heaven, *malkhut shamayim*, which is a technical designation of the tenth of the sefirotic emanations, *Malkhut* or *Shekhinah*, the immanence of God in creation.[57] The dual portion of Israel, this world and the world-to-come, is linked to the role of *Shekhinah* as kingdom of heaven, which signifies her capacity to exercise providential care over the universe. Conversely, idol worship consists of cleaving to the other god, the foreign dominion of demonic kingship, the other side (*siṭra' 'aḥra'*). If one cleaves to *Shekhinah*, *malkhut shamayim*, one attains a portion in the world-to-come, but if one cleaves to the "other kingship,"

---

[57] Scholem, *Major Trends*, 216, explains that the attribution of the first-person pronoun to *Shekhinah*, the last of the ten *sefirot*, signifies that this stage of the emanative process is characterized as the "true individuation in which God as a person says 'I' to Himself."

malkhuta' 'aḥra', one is destroyed in this world and has no portion in the world-to-come.

Kabbalists of the zoharic fraternity portrayed Christianity as the idolatrous religion that worships the demonic other side. It is possible that the zoharic authors have set up an analogy between Judaism and Christianity along the following lines: The holy nation cleaves to the masculine potency of God, designated as "heaven" (*shamayim*), through the *Shekhinah*, which is also called *malkhut*; the idolatrous nations are conjoined to the masculine potency of the other god through the feminine presence of the demonic realm, *malkhuta' 'aḥra'*. Although the names Samael and Lilith are not mentioned explicitly in the aforecited zoharic passage, from parallel texts it may be concluded that these terms can be applied appropriately to the masculine and feminine forces of impurity.[58] I surmise that the "other god" and the foreign "kingship" stand respectively for Jesus and Mary, the pair on the left side of impurity that corresponds to *Tif'eret* and *Malkhut* on the right side of holiness.[59] Even if we were to bracket this dimension of the Jewish-Christian polemic, it is evident that when the zoharic authors contrast the holy souls of Israel with the impure souls of the idolatrous nations, the distinction that is really being made is between Jews and Christians in the European landscape of the Jewish Middle Ages. Christians cleave to the demonic other side, the god who is foreign, for the spiritual root of Christianity is Esau or Edom, the nation to which is assigned the evil force of Samael and Lilith. As I have already

---

[58] *Zohar* 1:148a–b (*Sitrei Torah*); see Tishby, *Wisdom of the Zohar*, 376–79, 462, 467–68.

[59] The decoding of Samael as a symbolic reference to Jesus is enhanced by the adaptation on the part of the zoharic kabbalists of the aggadic theme that Samael is the archon of Esau, which is identified as the Christian empire. See *Midrash Tanḥuma'*, *Wayyishlaḥ*, 8; *Zohar* 1:146a, 170a; 2:11a, 111a, 163b; 3:124a (*Ra'aya' Meheimna'*), 199b, 243a (*Ra'aya' Meheimna'*), 246b (*Ra'aya' Meheimna'*), 248a (*Ra'aya' Meheimna'*); *Zohar Ḥadash*, 23d (*Midrash ha-Ne'elam*), 47a (*Midrash ha-Ne'elam*); *Tiqqunei Zohar*, sec. 69, 105a; Tishby, *Wisdom of the Zohar*, 464. On the association of Satan or the "other god" and Jesus, see Liebes, *Studies in the Zohar*, 234 n47 and 244 n92. Many of the images that depict Lilith—for example, the mother of the mixed multitude (*Zohar* 1:27b), the estranged woman identified as Se'eir (*Zohar* 1:172b), the woman of harlotry (*Zohar* 2:148b), and the evil maidservant (*Zohar* 3:273a)—suggest a clandestine reference to Mary. Worthy of further analysis are the implications of the congruence between descriptions of *Shekhinah* and Lilith on the Zoharic elaboration of the relationship between Synagogue and Church. On the complex relationship between *Shekhinah* and Lilith, see Scholem, *On the Mystical Shape*, 189–92; Tishby, *Wisdom of the Zohar*, 382–85, 468–69.

intimated, the tropological intent of the kabbalistic polemic can only be fully appreciated if one bears in mind that, in zoharic literature, the theological dispute with the idolatrous nature of Christianity cannot be separated from the moral struggle with sexual temptation, expressed as the Jewish man's desire to commit adultery with a Christian woman.[60]

III

By way of summary, we may conclude that the kabbalistic perspective, which may be culled from the zoharic text, accords special status to the Jewish people, who alone are endowed with a soul divine in nature; thus only to Jews is the term "human" accurately applied. By implication non-Jews are accorded an inferior status. The ethnocentric anthropology has exerted a major influence on kabbalists, pietists, and rabbinic preachers through the generations. What is especially noteworthy is that this orientation has figured prominently in writings that scholars have classified under the rubric of kabbalistic ethics, for example, *Re'shit Hokhmah* of Elijah de Vidas,[61] *Shenei Luḥot ha-Berit* of Isaiah Horowitz,[62] and *Nefesh ha-Ḥayyim* of Ḥayyim of Volozhin.[63] The persistence of the ethnocentrism is evident even in the work of Judah Loew of Prague, the towering rabbinic figure of the sixteenth century known as Maharal. Despite the effort on the part of Maharal to accord a divine status to all people, on the basis of the belief that human beings without qualification bear God's image,[64] in the end he, too, embraces an anthropological ideal that distinguishes in an

---

[60] See Wolfson, "Re/membering the Covenant," 221–22.

[61] Re'shit *Hokhmah ha-Shalem*, 3 vols. (Jerusalem: 'Or ha-Musar, 1984), Haqdamah 1:4; *Sha'ar ha-Yir'ah*, chapter 4, 1:92.

[62] Shenei *Luḥot ha-Berit ha-Shalem*, 2 vols. (Jerusalem: Yad Ramha Institute, 1992–97), 1:223–24.

[63] The kabbalistic anthropology adopted by Rabbi Ḥayyim in *Nefesh ha-Ḥayyim* is thoroughly ethnocentric in its orientation: The image of God relates to man's capacity to influence cosmic events, but this is a capacity that is realized only by Jews through performance of ritual commandments, especially study of Torah. See N. Lamm, *Torah Lishmah: Torah for Torah's Sake in the Works of Rabbi Ḥayyim of Volozhin and His Contemporaries* (Hoboken: Ktav, 1989), 73–87. For a universalistic reading of Ḥayyim of Volozhin's anthropology, see E. Levinas, *Beyond the Verse: Talmudic Readings and Lectures*, trans. G. D. Mole (London: Athlone Press, 1994), 151–67.

[64] See, for example, Judah Loew of Prague, *Be'er ha-Golah* (Benei Beraq: 1980), 121: "This image comprises all people, Israel and the nations, everyone who walks upright has the divine image."

essential way between Israel and the nations. The designation *'adam* applies most properly to the Jewish people, for only they truly possess the image of God in the most perfect sense since they alone have a divine soul that allows them to attain states of consciousness wherein spirit is separated from body.[65]

The price to be paid for the mystical conception of the Jewish people as the singular incarnation of the divine image is the ontological division separating Jews and other religious or ethnic cultures, which in both the medieval and modern context has led to a demonization of the cultural other. One might argue, however, that kabbalistic sources yield the possibility that this state of affairs will be overcome in a messianic future when the reintegration of all things back to the divine will signal the "othering of the other," i.e., the unification of opposites results in restoring the "other" to its original place so that it is no longer other, a de-othering[66] whereby the other becomes its other and thus remains the same. The monistic ontology undermines the logical antinomies, good versus evil, light versus dark, right versus left, male versus female. Prior to emanation of the various worlds, in the infinite, opposites are identical.[67] The ontological principle underlies the cosmological secret, linked exegetically in the *Zohar* to the verse "Who can bring forth a pure thing out of an unclean one, but the One" (Job 14:4): The pure comes forth from what is impure, for what was initially impure is purified in the manner of the ashes (*'efer*) that are turned into dust (*'afar*) by means of the raging fire (*Zohar* 2:237a–b). That the impure can become pure is possible for at root the pure and impure are not different; indeed, herein all opposites are the same.

As a consequence of this coincidence of opposites must not the ontological distinction between Jew and non-Jew also be transcended? If the impediment to a kabbalistic ethic is the xenophobic portrayal of the Gentile as asinine in contrast to the angelic Israel, then it follows that the possibility of genuine social reform emerging from kabbalistic symbolism would be linked to the metaphysical insight regarding the *coincidentia*

---

[65] Judah Loew of Prague, *Gevurot ha-Shem* (London: 1954), chapter 66, 311–12; *Tif'eret Yisra'el*, ed. H. Pardes (Tel-Aviv: Yad Mordechai, 1979), chapter 1, 91–92; *Derekh Ḥayyim*, ed. H. Pardes (Jerusalem: Yad Mordechai, 1993), 354–55; *Nesaḥ Yisra'el*, ed. J. Hartman (Jerusalem: Jerusalem Institute, 1997), chapter 11, 304–5.

[66] I am grateful to Sheila Delany for this locution.

[67] Zohar 3:80b. Citation and analysis of the text may be found in Wolfson, "Woman—The Feminine As Other," 183–84.

oppositorum within the uppermost aspect of the Godhead. In this state of mind, moreover, the polarities that shape the contours of the world in the everyday consciousness of the kabbalist are surpassed.[68] The eliciting of ethics by scholars from the kabbalistic teaching may profitably be linked to the utopian vision articulated by kabbalists themselves, a vision predicated on a radical transposition of the axiological framework of priestly codes and rabbinic halakhah so that there is no longer any ontological difference between Jew and non-Jew. For this transposition to occur, however, the Torah will have to realize its universal potentiality as moral imperative binding on all people without discrimination; this can only happen at the point when the law exceeds the limits of its own ritualistic prescriptions. The ethical ideal demands the equality of all people before the law, a view that stands in striking contrast to the repeated emphasis in kabbalistic tradition on the unbridgeable gap separating Israel and the nations. Venturing beyond the polarity of opposites is part of the rich eschatological legacy of the kabbalah, which is most fully expressed in effacing the difference between holy and impure, permissible and forbidden.[69] When the other can be truly felt as the same, then Jacob is Edom and Israel *'adam*.

New York University

---

[68] In the monograph that will include an expanded version of this article, I will enter into a much more detailed discussion of the ontological transformation (or what I have called the "othering of the other") occasioned by the messianic age, a breaking down of the barrier between holy and impure that is anticipated in the present by the phenomenon of the conversion of the non-Jew.

[69] See G. Scholem, *The Messianic Idea in Judaism and Other Essays on Jewish Spirituality* (New York: Schocken, 1971), 19–24, 49–141; idem, "Der Nihilismus als religiöses Phänomen," *Eranos Jahrbuch* 43 (1974): 1–50, especially 27–35.

Sexual Politics
in a Medieval Hebrew Marriage Debate

TOVA ROSEN

> *One of the great men built him a new house and wrote over the lintel: "Let no evil enter here." Diogenes, the philosopher, passed and saw the inscription, and then wrote underneath, "And how will thy wife enter?"*[1]

Based on a false syllogism, this witty anecdote aims to show how evil, i.e., woman, is unavoidably built into the familial-social system. The contradiction in terms inherent in the concept of "a house without evil" encapsulates two of the main concerns of medieval misogynist discourse: one is the discord between the negativity of woman and the positive postulate of marriage; the other is the contrariety between the philosopher's spiritual path and the indulgence in matter which is caused by family life. In the male philosopher's view, these were practical and indeed most excruciating problems.

In medieval ascetic thought (Christian and Islamic alike) the Male/Female difference was made to fit into a series of other Manichaean dichotomies (Good/Evil, Spirit/Flesh, Intellect/ Instinct, Order/Chaos).[2] Hence,

---

I wish to express my gratitude to Sheila Delany for her devoted reading and helpful comments. Thanks also to Deborah Bregmann and Ross Brann from whose reading I benefited during our stay at the Center for Judaic Studies, at the University of Pennsylvania, in 1999. I am indebted to the Center for their fellowship and for the excellent working conditions. Thanks also to the Israel Science Foundation for enabling me to carry out earlier stages of this research. The paper is part of my forthcoming book on genre and gender in medieval Hebrew poetry.

[1] The literary route of this anecdote is symptomatic of medieval intercultural contacts. Its earliest occurrence is in the third-century Greek work of Diogenes Laertius, *Lives of the Eminent Philosophers*, ed. R. D. Hicks (London 1925), 2:53. This and other anecdotes were recycled in Arabic, Hebrew, and European texts. For an Arabic version, see Fedwa Malti-Douglas, *Woman's Body, Woman's Word: Gender and Discourse in Arabo-Islamic Writing* (Princeton: Princeton University Press, 1991), 40. Joseph Ibn Zabara, a Hebrew author from Barcelona, late twelfth century, adopted from the Arabic several such anecdotes in his novella *Sefer Sha'ashu'im, The Book of Delight*, translated by Moses Hadas (New York: Columbia University Press, 1932), 67.

[2] For aspects of gender in Islamic asceticism, see Annemarie Schimmel, "Eros—Heavenly and Not So Heavenly—in Sufi Literature and Life," in *Society and the*

marriage, the place where male and female legitimately (though not unproblematically) meet, became a powerful metaphor for the paradoxical encounters of the two opposing metaphysical orders. Asceticism, in its extreme manifestations, preached the absolute dissociation of the male/spiritual from the female/material not only in the mind but also in the life of the true believer. Thus, "divorcing" matter entailed also avoiding matrimony. However, society and its religious institutions continued to advocate and sanction marriage and family life.

To what extent did medieval Jewish thinkers and writers participate in this contemporary discourse on women and marriage? And if they did, was there any Jewish cultural specificity to their rendition of the conflict between married and meditative life? The texts of medieval Jewish authors from Al-Andalus, and later from Christian Spain, show that they shared the discourse of their contemporaries, including also views on gender and sexuality. However, despite expressions of virulent misogyny occurring in many speculative and literary Jewish texts, marriage, together with the injunction to be fruitful and procreate, remained sanctioned cornerstones of the Jewish way of life and thought.

Given this unquestionable attitude towards marriage, the existence of a Jewish literary controversy over marriage is indeed surprising. This controversy, held in a series of Hebrew novellas written in Spain and Provence during the thirteenth and fourteenth centuries, is the topic of my article.

I

The earliest and most important in this series is an early thirteenth-century work titled *Minḥat Yehuda Sone ha-Nashim* ("The Offering of Judah the Misogynist"), written by Judah Ibn Shabbetai in Toledo in 1208.[3]

Sexes in Medieval Islam, ed. Afaf Lutfi al-Sayyid Marsot (Malibu: Udena Publications, 1979), 119–41.

[3] Printed in M.Y. Bin Gorion, *Mimekor Yisrael*, 5:102–19. Parts were reprinted in Hayyim Schirmann, *Ha-Shira ha-Ivrit bi-Sefarad uvi-Provens*, "Hebrew Poetry in Spain and Provence," (Jerusalem and Tel Aviv: Mossad Bialik-Dvir, 1961), 70–86. I relied on, and greatly benefited from, the texts, apparata, and discussions in Matti Huss's excellent doctoral thesis, *Critical Editions of "Minḥat Yehudah," "Ezrat Hanashim," and "Ein Mishpat" with Prefaces, Variants, Sources and Annotations*, 2 vols. (Jerusalem: Hebrew University, 1991). Huss printed the two versions of *Minḥat Yehuda* (one from 1208, the other probably from 1228). For problems of dating see Huss, 1:207–21. Parts of the work were translated (and introduced) by R.P. Scheindlin in *Rabbinic Fantasies: Imaginative Narratives from Classical Hebrew*

The twenty-seven extant manuscripts of this work attest to its popularity in the Middle Ages.[4] The story is saturated in misogyny and does explicitly declare its hostility to marriage. However, as its plot thickens, the story begins to display a growing ambivalence regarding the institution of marriage. The author, as I intend to show, speaks with both sides of his mouth, for and against marriage, transforming thus his ideological qualms into narrative devices.

On the other side of the controversy stand three other works reacting to *Minḥat Yehuda*'s apparent misogamy. Two of them, *Ezrat ha-Nashim* ("In Defense of Women") and *Ein Mishpat* ("The Fount of Law"), were written in 1210 as immediate responses to Ibn Shabbetai by a younger contemporary named Isaac.[5] The third work, *Ohev Nashim* ("The Lover, i.e. Defender, of Women") was written towards the end of the century by the Provençal Hebrew poet Yedaʿaya ha- Penini. All the works belong to the genre of the *maqama*, a form of eloquent rhymed prose adopted from the Arabic by Hebrew poets beginning in the late twelfth century. *Minḥat Yehuda* is in fact among the earliest examples of the genre in Hebrew.[6]

After expanding upon the literary interpretation of *Minḥat Yehuda* and exploring its ambiguities I will examine the responses of readers, medieval as well as modern. Finally I will suggest some conclusions about the social context of this controversy. But before that a brief synopsis of *Minḥat Yehuda* is in order:

> After being asked by friends, in the prologue, how he was lured into marriage and upon confessing his sin, the first person author, Judah, tells the story of Taḥkemoni and his son Zeraḥ, two victims of marriage as well as devotees of anti-marriage propaganda. Taḥkemoni, a dying old sage, adjures his son Zeraḥ never to marry.

Literature, ed. David Stern and Mark J. Mirsky (New Haven: Yale University Press, 1990), 269–94. My references follow Huss's edition of the 1208 text, by line number. Translations, unless otherwise stated, are Scheindlin's.

About Ibn Shabbetai, see Schirmann, 3:67–70 and Huss, 1:183–88.

[4] Huss, ibid., 1:190.

[5] Also published by Huss, ibid.

[6] Maqamas were intended mainly as entertainment; however, they range widely in style and purpose—from the rhetorical, allegorical, gnomic, didactic, to the humorous, narrative, and even lyrical. The insertion of poems within the prose is one of the genre's characteristics. About the Hebrew maqama and related genres, see Dan Pagis, "Variety in Medieval Rhymed Narratives," *Scripta Hierosolymitana* 27 (1978): 79–97.

After taking an oath of abstinence Zeraḥ with three noble friends establishes a fraternity to proselytize celibacy. Their success among both bachelors and husbands brings about a women's rebellion. The women, led by an old crafty hag, plot to undermine Zeraḥ. They will introduce him to a perfect lady whose charms he will be unable to resist, and then will replace her, at the wedding, with an ugly shrew. Once married, Zeraḥ reveals his bride's real face (and voice!). He regrets his error and sues for divorce. The shrew, aided by a host of women, persuades the judge to decree for Zeraḥ a death sentence. He is finally rescued only thanks to the author/narrator's direct interference in court, and with the latter's declaration that the whole plot was nothing but the figment of his own imagination.

Is this work misogynist or not? Is it misogamic or does it re-affirm marriage? How does it employ humor? In my opinion any attempt to reduce the work to a single message or an ultimate end misses the significance of its complexity. Combining a historical approach with an analysis of the narrative from a feminist perspective, my reading will focus on points of instability and ambivalence in the text, both narrative and ideological. The ambivalence felt in the author's culture towards women and sexuality (and expressed at the time in literary as well as non-literary works) is in my view a key to understanding its structure and thematics. The polemics interwoven in the work itself and the heated controversy it evoked attest to an atmosphere of public debate. Rather than identifying with either side, the work, in fact, thematizes the debate itself and dramatizes its different voices.

"How did the ocean of marriage overwhelm [an intelligent man like] you?" This question, addressed in the prologue to the narrator Judah, the author's namesake, by his good friends, determines the rhetorical as well as the ideological boundaries of the story: Intellect and marriage are considered to be diametrically opposed. The author, who is both enlightened and married, embodies a logically impossible state, an oxymoron. His friends beseech him to explain his erroneous deed and to write down—as a moral lesson for others—the story of his calamity. He is also encouraged by a divine spirit (who "came into me and stood me on my feet," as did the spirit to the prophet Ezekiel, Ezekiel 2.2) to perform this literary task. Hence, Judah writes this work as an offering (*minḥah*) to his friends and to man-kind in general. "Here is the life-story of a man whose soul was ensnared by a woman," he writes in the poem heading the work. The author expresses a hope that the history of his calamities ("his grief and gloom"), eloquently related, will be used as a reproach to and "exemplum" for all "men of wisdom and piety." Ibn Shabbetai's manifesto brings to mind the Latin subgenre known as the *dissuasio de non ducenda uxore*, dissuasion from taking a wife, advice given by a philosopher to a friend. This mode enjoyed a considerable popularity in Europe around the period when *Minḥat Yehuda* was written.[7]

The story of Zeraḥ and his father Taḥkemoni[8] takes place in a pseudo-biblical space, against a background of allegorical apocalypse. Folly and Evil (who are the supporters of marriage) have won the upper hand in their battle against Wisdom (who opposes it), and the world is about to collapse. Two survivors only, old Taḥkemoni and his son Zeraḥ, manage to flee to the mountains. Taḥkemoni is visited by an angel[9] who reveals the cause for the world's imminent upheaval: It is women who will soon turn the cosmos back into chaos. The angel's mastery of anti-feminist lore is quite impressive:

> "Who can undo the knots woven by women? They avert common sense and distort all truth. Their friendship and love are ephemeral.

---

[7] There are some differences between the Latin models and our work (in the Latin the philosopher is usually celibate; the address is in epistolary form; the addressee is a specific friend facing an imminent marriage, not mankind in general); however, the affinity cannot be denied. The relation to the Latin model is discussed by Matti Huss, *Critical Editions*, 1:55–59. The medieval examples follow a tradition rooted in antiquity. Famous examples are: Juvenal's *Sixth Satire* to his friend Postumus; St. Jerome's treatise *Against Jovinian* (quoting the *Liber aureolus de nuptis* by a certain pagan named Theophrastus); Walter Map's *Epistola Valerii* addressed by Valerius to his friend Rufinus, and many others. Even Heloise's dissuasions from marriage written to Abelard can be considered as part of this male tradition. For more examples and for further bibliography, see Katharina M. Wilson and Elizabeth M. Makowski, *Wykked Wyves and the Woes of Marriage: Misogamous Literature from Juvenal to Chaucer* (Albany: SUNY Press, 1990).

[8] This biblical name (2 Samuel 23:8) deriving from the root h.k.m. (wise, wisdom) denotes age-old patriarchal wisdom.

[9] The theme of angelic warning, typical of apocalypse, might come from the Jewish biblical or post-biblical apocalyptic tradition. But association between an angelic agency and anti-marriage propaganda (and of marriage as cause for doomsday) probably draws on a Christian theme. In an anonymous poem, *De coniuge non ducenda* (dated around 1222–50), three angels warn the poet against marriage (Wilson and Makowski, *Wykked Wives*, 124–32). Though the *De conjuge* is later than *Minḥat Yehuda*, it may reflect earlier traditions with which Ibn Shabbetai could also have been familiar. Other textual similarities between the two works corroborate this conjecture.

> They cause all quarrel and trouble. Many a man has been put to shame on account of them."[10]   122–24

These commonplaces are followed by a list of wicked women in the Bible.[11] Eve is blamed not only for Adam's but also for the snake's downfall; Rachel's theft of the idols caused the oppression of the Children of Jacob; Dinah and the concubine of Gibea (both rape victims) are held responsible for inciting bloody feuds; Delilah caused Samson's mishap; women's lust for gold motivated the making of the Golden Calf; Abraham was lucky not to have any daughters; and how clever was Pharaoh's ploy to persecute the children of Israel by killing the males and sparing the females (124–35)! Is the reader supposed to yield to the serious pathos of the visionary scene or catch onto the double entendres in the angel's misreading of the Bible?

Taḥkemoni initiates his son Zeraḥ into misogyny. In a lengthy admonishment he preaches to him the divine imperative:

> "Never take a wife. She talks peace and means trouble. Whoever touches her is destroyed. You will clothe her with fine satins and silks, and feed her with delicacies, then another man will come and sleep with her.... Do not covet her beauty in your heart, and let not her delights allure you. For she has cast down many wounded; all her slain are a mighty host.... Do not share the fruit of your toil and all your precious possessions with others. Do not let yourself become a pimp and do not give birth to any offspring.... My dear son, do not invest your wealth [and strength] in women, and let not evil inhabit your house. Better to keep company with wild wolves and bears than with a woman in her chambers. Ancient sages have already said their word: 'The storm will come from the [women's] ward!' Better to sit among thorns and thistles and not with a woman in her suite; between oven and furnace—not her breasts; among bramble and brier—not her curled hair; among nettles—not her necklets...! Do not let a woman's word fool you....

---

[10] My translation.

[11] This is the first occurrence of such a list in Hebrew literature. Lists of wicked women from the Bible and from antiquity are commonplace in the Latin tradition since St. Jerome's famous list in *Against Jovinian* "exercised a quasi-hypnotic influence on medieval anti-feminism"; Jill Mann, *Geoffrey Chaucer* (Atlantic Highlands, N.J.: Humanities Press International, 1991), 49. The first appearance of this theme in Arabic literature occurs only much later. See Malti-Douglas, *Woman's Body*, 55.

They are all erring at heart.... My son, lend your ear and listen to the words of the wise.... He who talks much with a woman paves his path to hell. She will be close to you when you are young and abandon you when you lose your strength.... Who can seize upon women's wiles and ruse? How many heroes have they let down? How many agonies have they caused?"[12]   141–233

With whom is the medieval audience of this work expected to side? Would they side with the fictional representatives of Wisdom (the Angel and Taḥkemoni) in totally rejecting marriage, or rather support marriage as do the fictional followers of Folly? How can the reader reconcile the fact that the advocating of marriage, which in the real social world is identified with rabbinical-communal norms, is here attributed to the vile and the fool? This perplexing reversal of norms built into the structure of the narrative throughout undermines any possibility of a univocal reading of the story.

It is noteworthy that Taḥkemoni's message, whose implementation is said to revolutionize the existing "order of things," is cast in a discourse devoid of any originality. Saturated with traditional misogynist clichés, his text is a pastiche of recycled fragments and tatters originating from "ancient wisdom." The sources of his "wisdom" are biblical phrases, rabbinic quotations, citations from Arabic misogynist literature, and sayings attributed to anonymous sages.[13] The effect of this "citational discourse" here is to adorn the message with an aura of legitimacy. Taḥkemoni utters no capricious newfangled ideology, but voices a sanctioned and authoritative tradition. The technique resembles that of Chaucer, of whose Wife of Bath Jill Mann writes: "In this vast echo-chamber of antifeminist commonplace the voices blur into each other, endlessly repeating the same message."[14] One example will suffice here to illustrate

---

[12] My translation. Scheindlin's translation does not include this passage.

[13] For the biblical and rabbinic sources of Taḥkemoni's speech, see Huss's commentary, *Critical Editions*, 2:192–95. This citational discourse is admittedly not exclusive to misogynist writings as such. Known as *shibbuz*, this technique is, in fact, one of the most characteristic stylistic features of both medieval Hebrew poetry and rhymed prose. For Arabic misogynist literature see Malti-Douglas's chapter "Sacred History as Misogyny," *Woman's Body*, 54–66.

[14] Mann, *Chaucer*, 50. R. Howard Bloch says about this tradition: "The ritual denunciation of women ... constitutes something of a cultural constant. Reaching back to the Old Testament as well as to ancient Greece [it extends] through classical Hellenic, Judaic, and Roman traditions all the way to the fifteenth century.... The discourse of misogyny runs like a vein throughout medieval literature"; Bloch,

the vastness of this "echo chamber" in Ibn Shabbetai's maqama. A large part of Taḥkemoni's address is built on the rhetorical formula "It is better to ... than to.... " This echoes the Solomonic dictum from Proverbs 21:9: "It is better to dwell in a corner of a housetop, than with a brawling woman in a wide house." This biblical formula, mediated by St. Jerome and other Latin sources, found its way also to Jankyn's Book of Wykked Wyves, which the Wife of Bath parodies.[15]

Taḥkemoni concludes his speech, and just before he dies Zeraḥ takes an oath of celibacy (235–39) and hurries to preach his doctrines to three noble friends. Together they establish a celibate brotherhood and search for a remote uninhabited refuge. After a long journey they find the perfect site for their utopia in the Valley of *Besor* ("Good Tidings"). There they rest, study and play. Theirs is an ideal world without women, an "ascetic paradise" where the masculine philosophic soul can finally find rest (257). Their refuge from sensual human nature takes place, ironically, amidst nature itself. Moreover, while the absence of women is celebrated, this pre-lapsarian asexual Eden swarms with symbols of femininity, fertility and sexuality. Fedwa Malti-Douglas makes an observation that can hold true also for our story. Discussing an Islamic male utopia, she maintains that though the author

> was able ... to cast aside the female, it would seem that woman's body was a permanent fixture of the world in which he set his tale.... The choice [of a far off and fecund island] manifests a tension between a philosophical ideal of a society devoid of sexuality and a geographical locus imbued with that very sexuality the philosophical ideal is fleeing. Sexual geography and a-sexual philosophy are two poles [brought together].[16]

Medieval Misogyny and the Invention of Western Romantic Love (Chicago: University of Chicago Press, 1991), 7.

[15] "Bet is" quod he, "thyn habitacioun
Be with a leon or a foul dragoun
Than with a wommaa usynge for to chyde.
Bet is" quod he "hye in the roof abyde,
Than with an angry wyf doun in the hous."

Chaucer, *Canterbury Tales* III.775–79, *Riverside Chaucer*, 3rd ed. (Boston: Houghton Mifflin, 1987), gen. ed. Larry Benson.

[16] Malti-Douglas, *Woman's Body*, 85. Chapter 4 of her book treats the problem of gender in Ibn Tufayl's (twelfth-century) masterpiece about an abandoned infant who grows up on an uninhabited womanless island. He is nurtured by a gazelle, rejects the opportunity of returning to "normal" society, and eventually chooses to

Similarly, in our maqama the valley is lush with flowing streams, "planted with the trees of Eden," every kind of fruit tree with branches spreading in all directions, "and in their branches nested birds of every wing ... every kind of fawn and deer took shelter there under every verdant tree" (258–73). A description of the garden's heavy fruitage as a sexy bosomy bride highlights this incongruity.[17] Also, ironically enough, Zeraḥ's fantasy of an ascetic haven is a replica of the Andalusian palace-garden, the conventional setting for love-making and flirtation in courtly poetry.[18]

As it turns out, Zeraḥ's utopia is not located in an entirely isolated valley, but alas, within the country of the Fools, who are committed to the business of marriage and reproduction. Despite their ascetic convictions, Zeraḥ and his company have no choice but to cope with the real world around them. So for one month each year they leave their haven and wander around the neighboring towns proselytizing their misogamic "religion" (284)—dissuading the young from marriage and persuading husbands to divorce their wives. Crossing the geographical—and symbolical—boundaries of Utopia will, however, prove fateful. What seems to be a successful mission—many men do "convert" (283) and abandon their wives—will turn upside down when Zeraḥ, the enlightened prophet of abstinence, blindly falls into the dark pit of marriage.

In every town where Zeraḥ comes to preach, the abandoned wives and young desperate maidens are filled with rage. They respond to Zeraḥ's propaganda with (stereotypically "female") symptoms of mass hysteria: they tremble like women in labor, "they tore at their skin in their fashion. Their cry and their wail waxed; great was their groaning, terrible their turmoil, and loud their lament" (286–88). Bodily reaction, accompanied by a series of uncontrollable animal sounds, comes first. The speech that follows, in which the women's sexual anxiety is artlessly spoken, heightens the nexus of female's voice and female's lust:

---

lead a life of meditation on his own island. In her chapter 5 she discusses the mythical island of al-Waq-Waq, devoid of women though its "trees bore women like fruit."

[17] It appears in a poem added by the author in the second version (lines 341–43); see Huss, *Critical Editions*, 1:72.

[18] For the Andalusian garden, see James Dickie, "The Hispano-Arab Garden, Its Philosophy and Function," *Bulletin of the School of Oriental Studies* 31 (1968). For gardens in Hebrew poetry, see Raymond P. Scheindlin, *Wine, Women and Death: Medieval Hebrew Poems on the Good Life* (Philadelphia: Jewish Publishing Society, 1986), 1–11.

"Not a man in the land will lie with us. Who indeed has a heart that would embolden him to touch us after this man has put us to scorn? The lasses languish, their wombs are waste, their fruit fails, all are virgins not known by man! Zeraḥ has turned us into objects of fear. And now one man has to be shared by seven women. See how great is our trouble! Every virgin is shut up and sealed off; no one enters, and none departs. Why should we lie here in our shame, covered by disgrace? Rouse yourselves, think what to do that the ladies may find lovers!"[19]   288–95

The effect of the women's language in this passage is double-edged. Since in real life Hebrew was the language of a male literate elite, the representation of a female and vernacular register of speech in a literary Hebrew text would have been thought of as an impossibility. Hence, Ibn Shabbetai has to let his women characters speak like men, using high Hebrew impregnated with biblical (often de-contextualized) allusions. Such grotesque parroting was probably entertaining for a male audience, but at the same time it touches upon men's fears of women's intrusion into their discourse. For medieval men the division was quite clear: sex is synonymous with woman's nature, but the discourse of sexuality and the control of sexuality are man's monopoly. These women's speech about their unsatisfied sexuality is not only funny; it exposes men's anxiety about a reversed world where women both usurp male language and employ it to express psychological and physical needs.

Women here become political agents too. They gain an independent voice and they act in the public domain, which, in real social terms, is exclusively men's territory. A political public assembly of women is thus a contradiction in terms; it can be a farce or a nightmare—or both. Men's derision of women's power is one way of dealing with the dread it arouses.

The panicky women's mob that is about to lynch Zeraḥ is finally

---

[19] This assembly of women, "young and old, widows and virgins, trembling with anger," brings to mind a possible analogy with Aristophanes's comedy *Lysistrata*. But unlike the Athenan women who refuse sex in protest against men's belligerent politics, our women are devastated at the menace of men's abstinence. In both works women's power is related to their alleged trickery, which they openly admit. Compare the women's words in our piece ("Where have all deceivers gone...? Where are women's ruse and their wiles and tricks and schemes and deceit and cunning?" 297–300) to Lysistrata's words in the Greek play: "Because the men account us all to be sly, shifty rogues," and to Calonice's reply: "And so, by Zeus, we are" (10–12, trans. B. B. Rogers, *Lysistrata* [New York: Putnam's, 1924]).

hushed by an old "shrewd woman ... a woman expert in sorcery and deceit" (303) named Kozbi bat Yeresha, the wife of Sheker. Her typological name denotes her hereditary deceitful nature.[20] Kozbi is thus the opposite of old Taḥkemoni: he represents patriarchal logic and intellect, she stands for matriarchal manipulation and conspiracy. Kozbi's plot—to tempt Zeraḥ into a marriage with a perfect irresistible bride—places Zeraḥ in precisely the situation against which he was warned by his father; his soul now becomes a battleground of two opposing powers: that of the righteous fathers and that of the dangerous tricky women.

While Kozbi urges the crowd of women to search everywhere for the perfect bride, Zeraḥ has two devastating premonitory dreams. In one he falls into a deep abyss; in the other he is surrounded by wild beasts, one of which mutilates his sex and is about to swallow him alive. His companions easily decipher the dreams: The abyss is marriage and the beast is a woman.

Kozbi furnishes the women with a detailed description of the ideal woman, which parodies men's common fantasies: She should be a girl of matchless beauty, an immaculate virgin, elegant and perfumed, a generous hostess, clever and resourceful (310–13). She must also be

> "A girl of culture and counsel, knowing poetry and rhetoric, speaking eloquently and composing verse, her speech sweet as honey and firm as a cast-metal mirror; a girl who can call on wisdom both esoteric and exotic ... who can play the harp and lyre so as to provoke the listener to laughter or lament." 313–16

In short, the ideal woman must also qualify for the title of ideal poet! This last requirement, strange as it is, will prove to be an important part of Kozbi's machination.

Kozbi's delegation has found the right match for Zeraḥ—a girl by the name of Ayala Sheluḥa ("a fleet-footed doe")—and Kozbi now prays to God "who chose man and rejected woman; who made flourish in men the beard and member for his fame and glory, and who gave the daughters of Eve the burning womb of desire" to blind Zeraḥ to the truth (374–79). Kozbi recognizes the reality of sexual politics: It is the difference in genitalia, she says, that determines the hierarchy of value and power. Later, though, when Kozbi and her husband Sheker try to talk Zeraḥ into mar-

---

[20] K.z.b and sh.k.r. are Hebrew roots for "deceit" and "lie"; y.r.sh. denotes inheritance or heritage. Thus, the pair are named "heirs of falsehood."

riage, they assume the role of mouthpieces of family values. Sheker's arguments are ideological in kind; he advocates tradition, the norms of the "generations of old" (412–14). Kozbi, on the other hand, lectures to Zeraḥ in the language of Genesis that "it is not good that the man should be alone; I will make him a helpmate for him." She enumerates the material benefits and comforts of a man's married life:

> "A Woman of Valor is her husband's crown. In a rainy day she is his shield and breast-plate, and in a cold day—his cover. She is a fort for the poor and the weak. Her eyes will guard you when you lie down to sleep, and she will greet you when you open your eyes. With her you shall know no fear."[21]   445–48

Zeraḥ insists in his refusal: "My youthful sins will never be wiped out if I let a woman enter my bed. I'd rather spend my nights on top of a dung heap and my days in the street. I'd rather eat my bread solitary than look at delicacies" (420–22). Finally he succumbs, but not before securing an attractive dowry, and beholding the girl's beauty with his own eyes: the "rose garden" of her body and her "untouched pomegranates" (478–81), imagery derived from the Song of Songs. Zeraḥ's fall, like Adam's, begins with this fruit, which is "pleasant to the eyes" (Genesis 3:6). Zeraḥ is caught in a confusing opposition of seeing and blindness. The moment he sees his future wife he stops seeing Kozbi's and Sheker's ploy. "For if a look engenders desire, desire, in turn, forecloses all future possibility of seeing."[22]

Hearing joins sight, and after hearing the girl, Ayala, play the harp and improvise songs, Zeraḥ exclaims, "This enlightened (*maskeleth*) woman was sent by God" (483). A poetic tournament now occurs with thirteen miniature love poems sung alternately by the couple. All poetic conventions of courtly love are followed here except for one—instead of the usual monologues addressed by a man to a woman, here the poetic dialogue is symmetrical. The prospective bride has mastered the male art of serenading. Her stylized epigrams describe Zeraḥ's beauty in superlative terms, similar to those employed in descriptions of women in male love lyric:[23]

---

[21] My translation.

[22] R. Howard Bloch, "Medieval Misogyny," in Bloch and Frances Ferguson, *Misogyny, Misandry, and Misanthropy* (Berkeley and Los Angeles: University of California Press, 1989), 15.

[23] Ayala's literary and musical endeavors do not reflect the situation of Jewish women in Muslim and Christian Spain, who were totally excluded from the artistic

> Why are your lips as red as blood?
> Ask the midwives at your birth—
> Did they tie a crimson ribbon
> round your wrist or on your lips?   508-9

And Zeraḥ, like an echo, responds to her *motif*:

> You chose your lovers' hearts
> as targets for your darts;
> Their blood cries from betwixt
> your lips and scares my heart.[24]   513-14

It is poetry—male love poetry sung by a woman—that leads Zeraḥ into the snare. Had Zeraḥ not been already blinded by the girl's looks, the fact that her speech equals (or even outdoes) his own—in elegance, in daring and in quantity—might have alerted him. Ayala's poems serve for him as a mirror in which he sees an erotic image of himself. Like Narcissus he falls in love with his own reflection. As the poems become more and more erotically daring Zeraḥ forgets all his reservations and invites Ayala to share his bed.

Zeraḥ is now consumed by lust and urges Kozbi to conduct the wedding instantly. In his eagerness he gives up the dowry and is even ready to pay a bride's-price. The fact that the ceremony takes place on the thirteenth of the month of Adar, Purim eve, heightens the carnivalesque features of the work.[25] A ridiculous *ketuba* (parodying the style of the Jewish marriage contract) is signed and Zeraḥ, the fallen saint, becomes the

---

scene. Two exceptions are recorded. One woman, perhaps the daughter of the famous poet Samuel ha- Nagid, was taught by her father to compose poems in Arabic; see James A. Bellamy, "Qasmuna the Poetess: Who Was She?" *Journal of the American Oriental Society* 103 (1983): 423–24. The other, the wife of another famous poet, left us a single Hebrew love poem; see Ezra Fleischer, "On Dunash ben Labrat, His Wife and His Son," *Scripta Hierosolymitana* 5 (1984): 189–202 (in Hebrew). In Andalusian-Arabic courtly culture, slave women served as musicians and singers, and some thirty Andalusian women poets are also known. On the absence of the female voice in medieval Hebrew literature, see Tova Rosen, "On Tongues Being Bound and Let Loose: Women in Medieval Hebrew Literature," *Prooftexts* 8 (1988): 67–87.

[24] Translations are mine.

[25] The theme of a "topsy-turvy world" is of significance in carnivalesque contexts. Talya Fishman argues convincingly that the work was designed to be read at the home of Ibn Shabbetai's patron on Purim eve, the only day on the Jewish calendar when the reading of comical texts was licensed. *Minḥat Yehuda* is indeed full of allusions to the scroll of Esther which is read on Purim in celebration of Esther's victory over the Jews' enemies. See Talya Fishman, "A Medieval Parody of Misogyny," *Prooftexts* 8 (1988): 101–2.

laughing stock of the event (562–80). Only upon unveiling the bride does Zeraḥ find out that an ugly crone with an ugly name (Ritzpa bat Aya, "Coal daughter of Vulture") has replaced the perfect bride:

> Kozbi took the girl and exchanged her for a quarrelsome hag, black as a crow, with lips like two inflated bladders—anyone who saw would gasp. The hair on her skin was like stubby brambles, and her face was covered with nettles—something to make infants and babes recoil. [583–85] Her days waxed old and her tits were shriveled. Her face was dark and her eyes dismal, her teeth long and her forehead harder than rock. She farted. She was plaintive, shrewish and contemptible.[26]

Seeing that "no gold and no beauty" remain, Zeraḥ cries "A plot! Deceit! A pack of lies!" but to no avail.

Besides its comic effect the "replacement device" betrays one of the deepest of men's fears, namely that the beloved maiden they marry may turn overnight into an unbearable spouse.[27] A popular medieval anecdote spells out this fear of transformation/deformation in a slightly different metaphor: "When Socrates's disciples gazed at a beautiful woman ... the master said, 'Turn her inside out; then wilt thou understand her ugliness.'"[28]

While Zeraḥ weeps, regretting his stupidity in "giving his soul into the power of its foes" (596), his wife makes the following shopping list:

> "Go and fetch me vessels of silver and vessels of gold, dresses and chains, bracelets and mufflers; a house and a flat, a chair and a lamp, a table and spoons, a pestle and groats, a blanket and spindle-weight, a mat and a tub, basket and spindle, a cauldron and bottle, a basin and clothespress, a broom and a kerchief; a pan, furnace, barrel, and

---

[26] The first part of the quotation is in Scheindlin's translation. The latter part (from Ibn Shabbetai's second edition, lines 740–43) is my translation. Judah Alharizi's sixth maqama in *Sefer Taḥkemoni* imitates and even surpasses the description of the wife's appalling portraiture. Compare also to the wife's physique in the *Lamentations* of the thirteenth century Matheolus: "Alas! Now my heart is very sad, for she is now so mangy, stooped, humpbacked and pot-bellied, disfigured and undone that she seems to be a deformed person. Rachel has become Leah, all gray ... rough, senile, and deaf ... her chest is hard and her breasts ... are wrinkled ... like wet-bags" (Quoted in Bloch, "Medieval Misogyny," 24 n45).

[27] The topos of the bride's replacement goes back to the biblical story of Jacob's wives in which Leah replaced Rachel (Genesis 29:25).

[28] Ibn Zabara, *Book of Delight*, 66.

shovel; a pot, vessels, goblets and charms; gowns, veils, turbans and robes; linen, nose rings, purses and lace; crescents, amulets and sashes, embroidery, headdresses, rings, checkered cloth, armlets and anklets and anklebands—and besides these: special clothes to wear on Sabbaths and festivals.... This is by no means all you shall have to provide." 609–16

Ritzpa's first act thus attests to two of woman's cardinal sins: her excessive speech and her greed for material possessions. A symmetrical dialogue between the sexes (as in Zeraḥ's and Ayala's courtship) is possible only as an erotic fantasy; marriage is presented as a semiotic battle over the domination of language and signification. When Zeraḥ begins an agonized monologue his wife stops him right away:

"Stop taking up your rhyme! Do not even raise your voice! I have no interest in wisdom or culture, only in bread and meat. Your poems and your lyrics mean nothing to me—'A poem does not buy a glass of wine.'" 787–88

In voicing her opinion of her husband's "literature" this wife anticipates the more overt and articulate Wife of Bath, who expresses her criticism by tearing three pages out of her husband's misogynist book. Moreover, when Ritzpa opposes man's "wisdom and culture" to "woman's bread and meat" does she simply reiterate hegemonic views about woman's crude nature, or does she mock them? Her text, like that of Chaucer's Wife, lends itself to more then one reading. According to one reading, misogyny, when voiced by a woman, is far more comical and thus more effective than when voiced by a man. According to another reading, the tension here between speech and speaker relativizes the message, and consequently subverts the male point of view.

Garrulousness (the wife's verbose monologues) and gluttony (her desire for bread and meat) are two female sins performed by the mouth; they become interchangeable as displacements of woman's excessive sexuality. Zeraḥ's nightmare had similarly equated woman's "upper" and "lower" mouths: for the mouth of the female beast that mutilated him is clearly a realization of the *vagina dentata* whose "lips are the gates of hell, and jaws—slaughterknives."[29] Ritzpa now pushes Zeraḥ to criminality, telling him what real manhood is:

---

[29] This is added in Huss's second edition, 2:76, lines 442–43.

> "Get up, take your plow and your plowshare, your quiver and bow, and go about the town from dusk to dawn, stealing and murdering and swearing falsely. As your household grows you will have to provide their daily bread. And you shall not appear empty-handed before me. Wasn't woman given to you to till her and to care for her? If you fail to bring me every single thing I desire—you will stay outside!"[30] 633-36

Having won the upper hand in language, she now also gets the upper hand in sex, controlling not only the household's economic affairs but also the ins-and-outs of copulation. Abstinence, Zeraḥ's abandoned ideology, becomes Ritzpa's strategy in controlling Zeraḥ's body; his phallus and its metaphoric replacements (his "plow and bow") are now, so to speak, in her hands. Using the phrase "to till and care for her" (borrowed from Genesis 2:15 where it is Adam's task "to till" the soil of Eden) this woman reverses the sanctioned order of things. She is no man's helpmate, but her husband's sovereign. And if he fails to care for her, she threatens to expel him from her (sexual) paradise ("stay outside!").

We may note that Ritzpa's ultimatum consists of three clauses: food (bread, meat, and wine), covering (veils, gowns, etc.) and intercourse. These three are, in Jewish marital law, the husband's obligations towards his wife and thus the woman's rights (*She'erah kesutah ve-'onatah*: "Her food, her raiment and her conjugal rights," Exodus 21:10). Ritzpa actually threatens to stop her husband from fulfilling his third duty (*'onah*) in case her first two demands are not fully met. But worse is still to come:

> "But all this is nothing compared with the day I give birth! Then you will really work! My brothers and my relations will be in your presence around your table, and you will provide a whole sheep for their daily delicacies. Nor will the midwife do without wine, bread, or meat. You will have to call a wet nurse for the children ... and buy slave women and maids to tend for them to eat their dung and drink their urine, for I will not touch them!" 636-40

As in the grotesque, the funny and the threatening meet here, in Ritzpa's rejection of all motherly functions. But did not Taḥkemoni warn Zeraḥ against "becoming a pimp" and having to support prostitutes and their children (166-67)? This picture of the tribulations of the paterfamilias has

---

[30] Scheindlin's translation slightly revised.

hardly any parallels in Jewish literature, but is matched in Latin literature in the theme of the poor husband who has to resort to crime to fill his family's insatiable bellies.[31]

While listening to his wife, Zeraḥ's hair turns white. Like Job he sits, bemoaning his fate, with three companions alternately rebuking and consoling him. His decision to eventually dissolve the marriage starts a heated debate among his townsmen. The townswomen, however, unite in support of Ritzpa. Everybody goes to trial in the court of "King Abraham."

Here historical reality trespasses on the confines of fiction. "King Abraham" is Abraham Ibn Al-Fakhkhar, Ibn Shabbetai's patron. A Hebrew writer himself, Ibn Al-Fakhkhar served as a courtier to Alfonso VII, and was a communal leader in Toledo.[32] As the guardian of societal norms, he is expected to elicit the truth. Upon listening to the accusations of the townswomen's advocate—Zeraḥ ruined families and disgraced women—the judge decrees a death penalty for Zeraḥ. Ambiguity dominates even this crucial point of the narrative: For the supporters of marriage the death sentence proves that Zeraḥ was the villain of the piece, but for those who oppose marriage Zeraḥ is convicted for betraying his own misogynist creed.[33]

Rescue comes unexpectedly. The author, Judah himself, appears in court like a deus ex machina and puts himself, instead of Zeraḥ, to the judge's trial (777). The author's defense is poetic license. Zeraḥ, he says, is only a fictitious literary creation. Unlike Zeraḥ and the misogynist narrator, he, the author, is a loving husband and father. Moreover, this piece is but an entertaining farce intended to please his patron, Abraham. It is a comic purpose, he says, which caused him "to reverse things" (785). What is now put on trial is Ibn Shabbetai's artistic achievement, not the moral of his tale. Hence Abraham, to whom everyone looked as the *arbiter morum*, becomes an *arbiter elegantiae*. His laughter is proof of the author's literary success. With the piece being dedicated to Abraham, and with Judah being generously rewarded—the contract between author and patron is fully completed and the maqama is happily brought to an end.

In my next section I will take up the question of interpretation and

---

[31] And compare to *De conjuge non ducenda* where "the husband always serves; the wife always commands.... [I]n order to fill their bellies, the husband is reduced to cheating and crime" (Wilson and Makowsky, *Wykked Wyves*, 127–28).

[32] For more data see Huss, *Critical Editions*, 1:263–73.

[33] See Huss's interpretation, ibid., 1:96.

ideology. How do modern critics interpret this complex and sophisticated work? How did medieval readers read it?

II

Among modern critics only Norman Roth reads *Minḥat Yehuda* as unequivocally misogynistic and misogamic: "The satire ... is clearly directed against woman in general and *any* kind of marriage."[34] Most other critics, however, have seen the misogyny as diluted or cancelled out by other aspects of the text: "The satire is directed against those who go to extremes. It is both a warning to the misogynist and a protest against hasty marriage.... This evidently is not only a satire on women, but also a reproach to those who despise them";[35] "Ibn Shabbetai did not mean in fact to preach women-hatred, but put it in the mouth of his protagonist.. All he intended was to please, entertain and divert his patron and audience";[36] "Its chief aim is indeed to divert, not to denigrate";[37] "It is hard to view 'The Misogynist' as a seriously misogynistic work ... [although] the author knows and enjoys the conventions and stereotypes of misogynistic literature."[38] "The ending alters the meaning of the central story line.... The author's ultimate exposure of the entire tale as illusory undercuts the work's misogynist content at the level of broad structure, just as his assertion that he loves his wife and children plays that role on a narrative level."[39]

By focussing on the author's intention these critics limit themselves to reading the work through the author's eyes, and thus fail to consider its diverse meanings for diverse readers. Adopting the author's perspective, critics fail to see humor as an ideological instrument by which misogyny is —inadvertently or purposefully, but always efficiently—disseminated. They see humor rather as a way of diluting or even disarming its virulence. My argument is that Ibn Shabbetai's disclaimer of seriousness at the end of his

---

[34] Norman Roth, "'The Wiles of Women' Motif in the Medieval Hebrew Literature of Spain," *Hebrew Annual Review* 2 (1978): 150.

[35] Israel Davidson, *Parody in Jewish Literature* (New York: Columbia University Press, 1907), 10.

[36] Schirmann, *Ha-Shira ha-Ivrit*, 3:68.

[37] Dan Pagis, *Hiddush u-Masoret be-Shirat ha-Hol* ("Innovation and Tradition in Hebrew Secular Poetry," Jerusalem: Keter, 1976), 192.

[38] Scheindlin, *Rabbinic Fantasies*, 271.

[39] Fishman, "A Medieval Parody," 94.

work does not itself have to be taken seriously, and his entertaining purpose does not necessarily mitigate anti-feminism. Nor does the defense of fictitiousness. Some critics argue that the ending (where Ibn Shabbetai admits that he concocted "the thing in order to turn it upside down") reverses the apparent meaning of the piece. This argument overlooks a structural pattern quite common in endings of maqamas: the self-referential exposure of the fictional nature of the tale.[40] Does the recognition of fictionality as such necessarily contradict the values of a discourse? Similarly, on the level of narration, does the narrator's avowal of loving his wife and children vindicate his expressed misogyny? Is not the proclamation of loving one's wife the last refuge of the male chauvinist?

Another position holds that the work is "egalitarian," i.e., as critical and satirical of men as it is of women. This ignores the double standard in this maqama. Men are censured here for acting stupidly (Zeraḥ) or falsely (Sheker), but women are deprecated simply for being what they are; men are judged for deeds, woman are incriminated on an essentialist basis. In addition, while men in the fiction are divided into two camps, the good and the bad, women are all bad; and if there is a good one, like Ayala, one finds that she was too good to be true. Lastly, some critics admit misogyny but assert extenuating circumstances: Jewish misogyny was product of the "bad influence" exerted by Islamic or Christian sources.[41]

In my view, Judah's misogamic message is contradicted in the story's conclusion, but its misogyny remains intact. The restitution of marriage as a societal norm does not logically alter the negative view of woman. An absurd, even tragic, aspect of the mentality of medieval men is thus disclosed: marriage is good, though it entails a union with an essentially evil partner.

While agreeing with Huss on many points of his comprehensive discussion, including his conclusion that no univocal conclusion can be

---

[40] The same device is employed also in Ezrat ha-Nashim, a pro-feminist response to *Minḥat Yehuda* discussed below. See also the ending of Ibn Saqbel's maqama (Schirmann, *Ha-Shira ha-Ivrit*, 2:565; trans. Scheindlin, *Rabbinic Fantasies*, 264). Judah Alharizi (the master of Hebrew maqama and Ibn Shabbetai's contemporary) ends many of his fifty *maqamat* with the discovery by the first-person narrator that he has fallen victim to the fabrication of his fictitious protagonist.

[41] As in Fishman ("A Medieval Parody," 93): "'The Misogynist' draws upon an established and vibrant eastern tradition of misogynist writing ... consciously ... distancing himself from [this] literary tradition." Or in Schirmann (*Ha-Shira ha-Ivrit*, 3:67): "The subject was in fact favored by medieval Moslem and Christian authors more than by Jewish ones."

drawn from this self-contradicting complex work,[42] I differ with him on the question of humor. Indifferent to the gendered aspects of humor, Huss writes: "Ibn Shabbetai makes it clear to us, as he did to his historical readers, that the sheer representation of absurd 'reversed worlds,' in which unexpected and illogical occurrences take place, is indeed very funny."[43] Who is Huss's "us"? Does the readerresponse as analyzed by Huss apply equally to the medieval reader and to the modern reader? Does it apply equally to readers of both sexes? Is the humor of these "reversed worlds" funny also from a woman's perspective?

There is no reason to believe that Ibn Shabbetai's audience, a literary circle at Abraham Ibn al-Fakhkhar's "court," was not exclusively male. Its ambience must have resembled those sessions in gentlemen's clubs where piquant jokes, not intended for a lady's ear, were told. Freud's definition of "smut" is relevant in this context:

> Where a joke is not an aim in itself—that is, when it is not an innocent one ... —it is either a hostile joke (serving for the purpose of aggressiveness, satire, or defense) or an obscene joke (serving the purpose of exposure).... We know what is meant by "smut": the intentional bringing into prominence of sexual facts and relations by speech.... A person who laughs at smut that he hears is laughing as though he were the spectator of an act of sexual aggression.... Smut is like the exposure of the sexually different person to whom it is directed.... It cannot be doubted that the desire to see what is sexually exposed is the original motive of smut.... Generally speaking, a tendentious joke calls for three people: in addition to the one who makes the joke, there must be a second who is taken as the object of the hostile or sexual aggressiveness, and a third in whom the joke's aim of producing pleasure is fulfilled.... Through the first person's smutty speech the woman is exposed before the third who, as listener, has now been bribed by the effortless satisfaction of his own libido.[44]

Shoshana Felman, in discussing this passage, calls attention to the essentially male structure of the sexual joke:

---

[42] Huss, *Critical Editions*, 1:100.

[43] Ibid., 102.

[44] Sigmund Freud, "Jokes and Their Relation to the Unconscious," *Standard Edition of the Complete Psychological Works of Sigmund Freud*, trans. J. Strachey (London: Hogarth Press, 1978), 4: 96–100.

Although originally seeking an exposure of the female body, [it] is in turn motivated in an exclusively male structure of address.... The act ... of joking is rhetorically addressed to male accomplices.... Women do not occupy the place from which the joke is funny. If the joke is an exchange of laughter or of pleasure between two men at the expense of women, women are completely justified to put themselves in a position to miss the joke.[45]

Not all medieval readers of *Minhat Yehuda* thought it to be funny. At least three literary responses written during the thirteenth century attack its misogyny. Two of them were written in 1210, just two years after Ibn Shabbetai's first version of 1208, by an author known only by his first name: Isaac, probably of a Provençal origin. *Ezrat ha- Nashim* ("In Defense of Women") closely follows *Minhat Yehuda*, but is a mirror reversing its model.[46] Here too the prologue is a revelation scene: an Angel orders Isaac to listen to the complaints of Jewish women about Ibn Shabbetai's disastrous influence on their husbands. The desperate women urge Isaac to take vengeance on their abuser, whereupon he undertakes to write a story in praise of conjugal love. Hence, the characters in Isaac's story are antithetic to those of Ibn Shabbetai's. A dying patriarch encourages his son to marry, and a young wife is a perfect lady, an ideal helpmate, and her husband's lifesaver.[47] In the prologue to his second work, *Ein Mishpat* ("The Fount of Law"), Isaac foretells the end of the world,

---

[45] Shoshana Felman, *What Does a Woman Want?: Reading and Sexual Difference* (Baltimore: Johns Hopkins University Press, 1993), 92–99, at 95–96.

[46] For the text see Huss, *Critical Editions*, 2:100–112; Schirmann, *Ha-Shira ha-Ivrit*, 3:87–96. For discussion see Huss, 1:10–14, 154–73. Isaac also attacks Ibn Shabbetai ad hominem, blaming him for hating all women on account of "the black woman" that he married.

[47] Here is the tale in brief: A dying father, Absalom, instructs his son Hovav to marry a virtuous, pious virgin. He adjures him never to betray her, and adds a list of biblical precedents in favor of marriage and procreation. Hovav marries his beloved Rachel against the will of her avaricious relatives, who conspire to kill him. On their escape the young couple encounter a series of dangers. It is only thanks to Rachel's resourceful trickery (which here is considered virtue not vice) that they are saved time and again from death. It is also thanks to her that they find a treasure, which enables them to return to town and be welcomed by her relatives. This happy ending is followed by an epilogue where the Angel reappears. It turns out now that the Angel is no other than Tadros ha- Levi ha-Nasi, Isaac's patron, who is very pleased with the tale, and claims that Rachel resembles his own wife. Upon declaring the fictitiousness of the tale the author dedicates it to the patron's wife, and gets his full reward.

which will be caused by husbands who followed Ibn Shabbetai's teaching and abandoned their wives. Isaac sees it as his mission to persuade men to rejoin their families.[48]

This literary marriage-debate was still current in 1295 when the eighteen-year-old Yeda'aya ha-Penini of Provence wrote *Ohev Nashim* ("The Lover of Women") as another pro-woman response to *Minḥat Yehuda*. One of ha-Penini's characters is Ibn Shabbetai himself, who is defeated in a literary contest in which the winner is the author, the defender of women and marriage.[49] In the heat of these rhetorical battles between woman-defenders and woman-haters one should not be deluded as to the nature of the "defense." The defending voices spring from the heart of patriarchy. The case for women is made by male voices. It is men who retaliate against other men for their misogyny. The admiration of "feminine virtue" is in fact a commendation of patriarchal feminine stereotypes. Rachel in *Ezrat ha-Nashim* is "good" because she is good for her husband: she is long-suffering, loyal and efficacious. The women in the other two "defenses" win male sympathy because they are abandoned and needy. As Alcuin Blamires observes in a book wholly dedicated to the medieval literary advocacy of women, this "profeminine discourse" has an "unfeminist quality."[50] R. Howard Bloch extends the definition of misogyny as to

---

[48] *Ein Mishpat* (text, Huss, *Critical Editions*, 2:113–21; discussion, 14–17) unfolds the allegorical- apocalyptic fiction of *Minḥat Yehuda* and takes place in a similar biblical ambience. In the assembly of the King of Demons and his allies (including the biblical foes of Israel, Ibn Shabbetai, and other enemies of wedlock), a pact was signed to invalidate the *ketuba* (the Jewish marriage contract), to humiliate women, and, furthermore, to eradicate them. Loyal husbands are lynched, but one escapes to warn the Israelite king Malkitzedek (literally: King of Justice). In the heat of the battle the two camps exchange hostile retorts for and against women and wedlock, giving examples of women good and bad. A referee, probably Isaac's patron, is chosen who decrees that "when women are good they are very good, but when they are bad they are horrid."

[49] *Ohev Nashim* was published by Adolf Neubauer in *Jubelschrift zum neunzigsten Geburtstag des L. Zunz* (Berlin: L. Gerschel, 1884), 1–19, 138–40. Here too an allegorical battle is fought between Wisdom and Folly. The Fools wish to annihilate marriage, and the women fight them. The women, saved by a virtuous heroine, celebrate their victory together with the narrator. Ibn Shabbetai descends from Paradise, indignant and armored, to defend his work. After a debate both authors go for a literary trial. The judges, respectful of both authors, refrain from a literary verdict; however, they decree that marriage should be sanctioned, whereby Ibn Shabbetai, who lost his case, returns to Paradise.

[50] Alcuin Blamires, *The Case for Women in Medieval Culture* (Oxford: Clarendon Press, 1997), 12.

include any "speech act in which woman is the subject of the sentence and the predicate a more general term [negative or positive]."⁵¹

In what way do *Minḥat Yehuda* and the works that responded to it reflect the culture that produced and consumed them? Is the debate between Judah and Isaac to be seen as a sheer literary tournament or does it indicate some real social tension? Is a debate over marriage plausible in a Jewish community guided by halakha? Prima facie the answer is negative: "Marriage is the positively marked term in rabbinic culture, while virginity is marked as negative."⁵² Where can a Jewish travesty of marriage, then, originate?

The possibility that Ibn Shabbetai may have been inspired by Christian culture is not implausible for an author whose patron was an important official at the Castilian court. Whether Ibn Shabbetai was acquainted with Latin language and literature is unknown. However, despite the difficulty in tracing the precise route of literary transmission, motifs and topoi culled from Latin literature may be readily recognized in Ibn Shabbetai's work (as indicated above). Moreover, it is likely that controversies around marriage which plagued Catholicism at this period were known to Ibn Shabbetai and other Jewish intellectuals.⁵³ David Biale refers to this socio-cultural unrest in southern France and Spain, and to its resonance in Jewish circles:

> Jewish intellectuals were undoubtedly aware of developments in canon law and scholastic theology.... Christian theologians of the High Middle Ages were deeply concerned with problems of sexuality and marriage. In precisely this period, southern France, Spain and Italy were gripped by the Catharist (or Albigensian) dualistic heresy, which preached renunciation of the material world. As medieval heirs of Gnosticism and Manichaeaism, the Cathars

---

⁵¹ Bloch, *Medieval Misogyny*, 5.

⁵² Daniel Boyarin, *Carnal Israel: Reading Sex in Talmudic Culture* (Berkeley: University of California Press, 1993), 46.

⁵³ Dates are not unimportant here: *Minḥat Yehuda* was first written in 1208 and *Ezrat ha- Nashim* in 1210. At about that time (in the reign of Pope Innocent III, 1198–1216) the struggle against clerical marriages reached its climax. It was also in the first decade of the century that several delegations of vagabond monks (including also a Spanish order) were sent to southern France to preach to the Cathars. Zerah's vagabond "order" seems to be cast in the mold of these mendicant preachers. However, in spreading his ascetic doctrines to all, he resembles more the Cathars who preached celibacy to laity and clergy alike.

vehemently rejected marriage and procreation. It is not unlikely that the challenge of these heretics prompted a renewed Catholic affirmation of marriage; at the same time ... church lawyers developed the medieval doctrine of marriage as a sacrament and of procreation as divinely decreed. During the twelfth century, though, the church also experienced a movement of reform that dissolved clerical marriages and unequivocally established clerical celibacy. As opposed to the Catharist desire to equalize clergy and laity under a common doctrine of celibacy, the church drew a sharp distinction between a celibate clergy and a married laity. The rabbinic class, which no doubt saw itself as the counterpart of the Christian clergy, must have felt the need to defend its own continuing marriages against the ideal of a celibate clergy.[54]

Thus it is legitimate to ask whether the internal Christian polemic over marriage touched a sensitive nerve in Jewish culture; whether *Minḥat Yehuda* reflects this polemic; whether it reflects similar discontent among Jews. I would like to argue that works like *Minḥat Yehuda* and its rejoinders could not have been written were there not some ambivalence towards marriage in the Jewish tradition as well as in the medieval Jewish milieu in and for which they were written. Although halakha is unequivocal in its positive valuation of marriage, this does not necessarily annul the possibility of other voices, of discontent and tension, within Jewish culture. Following Daniel Boyarin's advice to read talmudic culture "not as a monologic language but as a heteroglossic collection of dialects,"[55] I would apply the same perspective to medieval Judaism. In other words, the prevalence of halakha did not prevent the expression of non-halakhic tendencies, nor did it prevent the permeation of ideas and controversies from the ambient cultures.

A fascination with celibacy, created by the contradictory commitments to marriage and to the study of Torah, was already present in talmudic culture. Despite the sacred obligation to marry and procreate the Rabbis had still "to combat the attractiveness of celibate life ... [which] was the ideal of much of the ambient culture, both Jewish and non-Jewish."[56]

---

[54] David Biale, *Eros and the Jews: From Biblical Israel to Contemporary America* (New York: Basic Books, 1992), 97–98.

[55] Boyarin, *Carnal Israel*, 47.

[56] Daniel Boyarin, "Internal Opposition in Talmudic Literature: The Case of the Married Monk," *Representations* (1991): 87–113 (especially 87–88).

Following are several explicit ascetic pronouncements, made by eminent medieval authors, legal authorities and religious figures, which are not compatible with the spirit of halakha.

Saadia Gaon, the tenth-century leader of Babylonian Jewry, expresses repulsion towards sexuality but advocates it for procreation. Nevertheless, he is ambivalent in regard to raising children and lists the tribulations in providing for them, in health and in sickness, as well as in suffering heartache caused by their improper behavior.[57] Even more astounding are warnings against procreation itself, voiced in Hebrew poems of eleventh-century Al-Andalus. Samuel ha-Nagid, a halakha authority, a communal leader, the vizier of Granada, a master of love poetry and a dedicated father of four, writes:

> Men in their folly beget children
> in vain, and celebrate their birth.
> Had they known the world's end
> they would not rear children nor procreate.[58]

In a similar vein the celibate Solomon Ibn Gabirol (eleventh-century Zaragoza), poet and philosopher, writes:

> If you wish to inherit Paradise
> and if you fear hellfire,
> Loathe this world's values; be not tempted
> by riches, honor or offspring.[59]

Even if these epigrams are rhetorical exercises on an ascetic theme and not sincere utterances, still, the very fact that they were voiced in a Jewish milieu speaks for itself. The eleventh-century philosopher and moralist Bahya Ibn Paquda, although intellectually attracted to extreme Islamic ascetic celibacy, eventually yielded to halakha in matters of marriage and procreation.[60] More daring was Abraham Maimuni (Egypt), Maimonides's son

---

[57] Saadia Gaon, *Book of Beliefs and Opinions*, trans. Samuel Rosenblatt (New Haven: Yale University Press, 1948); see the chapters on abstinence, 366; intercourse, 371; children, 381–83. Saadia was the first Jewish philosopher to be influenced by Islamic thought, and one of the most revered rabbinic authorities of all times.

[58] The poem quoted is from Samuel ha-Nagid's collection of ascetic poems, *Ben Kohelet*, ed. Shraga Abramson (Tel Aviv: Maḥbarot le-Sifrut, 1953), no. 19. My translation.

[59] Solomon Ibn Gabirol, *Secular Poems*, ed. Hayim Brody and Hayim Schirmann (Jerusalem: Shocken Institute, 1974), no. 76. My translation.

[60] Ibn Paquda, eleventh century, was the author of an extremely popular moral

and Ibn Shabbetai's younger contemporary, who, influenced by Sufi mysticism, referred to the tribulations of family life, and praised the prophets for their abstinence from sex.[61] In their apologetic style both reveal their fascination with Muslim celibate ascetics, but ultimately align themselves with the Jewish consensus.

Most ambivalent on sexual issues was Maimonides. For him physical pleasure is an animal drive, adverse to meditative life, yet he admitted it as beneficial to health. Sex and the body are shameful, but marriage and children are primary postulates. The advantage of marriage, he added, is in that it dulls sexual desire. Like Islamic ascetics he recommended abstinence within the framework of family life. During intercourse it is commendable for a scholar to be restrained so that procreation is separated from desire. The commandment of *'onah*, that is the husband's obligation (according to the Rabbis) to ensure the woman's sexual pleasure, goes unmentioned by Maimonides.[62]

Rabbi Abraham ben David of Posquières (a rabbinical authority, ca. 1120–1198, usually referred to as Rabad) was Maimonides's vehement opponent. Criticizing Maimonides's opinions on intercourse, Rabad "restored the commandment of *'onah* as equally legitimate. The sexual rights of women now found a defender against the misogynist philosophers!"[63] In a "marriage manual" composed circa 1180 Rabad maintains that, though a husband should not indulge in his own sexual pleasure, he owes his wife not just the minimum of *'onah* as is required by the law but as much as she desires.[64] The protest of women in *Minḥat Yehuda* (repeated also in *Ezrat ha-Nashim*) and their insistence on fulfillment of their sexual pleasure may thus be a comical and exaggerated expression of this debate over the issue of *'onah*.[65]

---

treatise, *The Duties of the Heart*. For his ascetic views, see Josef Dan, *Sifrut ha-Musar ve-ha-Derush* (Jerusalem: Keter, 1975), 52–53.

[61] Biale, *Eros and the Jews*, 92.

[62] Ibid., 91–93.

[63] Ibid., 95–97.

[64] Underlying this statement is the assumption that the man's desire is more controllable by "intention" than the woman's. Biale, ibid., 97, maintains that Rabad's teaching reflected the intense debate that was going on simultaneously among Christian theologians.

[65] In real life, as shown by Y. T. Assis (based on court records and responsa), it was bigamy or the husband's business-trips which were most often the causes for the neglect of women's needs. However, there were many cases where it was "the woman's lack of enthusiasm about her conjugal life" which was the cause of a

§ § §

To conclude: Though ultimately guided by the consensus of official halakha, eminent Jewish leaders and thinkers did voice varied opinions on matters of marital life. Thus Ibn Shabbetai's *Minḥat Yehuda* is in all likelihood informed by the author's knowledge of contemporary Christian controversies. Yet there was enough of dissent in Jewish literature at the time to make the debate-theme effective in a Jewish context. Hence the perplexity of the reader transcends the realm of literary response to become a symptom of the qualms and ambivalence of the contemporary intellectual Jewish milieu.

Tel Aviv University

---

husband's complaint. See "Sexual Behaviour in Medieval Hispano-Jewish Society," in *Jewish History: Essays in Honour of Chimen Abramsky*, ed. A. Rapoport-Albert and S. J. Zipperstein (London: P. Halban, 1988), especially 31–33.

Alonso de Cartagena:
Nation, Miscegenation, and the Jew in Late-Medieval Castile

BRUCE ROSENSTOCK

Cartagena and the Imagination of the Spanish "Nation"

Perhaps the most influential intellectual figure in fifteenth-century Castile was Alonso de Cartagena (1385–1456), Castile's spokesman at the Council of Basle (1434–1439), Bishop of Burgos (1435–1456), and author of vernacular and Latin histories of Spain which set the tone for subsequent historiography. In addition, Cartagena composed one of the first defenses of the converso caste's prerogatives in the long history of the "purity of blood" dispute which erupted in 1449 when the Toledo rebels, seeking autonomy from Juan II of Castile, issued their anti-converso *Sentencia-Estatuto*. Cartagena was himself a converso, baptized in his early childhood together with father, Rabbi Solomon Halevi (Pablo de Santa María after his baptism.[1]

---

[1] For a discussion of the rebellion in Toledo and the following anti-converso persecution, see B. Netanyahu, *The Origins of the Inquisition in Fifteenth-Century Spain* (New York: Random House, 1995), 314–50. For biographies of Alonso de Cartagena, see *Intento de un diccionario biográfico y bibliográfico de autores de la provincia de Burgos*, ed. Manuel Martínez Añíbarro (Madrid: Manuel Tello, 1889), 88–115; L. Serrano, *Los conversos Pablo de Santa María y Alonso de Cartagena* (Madrid: C. Bermejo, 1942) and F. Cantera Burgos, *Álvar García de Santa María* (Madrid: C. Bermejo, 1952); for briefer accounts, see R. B. Tate, "The *Anacephaleosis* of Alfonso García de Santa María, Bishop of Burgos, 1435–1456," *Hispanic Studies in Honour of I. Gonzáles Llubera*, ed. Frank Pierce, (Oxford: Dolphin Book Co. Ltd., 1959), 387–401, and Netanyahu, *The Origins of the Inquisition*, 518–27. Pablo de Santa María was also a prolific writer, author of a *historia mundi* and of a full biblical commentary which was widely published together with that of Nicolas de Lyra. Pablo de Santa María was appointed to be the bishop of Burgos, the post his son took over at his father's death. The Cartagena family was truly remarkable; Pablo's granddaughter (Alonso's niece) wrote the first Spanish work of auto-consolation about living with a disability (she was deaf) and the first defense of a woman's equal claim to literary creativity (after critics denied she could have written the memoir by herself). On Teresa, see Alan Deyermond, "'El Convento de Dolonçias': The Works of Teresa de Cartagena," *Journal of Hispanic Philology* 1 (1976): 19–29 and Dayle

This paper examines Cartagena's defense of the conversos in relation to his conception of the national identity of Spain. We will find in Cartagena a profound tension between a conception of national identity as arising through productive miscegenation (between Jew and gentile) and a national identity legitimized through an unbroken racial lineage (that of the Goths). We may better understand this tension, I will suggest, if we frame it within the terms provided by recent postcolonial theory. Cartagena's recourse to the notion of productive miscegenation to defend the converso caste can be seen as exemplifying the discursive strategy of "cultural hybridity," unsettling the nation's representation of itself as possessing a homogeneous and integral identity. Before turning to postcolonial theory, however, it is appropriate to begin with Américo Castro's classic work, *España en su Historia* (translated as *The Structure of Spanish History*),[2] in which not only Cartagena, but the entire converso caste, play a central role in the construction of Spanish national identity.

When Américo Castro in the opening of his work wants to mark the first time that Spain comes to consciousness of itself as a nation with a distinct character, he chooses the speech which, in 1434, Alonso de Cartagena made to the Council of Basle asserting the precedence of Castile with respect to England. After describing Cartagena's "first and most faithful picture of the Hispanic soul," Castro goes on to state, "I do not believe that at the beginning of the fifteenth century any other European people had revealed such a complete and precise awareness of itself."[3] R. B. Tate, although he might disagree with Castro on this last point, has also stressed the decisive role of Cartagena in constructing the idea of the Spanish nation (*natio*):[4]

Seidenspinner-Nuñez, "'El solo de me leyó': Gendered Hermeneutics and Subversive Poetics in *Admiraçion operum Dey* of Teresa de Cartagena," *Medievalia* 15 (1981): 14–23. Teresa de Cartagena's writings, together with a short discussion of her family, are available in *The Writings of Teresa de Cartagena*, trans. Dayle Seidenspinner-Nuñez (Boydell & Brewer, 1998).

[2] A. Castro, *The Structure of Spanish History*, trans. E. King (Princeton: Princeton University Press, 1954).

[3] Ibid., 14.

[4] Tate, "The *Anacephaleosis* of Alfonso García de Santa María," 387–401, points out that the seating at the Council of Basle was by nation, not by dioceses or provinces. In Cartagena's successful defense of the precedence of the Castilian delegation over the English, "it is clear," Tate writes, that "the Castilians conceived of their representation in somewhat the same terms as the English" for whom the nation (*natio*) was a "microcosm of Church and State, a unit of imperium mirroring the sovereignty of its master" (391 n7).

The meteoric rise of Castile from a Peninsular kingdom, racked by civil discord for centuries, to a European and colonial power has always had a fascination for the historian. The credit for arousing this interest must naturally go to the historians of the *Siglo de Oro*. Yet they did not create *ex nihilo* their concept of the destiny and obligations of the "Spanish" nation that were to become current throughout 16th- and 17th-century Europe.... The *Anacephaleosis*, or epitome, by Alfonso García de Santa María, Bishop of Burgos is ... in fact one of the first explicit testimonies of Castile's awareness of her own past and the individual role she claimed for herself during the Late Middle Ages.[5]

Both Castro and Tate stress the fact that the idea of nationality in Spain was, in Tate's words, "the product of a slow elaboration."[6] Castro especially wants to explode the notion that Spain possesses a racially or ethnically defined character, and he insists that, whatever national identity Spain may have, it is the product of the cultural *imaginary*, as we might say today, and it "always already" calls itself into question. In the last analysis, according to Castro, Spain's "identity" has less to do with any fixed essence than with the effort to imagine an essence which could embrace (or perhaps homogenize) its geographic and cultural diversity and weather all historical vicissitudes. Every such imagined "Hispanic" essence was fraught with internal contradictions, and seemed always to be refuted even as it was offered up as the definitive summation of the nation's identity. In effect, Spain seems to be constantly creating itself anew. After having quoted from both Ortega y Gasset and a Fascist Phalanx propaganda pamphlet to the effect that throughout her history "Spain has not been herself," Castro writes:

> But what can the reality be of a present that is always felt as having its temporal foundations undermined, as being invertebrate? It can be nothing other than a recreating of itself as if the world were beginning anew in every instant, in a continuous process of creating-wasting.... The sustained consciousness of existence as a nonexistence, of putting to a test time and again the possibility of the

---

[5] Ibid., 387–88.
[6] Ibid., 387.

impossibility, is without parallel in either the Occident or the Orient.[7]

Castro's interpretation of the continuously self-deconstructing Spanish national identity (which he writes of as "vivir desviviéndose," "living by unliving") seems in many ways to resonate with recent postcolonial critiques of the idea of nationhood. Homi Bhabha, for example, has attempted to show that no nation has a seamless and integral identity, despite its best efforts at representing itself as temporally and spatially "plenitudinous."[8] Bhabha's critique of national self-representation lays great stress upon the "slippage" between the image of the nation's organic and unbroken connection to its past and the equally significant image of the nation as coming into being through a decision of the collective will, through a deliberate act of self-creation. The nation, more simply, represents itself as both old and new, ancient and youthful. For Bhabha, the writing of the immigrant and the colonial subject takes advantage of this temporal contradiction in the construction of the nation, generating confusion by playfully revealing the immigrant or colonial subject to be both "too new" (a latecomer to the nation) and "too old" (backward and tradition-bound). Unable (and unwilling) to be simply contemporaneous with the nation, the "foreign" other unsettles the nation's sense of its own present as a shared contemporaneity among a people who are "equally" old and new.

Bhabha's theorization of the temporal fault-lines, so to speak, in the construction of national identity can perhaps help to bring into focus Castro's formulation of "vivir desviviéndose" as the defining feature of Hispanic national construction. We might say that there are two moments in the construction of the idea of Spanish nationhood, namely, the discovery of a continuous tradition reaching into the past and the collective (re)dedication to a mission whose fulfillment lies in the future.[9]

In the fifteenth century, Alonso de Cartegena and others after him

---

[7] Castro, *The Structure of Spanish History*, 59.

[8] See, for example, Homi Bhabha, *The Location of Culture* (London: Routledge, 1994), especially chapter 8, "DissemiNation: Time, Narrative, and the Margins of the Modern Nation."

[9] While we may agree with Bhabha that this Janus-faced temporality is not unique to any nation, we may also agree with Castro that the fact that "a corner of the Peninsula, to subsist, had to destroy Islamized Spain, in which even the rivers had changed their thousandyear- old names" makes the temporal chasm between past and future all the greater, and the need to bridge it all the more pressing (*Structure of Spanish History*, 54).

hoped to discover Spain's identity in its people's unique mission to advance the Church Militant.[10] Cartagena returns to a thirteenth-century historiographic trope, namely, the divinely destined conquest of *Hispania* by the Goths who, he says, were as wellmatched to the Peninsula which they invaded as were the Israelites to Canaan. In Cartagena's "neo-Gothic" thesis, the Goths provide the ethnic base not only for the unbroken succession of kings whose titles are *Rex Gothorum*, *Rex Hispaniae*, and *Rex Castillae*, but also for the military valor which is a basic trait of the Spaniard. Tate summarizes Cartagena's use of Gothic history in the *Anacephaleosis* this way:

> The resumé of Gothic history before the colonization of Spain is framed in highly eulogistic terms. The foundation of their reigning house antedates the times of Hercules and their subsequent conquests are conceived as extending over the greater part of Asia and Africa. But their major achievement was the capture of Rome. This devastation of Italy, coupled with a dissociation of Spain from the Empire are topics which become an integral part of Castilian history. They prove the superiority of the Goths who, after this display of military skill, are able to settle down and practice the arts in just as civilized fashion as the Romans.[11]

For Cartagena, the Goths are the divinely chosen ethnic stock whose talents for military conquest and the arts of civilization make them fitted to cultivate and be nurtured by the soil of the Peninsula. The Goths, then, are imagined as the people who give the history of Spain its continuity throughout the past. In his classic study of the origins of the notion of "Spain" in the medieval period, Jose Maravall has demonstrated that the

---

[10] For a discussion of the general tenor of political philosophy in Castile in the fifteenth century, see John Edwards, "*Conversos*, Judaism and the Language of Monarchy in Fifteenth-Century Castile," *Religion and Society in Spain, circa 1492*, ed. John Edwards (Aldershot: Variorum, 1996), 17:207–23. Edwards does not see anything specifically "converso" or Judaic about the political thought of Cartagena and others, most of them conversos, in the fifteenth century. However, he does not consider the evidence of Cartagena's *Defensorium unitatis christianae* which, as I will argue below, gives us a different picture of the nation than the one foregrounded in Cartagena's other works.

[11] Tate, "The *Anacephaleosis* of Alfonso García de Santa María," 397–98. The *Anacephaleosis* is published in *Hispaniae Ilustrata*, ed. Andreas Schottus (Frankfurt, 1603–8), vol. 1. A new edition of the *Anacephaleosis*, with commentary and translation into Spanish, appears in *La Anacephaleosis de Alonso de Cartagena: Edición, traducción, estudio*, 3 vols. (Madrid: Universidad Complutense de Madrid, 1989).

"gothic thesis," whether in its thirteenth-century or in its later instantiations, was always a "creación historico-literaria."[12] Cartagena reactivates what Maravall calls a "myth" in order to justify the right of Castile to rule over the Iberian peninsula, the Canary Islands, and a portion of North Africa, demonstrating the point forcefully made by Homi Bhabha and other postcolonial critics, that the idea of the nation is always imbricated with a colonialist project. The "right" of "Castile" to become "Spain" is grounded in the unbroken continuity of its rulers with those of the Gothic kings who defeated Roman rule in the peninsula (and North Africa).

In one respect, however, Cartagena finds fault with the Gothic rulers from whom the Castilian royal line is allegedly descended. As we might expect given his own Jewish background, Cartagena is quite critical of Sisebut's forced conversion of the Jews in 613, and, although he otherwise relies on the thirteenth-century history of Jiménes de Rada, he omits that historian's description of Sisebut as "a wise man much dedicated to literature."[13] Cartagena has a very different idea about the way that the Jews will join the Gothic ethnic stock as the Spanish nation fulfills its divine destiny, and we will examine this below. I note here, however, that Gothic ethnic supremacy is in no way absolute or unqualified; Cartagena sees it as one element in a mixture, let us say hybridization, with the Jewish people. We will see that only this hybridization will ultimately "convert" the military valor of the Goths to a wholehearted dedication to their divine mandate, namely, the advance of the Church Militant throughout the world. According to Cartagena in his impassioned defense of the conversos (and the Jews) entitled *Defensorium unitatis christianae*,[14] the outbreak of what he calls the heresy of "paganism" in the mid-fifteenth-century anti-converso "purity of blood" statute in Toledo is, in fact, the greatest threat Spain faces to its mission.

It is no doubt remarkable that the construction of Spain's identity as a nation, with such emphasis placed upon the ethnic patrimony provided by the Goths, should be the work of a converso without any "Gothic blood" in his veins. It certainly does not escape Castro's notice that the first exponent of Spain's identity was a converso; indeed, for Castro, this fact is central to his general thesis in *The Structure of Spanish History*. The

---

[12] Jose Antonio Maravall, *El concepto de España en la edad media*, 2nd ed. (Madrid: Instituto de Estudios Políticos, 1964), 303.

[13] Tate, "The *Anacephaleosis* of Alfonso García de Santa María," 389.

[14] P. Manuel Alonso, S.I., ed., *D. Alonso de Cartagena: Defensorium unitatis christianae*, (Madrid: Consejo Superior de Investigaciones Científicas, 1943).

converso is someone who has refashioned his or her "given" identity and, from 1449 onwards (the first appearance of "purity of blood" legislation), lives in a society in which the "new" identity is called into question and problematized. When Castro describes Spaniards as "a people whose initial and constant problem is its insecurity and anguish concerning its own existence, its uncertainty, its living in a state of alarm caused by its doubt,"[15] he declares the paradigmatic nature of converso identity for all of Spain, and legitimizes his claim that conversos have been central to Spain's cultural self-definition.

The "Castro thesis" can be restated in terms of Bhabha's analysis of the disjunctive temporality of the nation. We may say that the converso writers as Castro understands them unsettle the image of a seamless national continuity from past to present because they place greater significance on the re-creation of the nation as "new" than on its perseverance on a course laid out for it in the past. The past is viewed not as the vital repository of the nation's strength, but as a process of degeneration and loss which needs to be reinvigorated through a rededication to the nation's mission. Whatever is vital in the past must be rescued rather than merely inherited.

This raises a problem about how and to what extent the projected future can be said to be a "natural" outgrowth of the past. The problematization of the organic connection between past, present, and future leads to that "uncertainty of existence" which Castro identifies as ongoing throughout Spanish history. Cartagena attempts to solve this problem in his *Defensorium unitatis christianae* by positing that the relationship between the past (the "old" nation which must be renewed) and the future (the "new" nation assuming the mantle of its divine mission) is mediated by the present as a time of conception, a time where two "parents" will disappear and be reborn as a new offspring. Cartagena identifies the national "father" as the Gothic race, the blood of whose kings and nobles continues to flow in the veins of Castile's kings and nobles, while the national "mother" is the Jewish people whose divine mission and priestly nobility can be revived if its aged body is provided a new form in a youthful child of "mixed" blood. Cartagena suggests that in their offspring, the features of both parents will remain discernible, though we will see that he hints that the Jewish physiognomy will be the more pronounced.

Cartagena's selection of miscegenation as the mediating bond between a Gothic past and a Spanish future is a strategy for envisioning national

---

[15] Castro, *The Structure of Spanish History*, 25.

identity which, according to Homi Bhabha and other postcolonial critics, is characteristic of the "marginal" writer who reconfigures the signs through which the nation is constituted (in the case of Spain, "Goth," "gentile," "Jew," "Muslim," "noble," "vulgar," "pure," "impure," "faithful," "infidel," "male" and "female," among others) and produces a "hybrid" representation of national identity which at once "renews" the nation and unsettles it. Although Cartagena is very serious about his project of renewing the Spanish nation through the mixing of two peoples, we will find that he also parodies his opponents' alternative project of renewing the nation by legislating against mixture.

In what follows I will examine in greater detail the intimate connection between Cartagena's construction in the *Defensorium unitatis christianae* of *Hispania* as a nation uniquely chosen to lead the Church Militant, a view which is prominent in his other historiographic works as well, and his understanding of the role of the Jew in the fulfillment of this mission, as the necessary "stock" with which Spanish-Gothic "gentility" can be productively hybridized. Although Cartagena's historiography of Spain is appropriated by later writers, his understanding of the role of the Jew will be roundly rejected in the later fifteenth century when "purity of blood" statutes begin to become the law of the land. Cartagena had discerned the "shape" which the Spanish nation was taking, and he hoped to provide a model for ethnic unity based upon the productive hybridization of peoples. His hopes were tragically unfulfilled as the nation stigmatized hybridity as impurity. By studying Cartagena's dream of productive hybridity we will be able not only to see with increased sharpness the tension between the idea of the nation and the idea of hybridity, but also to appreciate how the converso was, from the fifteenth century onward, the one who emblematized this tension at the very heart of the Spanish nation.

The Jew as Essential for Salvation in the *Defensorium unitatis christianae*

In order to appreciate the innovative nature of Cartagena's views on the Jews, we need to see it against the background of the normative Catholic doctrine, expressed for example by Augustine, that the Jewish people are no longer part of "salvation history," but are merely caught in a sort of temporal "limbo" until they will be erased from history at the Last Judgment.¹⁶ This view sees the Jews as "outside" both the Church and its "militant" mission to bring salvation to humanity. The Jews, on this view, rejected salvation and, as a people, are judged to be "cadavers" without vital connection to God. While a single Jew may always find salvation in Christ (something the racialists deny, taking the Augustinian view to its extreme), the Jews as a people cannot.

Cartagena argues that the Jewish people do remain part of redemption history, and we may see this first of all in his explanation of why they have not yet converted to Christianity. The explanation of the Jewish people's rejection of the Gospel comes first in an extended analogy which Cartagena offers for the spread of God's revelation. He compares revelation to the rising sun. The sun's noonday splendor is compared to the inception of the apostolic mission when the Holy Spirit descended, in the likeness of fiery tongues, upon the apostles' heads in Jerusalem on the first post-crucifixion Pentecost. Cartagena describes how the sun's rays extend to the farthest, coldest extremes of earth in circles radiating out from the center, which, in the analogy, corresponds to Jerusalem. Cartagena likens these widening circles of illumination and heat to the widening range of the Church Militant's preaching over the course of time. Using a verse from Isaiah as his proof text ("Lift up your eyes round about, and see; they all gather together, they come to you; your sons shall come from far, and your daughters shall be carried in the arms," Isaiah 60:4),¹⁷ Cartagena describes the final triumphant moment when all peoples shall be joined together as one people, as the homecoming of the most distant "sons" to the center point where the sun shines brightest, to the spiritual Jerusalem which is the Church. Cartagena states that the appellation "sons" is appropriate for the gentile nations, since the "masculine sex" characterizes best those who excel others by the "strength of their arms and extent of their lands" (1.9, 87).¹⁸ The daughters, however, "designate the Jewish people" who, like daughters in their paternal home, "have remained within the fixed limits of the promised land" (1.9, 87–88). Cartagena is using a

---

[16] Augustine explains in *Civitas Dei* 18:46 that the Jews are allowed by God to continue their existence as a people in order to serve as (hostile, and therefore credible) witnesses to the authenticity of the "Old Testament" prophecies which the Church interprets as referring to Jesus.

[17] Unless otherwise specified, translations from the King James Version.

[18] Translations throughout are my own. References are to part, theorem, and chapter divisions of the *Defensorium*, followed by page(s) in the P. Manuel Alonso edition; a Spanish translation appears in *Alonso de Cartagena y el Defensorium unitatis christianae*, ed. Guillermo Verdin-Diaz (Oviedo: Universidad de Oviedo, 1992).

phrase he used earlier in chapter 5, which begins:

> From these divisions [between Jews and gentiles], therefore, has arisen the difference among peoples which has lasted for so long. One group, few and peculiar, *remain within the fixed land of promise under the written law.* The other, great in number and grand in power, spread through all the regions of the globe, have lived *dispersed, without the law of god* contained in scripture.   1.5, 75

Given his apparently unqualified identification of the daughters with all the Jewish people, Cartagena intends the "fixed limits of the promised land" to refer metaphorically to the laws which fix the limits of the people's life in diaspora. And, remarkably, Cartagena understands these laws to hold the people within a single territory, even if it is only metaphorical, whereas the nations are "dispersed" which lack these laws, as all do until they have been brought within the Church. By thus reassigning the adjective "dispersed" to the gentile nations, Cartagena places the Jewish people at the center, in the paternal home, and the gentile peoples at the periphery. In his use of the Isaianic proof text, Cartagena gives pride of place to the Jewish people over the gentile peoples.

I would characterize this displacement of a trope associated with the Jews ("dispersed") to the gentile nations as a strategy of what Bhabha calls "hybrid writing" which "contests genealogies of 'origin' that lead to claims to cultural supremacy and historical superiority."[19] What Cartagena calls into question with his reassignment of "dispersed" as a predicate of the gentile peoples is any genealogy of origin for the gentile peoples. It is not where they have come from that is significant, but where they are heading. We may recall Cartagena's use of the Goths to anchor Castilian history in his *Anacephaleosis*. To choose the Goths over, say, the earlier Hispano-Romans is to privilege the mobile, conquering people over the sedentary natives, and this certainly serves Cartagena's purpose of justifying Castilian imperialism, such as it was in the mid-fifteenth century. However, the mobility of the Goths also indicates that they need to be "brought home," and this is done through their "marriage" to the Jewish people. The Jewish people have always been "at home" in the "fixed limits of the promised land," that is, within the limits defined by God's choice of them to bear a divine mission. As carnal Israel, however, they have been severed from their fulfilled future and reside only in the past of the "promise." Mixed

---

[19] Homi Bhabha, *The Location of Culture*, 157.

with the mobile people who always push away from their physical home to new territories, they will be carried over to their promised home, a "spiritual" Jerusalem. When the centrifugal impulse of the gentile peoples (outward to the ends of the globe) is finally married to the centripetal impulse of the Jewish people (return to Jerusalem), salvation history will have reached its telos.

In the image of familial reconciliation, the gentile "sons" enter the home of the father, the spiritual Jerusalem, by being joined to the father's daughters, with whom they will create a new people, "one true Jerusalem" ("ex utroque populo una vera Iherusalem," 1.9, 88). The Jewish people do not need to leave behind their identities in order to enter into the "true Jerusalem." It is almost as if the transformation will take place of itself, when the gentile peoples have all converted: "For Jerusalem has not converted to the gentiles, but gentile people are converting to Jerusalem.... Nor does Israel receive the gods of the gentiles, but the gentiles have received the God of Israel" (1.9, 88). The Jewish people, in other words, have no distance to traverse to achieve redemption; they only have to receive a fuller illumination from the meridian sun of divine love. Again, Cartagena is deploying a literary strategy best compared to that of the marginal discourses of hybridity: taking the term used for the minority ("converted," *conversus*) and reassigning it to the majority, thereby calling into question the integral self-image of the dominant group.

The subordination of gentiles to Jews at the consummation of history is the central thrust of Isaiah 60, the source of Cartagena's proof text. It seems likely that Isaiah 60 stands behind the entire extended analogy which Cartagena develops in this section of his work. The conclusion of Isaiah 60 invokes the image of divine illumination over Jerusalem, replacing the illumination of sun and moon: "The sun shall be no more thy light by day; neither for brightness shall the moon give light unto thee: but the Lord shall be unto thee an everlasting light, and thy God thy glory" (Isaiah 60:19). In terms of Cartagena's analogy, this prophecy refers to the time when all gentile nations shall be encompassed within the light of Christ, and the Jews will once more be the faithful "daughters" of God. No doubt, this means that the Jews will accept Christ, but it is important to point out that the Jews' conversion does not signify a loss of Israel's precedence over the gentiles. The gentiles (the "sons" in Isaiah 60:9), it should be remembered, will carry the Jews (the "daughters") back to Jerusalem in their arms.

But what is delaying the final redemption of the Jews as projected in Isaiah 60? Cartagena makes no mention of the clichéd "Jewish blindness" in order to explain why carnal Israel has not "seen the light" of the Christian faith. Rather, the implication is that the delay in full Jewish "enlightenment" is due to the continuing need for *two* streams to join in the building of the "true Jerusalem." Later in his *Defensorium* (2.3.6), Cartagena speaks of the gentiles and the Jews as two rivers that flow together into the single sea of the Church. He sees the end of the influx of water from the rivers to be a complete "drying up" of all faithlessness, both Jewish and gentile. At that time the Church will constitute a single, undivided people, in the image of a new Adam whose head is Christ. Significantly, the drying up of the two kinds of faithlessness is described as happening simultaneously. Humanity's unification requires both sons and daughters to come together, and, therefore, so long as there are unconverted sons, God's daughters can only partially be absorbed within the church. In other words, the Jewish people are playing a necessary role in the conversion of all the gentiles.

The proof text from the New Testament which Cartagena uses to justify his assertion that the Jewish people remain a part of redemptive history is Paul's Epistle to the Romans, in which Paul goes farther than he does in any other text to caution non-Jewish Christians against condemning the Jews for their rejection of Jesus as the messiah:

> Once you did not have faith in God, but now you have received mercy because of their lack of faith. Just as they now have not believed [in Jesus] for the sake of your mercy, so will they also receive mercy. God brings everyone into faithlessness so that he can bring everyone within his mercy.[20]   Romans 11:30–32

Paul makes the Jews' faithlessness an essential step in God's extension of mercy to the non-Jews. Furthermore he states that the faithlessness will be lifted, and in a verse just before the one just quoted he says, "Blindness has touched a part of Israel until the fullness of the gentiles enters [the faith], and so all Israel shall be saved." Cartagena quotes this passage twice, and he goes so far as to say that the numerous conversions of Jews in his own day are a sign that the final judgment is approaching when redemption will be fulfilled: "The more frequently and abundantly Jews convert, the more plausible it is that we are approaching the day of universal judgment" (2.2.3, 127). For Cartagena, the Jewish people, far

---

[20] For Paul's Epistle to the Romans, I have used the Revised Standard Version of the Bible.

from being enemies of Christ and locked out of salvation history, stand at its center and provide its driving force. The real enemies of Christianity, says Cartagena, are those who would claim a racial prerogative for the gentiles in redemption history. He calls such people "paganizers:"

> Those who, like the Philistines before, are now leaping to attack the Israelites who have become faithful Catholics, profess themselves in their actions to have remained up to the present pagans and ... to be battling the army of the faithful with their paganizing.
> 3.Prol., 270

Here is one of Cartagena's boldest moves. He takes the claim of the anti-converso party to be "pure blood" and stigmatizes this as the heresy of "paganizing"; he also denigrates the blood itself as tainted by "pagan," that is, low-born, blood. It could not have escaped his reader's notice that this word carried a connotation of non-noble origin. Indeed, Cartagena in this very passage explicitly drives home the point by saying, "I will not use the term 'gentilizing' because the word has acquired in common usage a certain appearance [*speciem*] of nobility." Renaming his opponents "pagans" rather than "gentiles," and even calling into question the genetic link between "gentility" and "nobility," Cartagena reveals the disjunction between the linguistic sign and its "common" referent, thus opening up a space for reinscribing or, better put, ingrafting a new people into the new nation he imagines. It should certainly come as no surprise when Cartagena says that the "nobility" of the Jewish people, marred by their "infidelity" over the centuries, can and will recover its prior glory:

> Such is the victory by which our faith conquers the world that those who have been conquered will themselves be conquerors too, and it is not unfitting that when they rise up again through the vigor of the faith, although they had been dead before, the cadavers, as it were, of their nobility which had been lying beside them will also rise with them.
> 2.4.9, 213

The renewal of the Jewish people will renew their nobility; in particular, their priestly nobility will be renewed, says Cartagena. Of course, his father and he are already proof of this, since they stem from the Levitical tribe and have, as Christians, returned to their ancestral role as priests.

The Hybrid Engendering of Jesus and the Gender of Israel

The Third Theorem of Part Two reads: "Both Israelites and gentiles, by entering into the Catholic faith through the gateway of holy baptism, do not remain two peoples or diverse nations [gentes], but, from two separately arriving groups, one new people is created" (131). Cartagena describes the conflict between the new paganism and the Church as one between the brutal power of the gentile nations and the meekness of Christ. Cartagena sees the new paganism as a recrudescence of the same gentile savagery which initially confronted the Church in its earliest missions. In the early history of the Church this gentile savagery was defeated by the physical meekness and passivity of the martyrs whose only defense was the word of God. Cartagena describes pagan brutality as arising from a valorization among non-Jews, both in antiquity and in his own day, of masculine physical prowess. He declares that Christ's ancestry, reaching back to Abraham, includes no male who was uncircumcised, a fact which signals God's own scorn for pagan virility in favor of a new virility which is self-abnegating (symbolized by the covenant of circumcision) and sublimated into a spiritual prowess in the realm of the word.

Cartagena points out, however, that among the female ancestors of Jesus's were two non-Israelites: Rahab and Ruth. Rahab, the prostitute who saves the lives of spies sent by Joshua to reconnoiter Jericho, was the grandmother of Boaz; Ruth, wed to Boaz after she leaves Moab with Naomi, is the great-grandmother of David. Gentile "blood" has thus already mingled with Israelite "blood" in Jesus's engendering. Cartagena sees the engendering of Jesus as a typological prefiguration of the conjunction of gentiles and Jews into one new people possessing a new spiritualized virility. Since Cartagena sees the oneness of humanity to be the culmination of redemption, it is Jesus' engendering rather than his death or his resurrection which, for Cartagena, holds the key to salvation history.

Christ for Cartagena represents the unity of gentile and Jewish peoples within the single body of the Church in virtue of his lineage. The fact that Jesus's genealogical relationship to the gentiles is mediated through women is "not lacking sacred mystery," Cartagena declares (2.3.2, 134). He offers as his first suggestion for why gentile women but not gentile men are found in Jesus's lineage the idea that only in this way can the covenant of circumcision remain unbroken from Abraham to Jesus. The unbroken line of circumcised males back to Abraham demonstrates that

Jesus came to "bring the law to its most complete fulfillment rather than to annul it."

Cartagena offers further reasons why women are the mediators of gentility; these relate to the difference between Jewish and gentile masculinity. Following Aristotelian embryology, Cartagena claims that the male seed is the active element in reproduction, while the female is passive material. In the context of spiritual reproduction, the male seed, which "proceeds from Israel as the active power of prophecy," is the "word of God, which the apostles and disciples of the Lord, and the many martyrs who arose from Israel dispersed by their diligent sowing" (2.3.2, 135). The passive material in which the seed bears fruit are the gentile nations. Dispersed throughout the gentile nations, the "seed-word" propagates sons. Cartagena uses Isaiah 60:10 as his proof text for this propagation: "And the sons of strangers shall build up your walls." But these new sons, offspring of gentile maternal passivity and Israelite spiritual paternity, will embody the spiritualized masculinity of Israel. In place of gentile "rage" (*rabies*) and "wildness" (*feritas*) which seeks to destroy the "walls" of the Church and which trusts in the strength of military armament, the new sons will defend the Church with "the indefatigable virtue of the sacred scripture." This new masculinity will reject the gentile valorization of physical and military prowess in favor of a feminine physical passivity coupled with the active, spiritually virile force of the word.

In an extended discussion of the Isaianic prophecy that "the wolf shall dwell with the lamb and the leopard lie down with the kid" (Isaiah 11:6), Cartagena finds further prophetic support for his claim that Israel's gentleness ("israelitica mansuetudo"), represented by the lamb and the kid, will triumph over gentile bellicosity, represented by the lion and the leopard. Cartagena contrasts the ferocity of an Alexander, Hannibal, or Caesar with the gentleness of Israel's David who "rules the wildness of his Caesar-like pride with the tempering of reason" (2.3.4, 141).

The critique of gentile masculinity must be seen in the context of what Cartagena elsewhere discusses, namely, the widespread belief that Jews are cowards and lack martial skill: "So great and notorious is the timidity of the faithless [infideles] Israelites, that whenever we want to describe excessive timidity we call it 'jewishness' [iudeitas], and we call an excessively frightened man, a 'Jew'" (2.4.20, 215).[21] In the passage which immediately

---

[21] The prevalence of the stereotype of the cowardly and effeminate Jew is amply documented by Louise Mirrer who, in her reading of *Cantar de mio Cid*, writes: "In

follows upon this, Cartagena rejects the negative cultural image of the Jew as coward, and he goes on to claim that the converted Jew can overcome the long habit of military ineptitude and its consequence, timidity. But in the earlier passages which we have just been considering, Cartagena adopts a different and more challenging line of defense. He turns the cultural stereotype of the Jew as effeminate and timid against itself, viewing timidity as rather "gentleness," and declaring that gentile masculinity has no share in the constitution of Jesus's humanity. When Cartagena declares that the blood of gentile males was not present in Jesus, he is surely striking at the racial pride in "blood purity" on the part of the anti-converso party in Spain. And when he says that Christ rejects the virility of the pagans in favor of the meekness revealed by Israel's heroes and the early Christian martyrs, Christ's "sons from among the strangers," he is also attacking the cultural stereotypes which identify the Jew as a coward, and the "pure blood" Christian as a valiant warrior.

Once more we find Cartagena engaged in the disruptive strategy of hybrid writing. The vaunted strength of the gentile male is turned into a despised and discarded violence, having nothing to do with Jesus's masculinity. Previously we have seen how Cartagena unsettles the assumption that "gentility" means "nobility"; now he questions whether either of those terms has anything to do with "virility" as properly understood. Cartagena is redeploying the terms through which the nation views itself in order to reassemble them in the image of a nation where "hybrid blood" rather than "pure blood" is valorized as true nobility and true virility.

---

this context of exalted male aggression and extroversion, the 'otherness' of Jewish men could not have been plainer. Over and over again the text makes the point that the Jews' locus of activity is the home, while that of Christian Castilian men is the battlefield"; see *Women, Jews, and Muslims in the Texts of Reconquest Castile* (Ann Arbor: University of Michigan Press, 1996), 78. Is it possible that Cartagena's likening of the Jewish people to daughters within the home of their Father is a revaluation of the image of the "homebound" Jewish male? A parallel revaluation occurs in earlier rabbinic culture in which Torah study was viewed as a retreat into a secluded, "feminine" space and away from the public, "out-of-doors" military pursuits of the Roman male; however, the "feminine" space of Torah study is given precedence over the "masculine" space of the battleground. See Daniel Boyarin, *Unheroic Conduct: The Rise of Heterosexuality and the Invention of the Jewish Male* (Berkeley: University of California Press, 1997), chapter 3. For an examination of the effect of this stereotype of the Jew as effeminate on a sixteenth-century Sabbatean and former crypto-Jew, see Bruce Rosenstock, "Messianism, Machismo, and 'Marranism': The Case of Abraham Miguel Cardoso," *Queer Theory and the Jewish Question*, ed. Daniel Boyarin and Daniel Itzkovitz (New York: Columbia University Press, 2003).

We have seen previously how Cartagena compares Israel to daughters waiting for "foreign" sons to join them in marriage within their father's home, the New Jerusalem. Although this may seem to contradict the idea of a female-mediated gentility in the lineage of Jesus (foreign women, not men, join Israel), in fact there is perfect consistency here. Just as a gentile male when he would marry a Jewish woman according to the "law of Moses," must convert and be circumcised, so when gentile males enter the New Jerusalem and join with "faithful Israelites" as one people, they must convert to the God of Israel, as we have seen Cartagena expressly state, and be "circumcised" (symbolically, of course) of their gentile virility. The Jewish male who enters the New Jerusalem does not "leave his father's home" to do so, but only needs to acknowledge the spiritual nature of his physical circumcision, and this acknowledgment is the fullest expression of circumcision, not its annulment. The transition from "faithless" to "faithful" Israelite is paralleled by the Christian's transition from unmarried daughter to wife.

In rewriting the meaning of "conversion" and reinscribing it within a scenario of return to the paternal home (spiritual Jerusalem), Cartagena unsettles the cultural binarisms which, in his view, threaten to destroy the Church and, with it, the nation which is carrying forward its mission. All the terms seem to cross—the Jew is not the convert, but the gentile is; the Jew is the female, but the gentile must be feminized in order to marry her; the Jew is at home, and the gentile is "dispersed"; whereas "gentility" and "nobility" are not co-extensive, the nobility of the Jewish people will return again. Cartagena has unsettled these cultural binarisms in order to re-imagine a national community in which hybridity is sacralized and "blood purity" is viewed as the return of the pagan past.

Conclusion

Postcolonial studies dealing with "nation and narration" have claimed that the "normative" construction of national identity projects an image of seamless historic continuity leading to an ever-new and youthful present which embraces the people in a plenitudinous contemporaneity. In this normative construction of national identity, all the traces of the nation's hybrid origins are obliterated, and all contravening discourses of hybridity are repressed. Cartagena seems to straddle the normative and the hybrid ideas of the nation and, if we accept Castro's reading of Spanish national self-construction, Cartagena is the first in a long line of writers marked by such ambivalence. As an exponent of the right of Castile to rule the

Peninsula, Cartagena reactivates the "neo-Gothic thesis" which becomes definitive for later Spanish historiography. As a converso, however, Cartagena is committed to a principle which runs counter to the ethnic singularity of the nation, namely, the hybridization of Jew and non-Jew in fulfillment of each people's divine mission. As an exponent of the latter principle, Cartagena exemplifies the very discourse of hybridity which the nation typically seeks to suppress. Thus, Cartagena allows us to see the dynamic tension between the discourses of nation and of hybridity, typically represented in postcolonial criticism as characteristic of the conflict between the modern imperial nation and its colonial subjects. It seems that the "postcolonial" and "postmodern" may be prefigured in fifteenth-century Castile; perhaps this would have come as no surprise to Américo Castro.

One last observation is in order. In his path-breaking study of the origins of the nation, Benedict Anderson points to the beginning of ethnically defined nationality among the "creoles" (Spaniards marked as different by the accident of their birth in the colonies) of the newly independent countries of the former Spanish empire. But in the fifteenth and sixteenth centuries there arose an internal "creole" class within the Peninsula, namely, the conversos: Spaniards and Portuguese marked as different by the accident of their descent from one or more Jewish ancestors. When at the close of the sixteenth century members of this creole caste settled in Amsterdam, they described themselves as "the Nation" and constructed an image of a diasporic community with a shared culture, language, and hybrid ancestry (though not a shared religion, since some of its members continued to live as Catholics) which distinguished them not only from other *peninsulares*, but also from other Jews. These creoles often prided themselves on their "noble" hybrid ancestry. Many of them displayed a messianic fervor in their religiosity, manifesting itself in their particular attraction for Sabbateanism.[22] It may well be that this creole diaspora "nation" comes closer than any other to embodying Cartagena's dream of a hybrid people with a unifying divine mission.

University of California at Davis

---

[22] For a detailed discussion of the Amsterdam community of former conversos and their communal self-definition, see Miriam Bodian, *Hebrews of the Portuguese Nation: Conversos and Community in Early Modern Amsterdam* (Bloomigton: Indiana University Press, 1997).

Cultural Hybridity, Cultural Subversion
Text and Image in the Alba Bible, 1422–33

SONIA FELLOUS

The *Alba Bible* is an illuminated manuscript containing a translation of the Hebrew Bible from both Hebrew and Latin into Castilian. It is accompanied by abundant marginal glosses and by 324 miniatures illustrating the text. A long prologue precedes, which relates the history of the production of the manuscript, including correspondence between the principals. Commissioned by a Catholic and executed by a Jewish scholar supervising the painters, the manuscript testifies to cultural interpenetration in the Iberian peninsula. Though Jewish-Islamic reciprocity is well known in architecture, textile design and literature, Jewish-Christian hybridity is less well documented. The Alba Bible is an effort of communication between cultivated Jews and Catholics during a rare moment of détente in the tormented fifteenth century. It also witnesses to the penetration of Jewish sources into Christian religious literature and artistic creation, for despite supervision by Catholic scholars, the Jewish translator ensured that his version of the Hebrew Bible remained, as far as possible, a profoundly Jewish work.

§ § §

The manuscript was commissioned on April 22, 1422, by Don Luys de Guzman, Grand Master of the Order of Calatrava, in an order to his "vassal" ("nuestro bassallo," fol. 2r), Rabbi Moses Arragel (some time between 1385 and September 21, 1456)[1], who was to translate, provide

---

This article combines and condenses two others by the author, previously published in French; translation and redaction by Sheila Delany. They are "Prologue et dialogue dans *La Bible d'Albe*," in *Entrer en matière: Les prologues*, ed. Jean-Daniel Dubois and Bernard Roussel (Paris: Cerf, 1997); and "*La Biblia de Alba*: L'iconographie ambigüe," in *Creencias y culturas* (Salamanca and Tel Aviv: Universidad Pontifica de Salamanca/University of Tel-Aviv, 1998). I thank the editors for permission to translate and use the material, and the Casa de Alba for allowing me to see the Bible. Photos by Sonia Fellous, taken and reproduced with the kind permission of the Casa de Alba. For a facsimile, see *The Hebrew Bible of the Jews*..., ed. J. Schonfield (Madrid: Fundación Amigos de Sefarad, 1992). Much of the material is taken from the author's dissertation, *La Bible de Moïse Arragel* (Paris: EPHE, 1993).

[1] We know little about Arragel. He came from Guadalajara, whence he moved to

Fig. 1. Moses Arragel, his back turned to the reader, between Frey Arias deEnçinas, Father Superior of the Monastery of St. Francis of Toledo to the right, and Frey Johan de Zamora, the Dominican supervisor, on the left. Their forefingers are raised in instruction while the rabbi points towards them, discussing the work he is to write, in front of a book open on the desk. Alba Bible, fol. 1vb.

glosses from rabbinical commentary, and oversee illustrations ("una bibliaen rromance, glosada e ystoriada," fol. 2ra). The rabbi was to be supervised by a cousin of the Grand Master, Don Vasco de Guzman, archdeacon of Toledo, and by representatives of the two main politico-religious forces of the day: the Franciscan Arias deEnçinas, superior at the convent of Saint Francis of Toledo (and a cousin of the Grand Master), and the Dominican scholar Frey Johan de Zamora (see fig. 1).

Maqueda (about twenty-five miles from Toledo), perhaps after the murderous anti-Jewish preaching of Vincent Ferrer in Guadalajara during 1419. Apart from the Bible, there remains no other signed work by him. He gives some information in the prologue to the Bible, and his son Isaac gives some in the colophons to two illuminated Hebrew manuscripts that he copied. They are Vatican Library Urbinate Ebreo 7 (fol. 122r) and a manuscript in Sotheby's catalogue (London), June 22, 1993, notice #78.

At first the rabbi refused to work under such constraint and to take charge of the illuminations; he could not be faithful to Jerome's (Vulgate) translation or to Christian theological notions of the Hebrew Bible, nor could he countenance the anthropomorphic representation of God. But these objections were overruled. Arragel did eventually direct the painters;[2] most of the scenes represented in his Bible do not appear in the limited number of extant Hebrew manuscripts, in illuminated *haggadot* (Passover service books), or in Christian manuscripts of the Bible. As for the glosses, a compromise was reached: in cases of doctrinal divergence, both Jewish and Christian commentary would be included, the Christian glosses supplied by Arias (fol. 12rb). Thus the translation became a work of comparative doctrine, a duality marking its imagery as well as its text. This deviant text resembles no other; it follows no known model; it is faithful to the original Hebrew while using Jerome's vocabulary; often its translation is completely original.

§ § §

What motivated this unusual collaboration?[3] The Grand Master's explicit impulse was scholarly: to have an accurate translation into good Castilian, and to provide himself and other learned ecclesiastics with an explanation of obscure passages (fol. 2ra). That this explanation was to come from rabbinical sources was implicit recognition of the *hebraica veritas*. The Franciscan Arias, reproaching Arragel for obstinacy, urged him to accept the commission in order to serve God and save both nations (fols. 11v–12r). The point was to establish an official text of Hebrew scripture in the vernacular, as the terrain if not of agreement at least of serene discussion between Christians and Jews who might be converted more easily with an ecumenical version of the Bible.

---

[2] There are two *ateliers* represented in the manuscript, one responsible for the prologue and the second part of the manuscript, the other for the Pentateuch and historical books. Their styles and dominant colors differ; cf. Th. Metzger, "The *Alba Bible* of Rabbi Moses Arragel," *Bulletin of the Institute of Jewish Studies* 3 (1975): 131–35 and S. Fellous, "The artists of the *Biblia de Alba*," in *La Biblia de Alba, an Illustrated Manuscript Bible in Castilian*, ed. J. Schonfield (Madrid: Fac-Simile Editions, 1992), 65–77.

[3] There is also a psalter of English provenance, written in Hebrew at the end of the twelfth century, commissioned by a Christian from a Jewish scribe for the purpose of studying Hebrew; cf. M. Garel, *D'une main forte: Manuscrits hébreux des collections françaises* (Paris: Seuil, 1991), 90–91. But the case is scarcely comparable.

Both Grand Master and supervisor were taking advantage of an unusually pacific moment in Spanish ecclesiastical history, during a period when the Catholic appetite for, and confidence in, *reconquista* was in full flood. The early years of the century were marked by the enactment of many repressive laws in Castile lowering the legal status of Jews and limiting or abolishing their traditional rights and privileges. In 1411–12, the travelling preacher Vincent Ferrer mobilized popular anti-Jewish sentiment and lobbied for anti-Jewish legislation. In 1413–14, the infamous Tortosa disputation took place at the papal court in Tortosa. Instigated by a convert from Judaism to Catholicism who wanted to convert the rest of the Jews through a series of discussions, this event resulted in new ordinances, new persecutions both individual and communal, and many conversions.[4] But with the accession to the Aragonese throne in 1416 of the humanist Alfonso V, and to the papacy of Martin V (1417–31), a certain level of reversal was achieved. Between 1419 and 1422, the new pope and king nullified the anti-Jewish edicts of the previous era. "Our will is that Christians should treat Jews with humanity and kindness, and not offend them either in their persons or their property, so that Jews and Catholics may communicate and be of mutual help," wrote the pope in February, 1422, in a bull directed to the Christian world confirming the Church's protection of Jews.[5] The date of the Alba Bible commission, just two months later, is in my view closely connected with this papal remonstrance. The relation is all the more likely when we recall that the powerful and illustrious Order of Calatrava (of which the commissioner, Guzman, was the Grand Master) sheltered on its Castilian territories the most important Jewish community in the country, from which—as well as from other Jewish communities, or *aljamas*—the Order collected the tax.

How, then, do the text and its iconographic program exemplify the renewed papal will to coexistence? How does the Jewish director of the project ensure the presence of a Jewish voice and above all the integrity of the Jewish vision?

---

[4] See A. Pacios Lopez, *La disputa de Tortosa*, 2 vols. (Madrid and Barcelona: Instituto "Arias Montano," 1957); Y. Baer, *A History of the Jews in Christian Spain* (Philadelphia: Jewish Publication Society, 1966), chapter 10; Blasco Martinez Asuncion, "Los Judios del reino de Aragon" and Elisenda Casanova I Querol, "Estado sobre los judios de Tortosa (XII–XV)," both in *Actes 1r. Colloqui d'Historia dels Jueus a la corona d'Arago* (Lledia: 1991), 37–41 and 393–400 respectively.

[5] See J. Vernet, "Le pape Martin V et les juifs," *Revue des questions historiques* 51 (1892): 373–423.

The Prologue

The prologue of Moses Arragel can be placed in the tradition of prologues by Jewish translators or commentators: it presents the purpose and intention of the work commented or translated, its structure, its place in the course of study, its utility, its parts, its method and relation to various fields of knowledge, as well as its title, author and collaborators.[6] In this case, the translation and glosses are meant to resolve ambiguities of the original text and judge between true and false interpretations. How can a Jew do this when he writes, with the aid of two ecclesiastics, a Bible destined for Christian readers? Arragel is prudent: he relies on the protections he enjoys and justifies his decisions in a scientific manner. In announcing his exegetical principles at the outset, he writes a veritable *discours de la méthode* and gives a key to reading the manuscript. In so doing he exceeds by far the limits of his initial intent and manifests a genuine autonomy.

The length of the prologue is untypical. It occupies twenty-five leaves written in double columns of forty-five to fifty-four lines each; other prologues to Hebrew manuscripts take up two to ten leaves at most. The lettering is suspended from the upper ruled line (rather than placed on the lower) as is typical for Iberian Hebrew scribes (figs. 5, 6, 7).

The copies of all letters exchanged between the protagonists give the prologue the direct style of dialogue. Thus the author prepares the reader to encounter the commentaries as a debate between equals, and in fact the commentaries are structured like the prologue. In both, when the author approaches a new problem, he employs the same method: he clearly exposes the gist of the question, then cites Jewish commentaries on that problem before citing Christian glosses (on which he rarely expatiates). He comments on Christian glosses only when there is a question of a literal explication of a Latin text. He always returns to Jewish opinion, concluding with an affirmation of fidelity to the principles of Judaism and with a diplomatic refusal to be engaged on polemical terrain.

---

[6] Jean-Pierre Rothschild has studied about a hundred prologues of translators in "Motivations et méthodes des traductions en hébreu du milieu du XIIe à la fin du XVe siècle," *Traduction et traducteurs au moyen âge* (Paris: CNRS, 1989), 280–302. Also see Jean-Christophe Attias on commentators' prologues: "L'âme et la clef: De l'introduction comme genre littéraire dans la production exégétique du judaïsme médiéval," in *Entrer en matière*, ed. Dubois and Roussel, 337–58. Arragel blends the two types.

Certain passages constitute valuable historical testimony, for Arragel specifies the social and political context of his work. He praises the virtues of the order of Calatrava, describing the antagonism between it and the nobility; he criticizes the mores of the nobility who devastate peasant land for mere pleasure, the civil wars that divide the nobility and ruin the kingdom, the social and economic problems created by these wars; he writes of the situation of the Jews. In another rare testimonial, the author tells what happened after the completion of the translation, for in the third and last part of the prologue (fols. 20r–25r) he treats the critical examination of his book by theologians at the Franciscan convent of Toledo.

Finally, the prologue contains an iconography that could be termed "commemorative-historical"; it shows the personages involved in the commission of the manuscript. The role of each is clearly illustrated: Don Luys de Guzman sending the commission letter to the rabbi (fol. 1v); Moses Arragel instructed by the Dominican and the Franciscan (fol. 1v, fig. 1) then accepting the gloss-registers from Frey Arias (fol. 11r). The miniature showing Moses Arragel kneeling before Juan II of Castile (1406–54; fol. 11r) suggests that the commission of this Bible is to be inserted in a political project that surpassed the scientific project. This hypothesis is supported by the sumptuous miniature representing the ceremony of transmitting the manuscript to the Grand Master of Calatrava; this painting closes the prologue and confers an official character upon the enterprise (fig. 2).[7]

The prologue has three sections, each divided into chapters. The first section evokes the political context in which the commission is situated; it then approaches the content of the text, the clerical criticism of which could have disastrous consequences for the author and for the community whose spokesman he had become. The second part treats the content of glosses and the hermeneutic problems of the biblical text. The third takes up the revision of the work by Christian religious authorities.

The first part, composed of fifteen chapters, takes the form of dialogue by correspondence among the Grand Master, Frey Arias, and Moses Arragel. It is subdivided into three sections, all treating the nature of the commission as approached by each of the three protagonists. It begins by situating the executor of the work intellectually and religiously, combining Aristotle and Holy Writ with no sense of contradiction:

---

[7] This last scene is probably fictive, as there is reason to think that the Grand Master did not receive the manuscript personally.

Fig. 2. The ceremony (probably fictitious) at which the manuscript is presented by Moses Arragel (kneeling at the very bottom of the scene) to the Grand Master of the Order of Calatrava, Don Luis de Guzman, before the dignitaries of the Order. Placed at the end of the prologue. Alba Bible, ill. 5, fol. 25v.

It is proper at the start of all our actions to magnify the true God: final cause, end without end, origin without origin [Aristotle, *Metaphysics* 4.2].... God who above all the prophets elevated Moses to great excellence; God who gave him the law in heaven.

God is one, his deity is without equal either in kind or in species.... And thus I, Rabbi Moses, ask and desire the aid of the aforesaid God, saying as says the psalmist: "May the grace of Adonai, our God, be on us, etc." [Psalms 90:17].   Fol. 1va

The introduction then presents the commissioner, Guzman, and the three Christian supervisors, situating them socially. Next comes a copy of the official commissioning letter with Guzman's motivation and purpose, along with high praise of the rabbi's scholarly reputation.

The rabbi's reply is a long, polite, and erudite refusal. Chapter 1 invokes the well-known modesty topos, insisting that the author's reputation for erudition is surely exaggerated; chapter 2 praises the virtue of noble patrons in supporting scholars; chapter 3 discusses hunting, as a critique of the less worthy nobility, and segues into a long argument justifying the rabbi's refusal of the commission. To this end he produces an exposé of the differences between Judaism and Christianity, comparing Maimonides's thirteen articles of Jewish faith and fourteen of Catholic faith, concluding that his work could not be used by a Christian and would thus be in vain (fol. 4r). Next the rabbi turns to the problem of translation itself. Jews, he argues, have transmitted their scripture in an unbroken chain, both oral and written, without changing so much as an *iota* (fol. 4r), whereas the Latin, in Jerome's translation, is not always exact. Unless he were able to translate direct from the Hebrew, the rabbi would not be able to work under Christian supervision—particularly since a divergent translation would cause him injury (fol. 9r).

In reply to this refusal, the Grand Master only confirmed his commission, ordering Arragel to contact Arias immediately. For his part, Arias was willing to transform the thrust of the commission by establishing another modality of collaboration, particularly for exegesis and iconography.

The second section of the prologue reveals its originality and the creative role of the rabbi. It constitutes a discourse on method in four chapters, in which the author develops the problems of translation, interpretation, exegesis, and philology. Arragel's analysis of the aptitudes basic to translating are standard in translators' prologues: good knowledge of both languages and of the subject; to these he adds the thirteen virtues of a translator enunciated by Ibn Ezra. In translating Hebrew, he writes, it is especially important to know how to read the signs (points) corresponding to vowels; here Jerome is at fault, along with other translators into Latin. Thus Arragel writes that he intends to try to harmonize divergent readings as far as possible, but when he cannot, he will follow the Hebrew, "conforming to Jerome's own recommendation." For this he begs mercy from those who read the translation and its commentaries, asking to be judged by his good intention (fol. 14v).

For exegesis, Arragel chooses the juxtaposition of sources when they diverge, but if there is no divergence between Latin and Hebrew commentators, he proposes to establish a unique reference text that will be able to be supported by both nations, Christians and Jews: a summa of agreement. Of course it is divergence that has the potential for personal and collective disaster, so Arragel is very clear in his instructions as to how the work is to be read:

> So that neither Christian nor Jew be led into error, wherever the Christian may feel that a point or gloss is in opposition to the articles of his faith, let him take it for a Jewish interpretation brought in to report, not to undermine. The same for the Jew: if he finds a gloss that would go against the articles of his faith, let him take it for an opinion of the Roman Church, coming from the register given me by the reverend master Arias, and not from a Jewish commentator or a rabbi.... Everything having been examined by the Christian and by the Jew, this will lead them to not cry abomination or say that there are heresies or erroneous opinions; and everyone, Christian or Jew, will not abandon the articles of his faith because of the opinions assembled here, and will believe firmly in the principles of his faith which, in this work, are presented as opinions, reported without being determined or affirmed, in the form of a question. For my part, I am a Jew, I believe Hebraic opinions, just as the Christian believes in his, and I do nothing other than relate and recall the Hebrew opinions produced by Jewish scholars, the best that I have been able to find, ancient and modern.... Now that we have shown the nature of this work, it seems reasonable to me that its name should correspond to what it is for the advantage that it may bring. This is why it is appropriate that its name should be: The Memorial. fol. 14vb

The end of this second portion of the prologue is devoted to semantic and linguistic questions, with a historical-comparative study of the two languages involved: etymology, dialectology, grammar, lexicography, morphology, and rhetoric are covered. A glossary concludes this discussion; composed of learned words both Latin and Hebrew, and of new words, it aims to eliminate any confrontation based only on a linguistic misunderstanding.[8]

The third and last part of the prologue records the speeches of Rabbi Moses and Frey Arias upon the official presentation of the manuscript for its detailed examination by Arias and his erudite colleagues. On this examination depends the payment of the salary that Arragel claims in his speech and that had not yet been paid after eleven years of work. The work of examination and correction would take place in public, before a multi-confessional and multiclass audience ("masters in theology, doctors from other orders, lords of the Church, numerous knights, squires, Jews and Moors," fols. 24v–25r). We do not know whether Arragel's Bible was finally accepted or refused, nor do we know how much, or whether, the rabbi was paid.

The Commentaries

The commentary in the Alba Bible is very dense, up to eighty-four lines per page. Every lemma is underlined in red ink. The glosses sometimes occupy all four margins, though sometimes a comment may consist of only a phrase, as when Arragel reports the literal meaning of a word. In general, the commentary treats the literal sense first, and its style—unlike that of the expansive and rhetorically elaborate prefatory letters—is marked by extreme precision and economy as the rabbi seeks to avoid all confusion.

Though the glosses follow known models, they are exceptional in their abundance of Jewish sources and in their presentation as comparative doctrine. Ancient, modern and profane sources appear as well as the expected ones: Aristotle, Virgil, Hippocrates, Ptolemy, Euclid, Pliny as well as Jerome, Augustine, Nicholas of Lyra, St. Bernard, and various recent or contemporary scholars of both faiths, not all of whom have been identified. The rabbi did not limit himself to theology; his culture extended to all the sciences of his time: history, medicine, philosophy, geometry, astronomy—the latter especially in matters of messianic calculation. Of Jewish sources, Rashi, Maimonides, Abraham Ibn Ezra, and David Kimchi

---

[8] This was also the concern of the converso Pablo de Santa María (1415–35); cf. Nicolas Lopez Martinez, "Sinodos burgalese del siglo XV," *Burgense* 7 (1966): 305–6 and J.-M. Soto Rabanos, "Disposiciones sobre la cultura del clero parroquial...," *Anuario de estudios medievales* 23 (1993): 257–356.

are the most often cited (without always being mentioned by name); then Midrash, Talmud, and authors such as Nachmanides, Levi Ben Gershom, and Moshe ha-Darshan. Jewish literary references are numerous and varied, giving important information about Spanish Jewish literary currents of the period. The general point of the gloss is to permit the re-establishment of literal translation, especially when this brings the rabbi closer to rabbinic commentary than to the Christian point of view. Arragel's aim is always to return to the original Hebrew and to Jewish interpretation of the Bible. Where he had to, the rabbi limited himself to saying that Christians had a different opinion than Jews and to a brief summary. Thus the Jewish commentaries are more numerous and more explicit than the Christian ones, so that the corpus becomes a Jewish text by its treatment. It is a case for Judaism, hence a subversive text and a deviation from the recommendations of Friar Arias.

The iconography displays the same characteristics: most often it is a vehicle for the Hebrew text or Jewish sources even though certain images may feature human representations of God, or though a Christian reading of the text shows through the image. The examination of the images shows that the Jewish scribes worked at the same time, indeed alongside, the Toledan artists who executed the illumination.

Conception and Execution of the Iconographic Program

In the rabbi's letter to the Grand Master, one chapter is devoted to iconography: he declines to participate in any way in its execution, and particularly of anthropomorphic images of God: it would be a sin against his law even to direct the painters thus (fol. 9rv). Faced with this *endurescido judio* (hardened/stubborn Jew), Arias decided to have the miniatures copied from those of a Bible kept in the treasury of the Toledo cathedral. He would indicate the passages to be illustrated and send the pictorial models for review; then the rabbi would leave a blank space where an image could be inserted. The manuscript Bible that served as model has not been identified.

All the biblical books are illustrated excepting Psalms, Proverbs, Ecclesiastes, Lamentations, and Chronicles. At first view the paintings seem to be of Christian inspiration, because the representation of God agrees with Christian iconographic tradition in some of them; nonetheless, many images reveal details and concepts originating in Jewish literary sources. Five principal types of miniatures have been catalogued (though some may belong to two categories):

1) miniatures faithful to the Hebrew text. These are the most numerous, more than half the total; I will not discuss them here.
2) miniatures of Christian type (about 50);
3) miniatures of Jewish type, of two kinds (nearly 60): a) ritual, b) supported by rabbinic sources;
4) miniatures of syncretic type, combining Jewish sources and anthropomorphic representation of God or typological figures (about 20);
5) miniatures with ideological aim: a) the exploits of the Hebrews, presenting the historical books as epic narrative (about 50); b) caricature: the representation of the Jew according to Christian polemic: humpbacked, hook-nosed, with moneybag hanging from his belt (under 10).

Of course, these ideological images are completely opposite.

Christian type. In this category I include images whose conception or execution supports Christian theory or practice; these include anthropomorphic figures of God, typological images, attributes such as nimbuses aureoling the faces of holy persons, or simply a gesture similar to that of Christian prayer—hands joined and kneeling—or the gestures of priests administering their office (notably the desert tabernacle, fol. 88v).[9] Christ, represented twice in Genesis (fols. 28r and 29v, with Adam and Eve, then with Cain and Abel) wears a twopart robe, symbolic of his two natures. Aaron's rod is represented as an episcopal cross (fols. 236v, 340r). In the desert tabernacle (fol. 88v), the horizontal form of the table is modeled on the *Postilla* of the fourteenth-century Franciscan Nicholas of Lyra rather than on the Biblical account, which makes the table vertical. In the book of Isaiah, God is always in majesty, represented with a cross-shaped nimbus, making the Latin sign of benediction with trinitarian meaning.

In the book of Isaiah (cf. 7:1, 13–14), the siege of Jerusalem by the kings of Israel and Syria is illustrated along with the prophet's prophecy of

---

[9] See S. Fellous, "Catalogue raisonné" in "*La Biblia de Alba*," 98–99, 114; François Garnier, *Le langage de l'image au Moyen Age: Signification et symbolique* (Paris: Le Léopard d'Or, 1982); Michel Pastoureau, *Figures et couleurs: Étude sur la symbolique et la sensibilité médiévales* (Paris: Le Léopard d'Or, 1986).

victory: a young woman will bear a child, to be called Emmanuel (God is with us), in whose childhood the victory will be won (fol. 267vab, fig. 3). The chapter heading reads: "How it was announced to King Ahaz, encircled in Jerusalem by the king of Israel and the king of Syria: the young woman will conceive." What ideological coherence is there between the two parts of this illustration? The image represents a city surrounded by towers and ramparts, assailed by knights and soldiers. In the exterior margin, a kneeling Isaiah, his head aureoled in a starred nimbus, addresses Ahaz, who stands near the city ramparts. However, a seated and aureoled pregnant woman located in the margin is obviously meant to be the most important person in the miniature because of the large dimensions of her image. She wears a blue cape: the Virgin Mary's color; she holds a little book in one hand while the other hand points to the scene occurring at the right, palm open to signify acceptance of her mission. As a representation of Mary, her presence attests the Christian interpretation of Immanuel as Jesus. Moreover, illustrations of the Annunciation often show Mary reading a book inscribed with Isaiah's verse 14. Mary herself, as daughter of Zion (Luke 2:33–35), symbolizes Jerusalem; the attack on Jerusalem reciprocally prefigures the passion of Christ, Mary's son. Lastly, the destruction of Jerusalem was considered punishment for the Jews' part in the crucifixion of Jesus (figuralism of course renders anachronism perfectly admissible).

Arragel's commentary presents a Jewish viewpoint, explaining the young woman as the prophet's wife or the king's wife, as in commentaries by Rashi and David Kimchi. Though conceding nothing to the Christian (mis)translation of the Hebrew *'almah* as "virgin" rather than simply "young woman," he avoids a discussion of this contentious word (which had been extensively debated during the Tortosa disputation as a fundamental doctrine in Catholic theology). Instead, he dwells on the patristic identification of the young woman as the Virgin Mary, and repeats at beginning and end of the gloss that the difference between Jews and Christians on this point is immense. Fierce defender of his faith, Arragel avoids lengthy consideration of a subject he knows to be dangerous.

The illustration of Ezekiel's vision (Ezekiel 1:1–13; fol. 320r) integrates anthropomorphic representation of God and typological figures. The assimilation of Ezekiel's four syncretic creatures (part lion, ox, eagle, and human) to the four evangelists was current in Christian manuscripts, in accordance with Apocalypse 4:7–8, as is suggested in this illumination.

Fig. 3. The siege of Jerusalem by the kings of Israel and Syria and the announcement of Emmanuel's birth (Isaiah 7:1, 13–14). Alba Bible, ill. 224, fol. 267vab.

However, it is not the New Testament interpretation which underlies Arragel's commentary or the depiction of the vision. Rather the arrangement of the four creatures corresponds to that in the Talmud (Hagiga 13b).

Jewish type. Here, no anthropomorphic representation of God appears, though divine manifestations are represented as angels or clouds, usually in conformity with what is indicated in the original Hebrew. The large number of illustrations of Exodus and Numbers, as well as Jewish ritual details, are surprising in a manuscript destined for Christians. Apparently Moses Arragel contributed significantly to the choice of illuminations and to their execution through the guidelines he gave the painters. The twenty-nine miniatures of Exodus could have been conceived on the basis of the iconographic program of Spanish haggadot; those of ritual might have had a Jewish iconographic model, not necessarily written in Hebrew, but destined for Jews who, in these troubled times, knew little of their rituals and required instruction in it. The rabbi's glosses refer to the miniatures, and the rigor with which the painters illustrated the text show that Arragel did supervise the work of copyists and painters despite his initial refusal to do so.

When Moses is shown before the burning bush (Exodus 3:3, fol. 60rab), the bush reveals an angel within it. This is in accordance with the Hebrew but not with Jerome's translation, which has God himself being revealed. The difference is noted in a vertical inscription, along with the observation that Jerome's translation is believed by *la santa madre egleja romana*. In Daniel's vision (Daniel 7:3–8, fol. 465r, lower margin), the bear is shown with three fangs in its mouth, not three rows of teeth as Jerome has it; again this is acknowledged in a vertical inscription next to the bear. Thus it is Arragel's translation that served as a reference for the illustration and not Jerome's. Of the 107 miniatures ornamenting the Pentateuch, fourteen scenes show rituals associated with Yom Kippur, Sukkot, and Shem ini Atzeret (the last day of Sukkot, Simchat Torah). Passover and Purim are presented in the historical episodes associated with them. Numbers contains eighteen illuminations, including the high priest in Solomon's Temple and the Ark of the Covenant. The high priest's costume and mantle, described in Exodus 39:33, is complete in every detail down to the ritual curls (*pe'ot*) prescribed in Leviticus 19:27 and taken up extensively in the Talmud. Similarly, the priest shown sacrificing the red cow (Numbers 19:2–3; fol. 123vb)—a ritual linked to the Yom Kippur liturgy—is also shown with the ritual curls on each side of his face. The illustration of these and other themes was probably decided by Arra-

Fig. 4. Moses's rod (Exodus 4:1–7); cf. Pirkei of Rabbi Eliezer, ch. 50. Alba Bible, ill. 54, fol. 60vb.

gel, with their minute representation of ritual detail. Often from the hand of a less skillful artist, these ritual paintings suggest that they may have been executed by the rabbi himself or by a Jewish amateur artist rather than the professional Toledans mentioned by Arias.

More than fifty miniatures are supported by Jewish literary sources. Outside those illustrating the epic of the exodus (current in contemporary haggadot), most of them reproduce scenes rarely represented, even unique, in medieval iconography whether Jewish or Christian. Four examples will demonstrate the method: two from each of the two main artistic teams.

The first illustrates an episode from Exodus in which Jahweh turns Moses's rod into a serpent and back again in order to encourage Moses to speak to the Jews as Jahweh's spokesman (Exodus 4:1–5). The origin of this rod is not mentioned in scripture, but only in certain literary sources. According to the *Pirkei of Rabbi Eliezer*,[10] Moses found this rod in the garden of Jethro, his father-in-law. Thus the illustration (fol. 60vb, fig. 4) proceeds from right to left in the manner of Hebrew, showing (in that order) the rod planted on a heap of green leaves designating the garden, then transformed into a serpent, and finally in Moses's hand. The *Pirkei*

---

[10] See *Leçons de Rabbi Eliézer*, trans. and annotated by M. A. Ouaknin and E. Smilevich (Paris: Verdier, "Les Dix Paroles," 1983), chapter 40.

also says that on this baton were inscribed the initials of the ten plagues that Moses would inflict on the Egyptians; the illustration shows these initials, in Hebrew characters and in Latin letters (though the latter represent not the initials of corresponding Castilian words but those of phonetically sounded Hebrew words). Though the transformation of the rod into a serpent is not infrequently represented in Hebrew manuscripts, that of the rod in Jethro's garden, bearing the initials of the plagues, is exceptional; clearly it was influenced by the Pirkei.

Another painting shows the death of Ahasuerus's first queen Vashti, who refused to appear before him at his command (Esther 1:10–20). Though the book of Esther says little about Vashti, she is portrayed here (fol. 390v) nude, wounded to death, and with two tails, one growing from her spine, the other from her forehead. The literary sources here are *Midrash Esther Rabbah* and Talmud (Megilla 12b)—but the latter accounts for only one tail, and we do not know what text might have inspired the second tail, a variant unique to this manuscript. A second instance shows Ahasuerus listening to the reading of annals of past events and the honoring of Mordechai for having prevented the murder of the king (Esther 6:1, 10; fol. 393 lower margin). The scene includes a winged angel pointing at the passage about Mordechai's heroic act. This angel is not mentioned in the biblical narrative but in the *Targum Sheni*, where its function is to keep the king awake during the reading of the annals until the mention of Mordechai is reached. The Bible illumination also depicts the villain, Haman, being trod on by Mordechai and then having a chamber-pot emptied on his head by a woman in an upper-floor window. These details come from the expanded accounts in the *Pirkei of Eliezer* (chapter 50) and the Talmud (Megilla 16a) respectively. Lastly, there is the depiction of the death of the Chaldean king, Balthasar (Daniel 5:30; fol. 464rb). The king is assassinated by two men while seated, pants down, on a toilet. The only known commentary that mentions the digestive troubles of Balthasar is the *Midrash Rabba* on the Song of Songs; here he is assassinated while returning from the toilet, and if there is a textual source for Arragel's variant, it has not been identified.

The book of Esther is the only one unaccompanied by commentaries. Nonetheless we may suppose that Moses Arragel furnished the Jewish iconographic models, for in several instances no other example of his iconography is found in surviving manuscripts. Possibly a local Jewish literature which has not survived transmitted the iconographic models for the pictures influenced by literary sources, but in its absence we may assume the personal direction and perhaps invention of Arragel.

Fig. 5. The discovery of Moses's basket (Exodus 2:5, 9).
Alba Bible, ill. 52, fol. 59va.

Syncretic illustrations. These combine Jewish sources with Christian iconography. Some are of a typological character, such as the portrait of a haloed and crowned infant Moses in the arms of a bluecaped woman (fol. 59va, fig. 5). The rubric identifies her as Pharaoh's daughter, as in the Talmud (Sotah 12b) and the *Targum Pseudo-Jonathan* on Exodus 2–6, rather than as in the Bible, which identifies her as a servant;[11] but the picture

---

[11] This scene is illustrated according to the same rabbinic sources in the synagogue of Dura-Europos (enlarged and repainted between 230 and 245, destroyed in

itself strongly resembles a Virgin and Child. Similarly, Moses addressing the Jews again becomes a type of Christ (fol. 84ra); the model may have been fairly close at hand in the "Jesus addressing the Jews" motif found in a manuscript of the *Castigos del rey Sancho IV* executed in Toledo in 1391 (Madrid, Biblioteca Nacional, MS 3995, fol. 19v).

Divine anthropomorphism occurs in the illustration of Moses's death (Deuteronomy 39:5–6; fol. 163r), where the bust of God in a cloud has been added by another hand than the one that painted the rest of the image. This might have been the initiative of one of the Christian artists, or of the supervisor Arias wanting to "christianize" certain important miniatures; it is improbable that Arragel would have urged the insertion of a divine image. The illustration of the murder of Abel gives a typical case of insertion of a rabbinic element in a Christian model (Genesis 4:3–8; fol. 29vab, fig. 6). The sequence has four scenes showing the two offerings, the murder, and God's reprimand. God is given the attributes of Christ, and the offering is made in a kneeling position as was current in Christian, not Jewish, ritual. The Bible does not indicate how Abel is killed; this is found in the *Zohar*, which specifies that Cain bit him like a serpent (1:54b).[12] This is the option chosen by the illuminator, blending a Jewish literary source with Christian iconography of God. Cain's posture—extended over the fallen Abel, bared teeth in the victim's throat—resembles that of an animal and might owe something to the representations of animals killing their prey, a common motif in bestiaries. Interestingly, a bas-relief in the Toledo cathedral, dating from the late fourteenth century, is identical to that in the Arragel Bible. Thus the painter could have used

---

256) and the Sarajevo Haggadah (fol. 20r) of fourteenth-century Aragonese provenance. The Dura synagogue was discovered in 1932 by British soldiers; it is the earliest example of Biblical iconography and the first to use rabbinic literary sources in illustrating Biblical scenes. This discovery posed the question of the origin of iconographic models found in Christian art. See C. H. Kraeling, The Synagogue: The Excavations at Dura-Europos (New Haven: Yale University Press/Ktav, 1979) and E. R. Goodenough, *Jewish Symbols in the Greco-Roman Period IX-XI: Symbolism in the Dura Synagogue* (New York: Pantheon/Bollingen Foundation, 1964). The Sarajevo Haggadah contains a large number of miniatures; its iconographical program extends from creation to the exodus and ends with scenes from contemporary Jewish life. It served as model for other haggadot and probably also for non-Jewish works; cf. Angela Franco, "El Genesis y el Exodo en la cerca exterior de la cathedral de Toledo," *Toletum* (1987): 53–160, especially 129–34.

[12] *Zohar* is the central work of Jewish esoteric literature (the Kabbala); supposedly compiled in the second century, it was "revised" about 1270 by the Spaniard Moses de León.

*Fig. 6. Cain and Abel cycle (Genesis 4:3–8); cf. Zohar 54b.
Alba Bible, ill. 8, fol. 29vab.*

this nearby Christian model, but one may ask where the cathedral sculptor found his inspiration. Perhaps Jewish culture had sufficiently impregnated the Iberian peninsula that certain literary or artistic sources had passed into the national heritage. Indeed, the profusion of scenes from Genesis and Exodus in the Toledo cathedral and in the Alba Bible could come from the same current of deluxe Hebrew manuscripts, especially haggadot, taken up by Christian artists as models for moments when those themes played a major role in Christian ritual.

Ideological images: the Hebrew epic. The manuscript, scattered with war scenes, could not have lacked social or artistic models for this type of representation. War was considered a good thing, especially if it were a just war, such as one waged against heretics or pagans, or for territorial defense—particularly in this troubled period, as specified in the colophon to the manuscript. Illustrated historical epics were a fashionable genre of the day. Moses Arragel's Bible has thirty-seven battle scenes (as well as numerous others of murder and scatological episodes, heralding the birth of picaresque literature).

The rabbi followed clear ideological principles in directing this part of the iconographic program of his Bible. He had the history of his people illustrated as *res gestae*, changing the image of scapegoat or victim into that of the conquering warrior and champion of the Mosaic faith. This image, highly privileged in contemporary Hispanic society, seems to aim to efface that of the "degraded people" which the Church sought to give the Jews, guilty as they were of failing to recognize the true faith.

Ideological images: caricatural figures. On the other hand, what can we make of those miniatures in which someone is represented caricaturally? It is unlikely that Jewish artists themselves would be so accustomed to these anti-Jewish models that they would automatically repeat them. Clearly the rabbi either approved in some way these Christian insertions, or was unable to intervene in time to prevent such representations. The same dynamic appears to be at work in representations of circumcision, whether that of Abraham (fol. 37rb) or of the Israelites by Joshua (fol. 176vb, fig. 7), in which the ritual is represented as a bloody, barbaric act on an organ of monstrous dimensions.

Fig. 7. Joshua circumcises the Israelites (Joshua 5:2–3). *Alba Bible*, ill. 110, fol. 167vb.

In three cases, the Jews wear the *rouelle* or identifying badge imposed first at the Fourth Lateran Council (1215) and again, locally and very currently, in the Statutes of Valladolid (1412). The badge, on the cloaks of the prophets Eli and Elisha (fol. 248r, fol. 250v), appears green in one and perhaps red in the second, where it is indistinct as if it had been added. However, the badge is quite systematically represented in the portraits of Arragel in the prologue: in conformity with Article 18 of the new Statutes, the rabbi is humbly dressed and coiffed, beard and hair uncut, wearing a mantle of coarse weave on which appears the red badge (figs. 1, 2). All of these instances are from one of the artistic teams, the so-called "Parma painter" and his studio.

In paintings by the other team, that of the so-called "bright-yellow painter," physiognomic characteristics are used to designate at least one man in a group as Jewish and thus, by association, the entire group. This caricature appears five times: when Moses brings down the tablets of the law, a hunchbacked, hooknosed man is shown in the crowd of Hebrews (fol. 72v); when Moses explains the commandments, the group of Israelites are shown as obese, with hooked and snub noses, carrying moneypurses at their belts (fol. 84ra); hooknosed individuals appear in two scenes from Joshua and one in Judges (fols. 167v, 170v and 179r).

In sum, then, of 324 miniatures, twenty-two represent God or Christ, twenty-three evoke a Christian interpretation of scripture, there are six Marian figures, and perhaps a half-dozen could be described as caricatural. It appears that the iconography of the Alba Bible is much more faithful to the original Hebrew than to Christian interpretation. Whatever the truth about the process of production, the Catholic supervisors apparently found nothing to censure, although they evidently added a few divine images and a few interlinear and marginal remarks.

§ § §

Moses Arragel of Guadalajara finished his manuscript of the Bible on Friday, June 2, 1430, in Maqueda, with the exception of the prologue and corrections, which were completed in 1433. Although he does not name himself at the end (as he had done in the prologue), everything indicates that he did complete the manuscript. The messianic theme with eschatological overtones that appears in the two last illustrations (Ezra reading the law and the celebration of Sukkot, fols. 478v and 479rab, from Nehemiah 8:16) can scarcely be accidental. They seem to me to be a deliberate choice of the rabbi addressing a message of hope to his people, who were trying to recover from the damage of the great 1391 persecution and that of 1413 following the Tortosa disputation. Moreover, in his speech at the official presentation, copied out in the prologue, the rabbi mentioned the "mill doblas" spent during eleven years of work; thus he did complete the work and brought the book himself before the Catholic censors who would study it, have it read aloud publicly, and declare it acceptable or heretical. We have no documentation of the official response. Arragel lived in Toledo until his death about 1456.

The Alba Bible remained in the convent of Toledo for nearly two centuries after its presentation. It next appears in an Inquisition document of 1622 ordering its confiscation. In 1624, the Grand Inquisitor Don Andres Pacheco gave it to the Prime Minister, Count Duc d'Olivares, in recognition of the latter's service to his nation, and because the manuscript had belonged to Olivares's ancestor. Olivares had acquired some notoriety as a protector of New Christians (i.e., those converted from Judaism) and even of Jews. The restitution of the Bible to a relatively enlightened man probably saved the manuscript from destruction. It remains today in the Library of the Dukes of Alba, the descendants of Olivares, in the Casa de Alba.

Institut de Recherche et d'Histoire des Textes, C.N.R.S., Paris

Women, Demons and the Rabbi's Son
Narratology and "A Story from Worms"

CHANITA GOODBLATT

The Yiddish folk tale "A Story from Worms" ("Mayse fun Vorms") was written down in Northern Italy at the beginning of the sixteenth century, having probably originated in the earlier folklore of the Jewish community of Worms,[1] a major medieval center of Jewish learning on the banks of the Rhine river, along with Speyer and Mainz. My English translation of this tale (see Appendix) was made from a transcription of the original Yiddish story, first published by Sara Zfatman in 1987[2] from a unique manuscript (MS F.12.45 Trinity College, Cambridge, fols. 24r–31r) dating from the 1520s. "A Story from Worms" tells the tale of a young man's inadvertent marriage to a female demon and his subsequent release from this bond through the efforts of his poor but pious wife.[3]

Curiously, a real-life version of "A Story from Worms" appears in the records of the Jewish community of nearby Mainz,[4] involving a young

---

An earlier version of this essay appeared in Hebrew in Jerusalem Studies in Jewish Folklore 15 (1993): 83–95. I would like to thank the editors for permission to reprint this essay, as well as the story itself, in English translation. I would also like to thank Sheila Delany for her important contribution to this essay, through her careful and sensitive editing.

[1] For discussion, in Hebrew, of the dating of the story and the manuscript, see Sara Zfatman, *The Marriage of a Mortal Man and a She-Demon: The Transformation of a Motif in the Folk Narrative of Ashkenazi Jewry in the Sixteenth-Nineteenth Centuries* (Jerusalem: Akademon, 1987), 19-20 and vii.

[2] Ibid., 118–127.

[3] As an example of the motif of the demonic marriage, "A Story from Worms" comprises a link between medieval Christian and later Jewish tales (both Yiddish and Hebrew). For a comparative analysis, see Zfatman, ibid.; and Joseph Dan, "Five Versions of the Story of the Jerusalemite," *Proceedings of the American Academy for Jewish Research* 35 (1967): 99–111.

[4] In the *Responsa of Maharil*, chapter 96. This document contains the questions and answers of the German-Jewish Rabbi Jacob Moellin (1360?–1427; called "Maharil," a word composed of the first letters of his Hebrew title and name: "Morenu ha-Rav Ya'akov ha- Levi ben Moshe Moellin) regarding religious matters. See Solomon B. Freehof, *The Responsa Literature* (Philadelphia: Jewish Publication Society of America, 1955); Sidney Steiman, *Custom and Survival: A Study of the Life and Work of Rabbi Jacob Molin* (New York: Bloch, 1963); *Encyclopedia Judaica* (Jerusalem: Keter, 1971), 12:210–11. As the Rabbi of Mainz, the Maharil was consulted

Jewish scholar, the son of a rich man, who later became known as Rabbi Natan Halevi Epstein, the Rabbi of Frankfurt. On the night of November 29, 1414, he jokingly recited the marriage benediction to his teacher Rabbi Zalman's maidservant (a woman of about forty), causing a great uproar and requiring an annulment. The annulment was all the more necessary because the young man in question, already a widower, was about to be married for a second time; as the records explain, "that same day a letter had arrived from his father, and because of his great happiness and longing for his bride he could not take his mind off marriage, and his words betrayed him, causing him to jest in this manner."[5] The maidservant attempted blackmail; the Rabbis wanted to permit the young man to take a second wife without divorcing the maidservant; and the maidservant insisted upon attending the wedding ceremony to ensure the annulment of her "marriage."

A comparison of this incident with the tale shows how art can function subversively. As Tamar Alexander has observed, Jewish tales such as "A Story from Worms"

> have enabled a man living in a traditional society, often married to a woman not of his own choosing, to fulfill his fantasies of living with two women and having, in addition to his wife, a beautiful, sexually active and indulgent woman who will stop at nothing, including killing her human rival, in order to have him.[6]

In turning to the maidservant, did the young scholar Natan Halevi Epstein express his sexual desires, or was it rather a wish to escape from the parental authority and nuptial commitment sanctioned by the community? Thus, besides our interest in psychological issues, an effective reading of both the historical record and the folk tale can also reveal the ways in which late-medieval German-Jewish society was stratified by class and gender.

Even the spare details of the historical event point to such stratification. The efforts made by famous Rabbis to protect the young scholar's ability to marry a woman of his own class and age; the attempts of the maidservant to profit from the wealthier members of the community; and

---

about the event. For an account, in Hebrew, of this event, see Israel Jacob Yuval, *Scholars in their Time: The Religious Leadership of German Jewry in the Late Middle Ages* (Jerusalem: Magnes Press, 1998), 115–17, 208 and 228–30.

[5] Yuval, ibid., 229. My translation.

[6] Tamar Alexander, "Theme and Genre: Relationships between Man and She-Demon in Jewish Folklore," *Jewish Folklore and Ethnology Review* 14 (1992): 60.

the condescending attitude of the male religious establishment towards the (not entirely blameless) maidservant all emphasize issues of social stratification. In much the same way, the folk tale presents the story of the reprehensible attempt by an unsuitable and more (sexually) mature woman to stay married to a young and wealthy scholar, and the corresponding attempt by the religious establishment to provide him with a more suitable match. Unlike the historical event, though, the tale presents the ultimate victory of a poor but pious woman over both the wealthy religious establishment and the demonic realm. Taking this difference into account, I suggest that in "A Story from Worms" not only is the ordinary social situation overturned, but the traditional explanation of the means by which such victory is won is challenged: namely, that the piety and modesty of a Jewish wife releases her husband from his demonic marriage. The narrative can be interpreted as offering a more subversive view of female agency.

In order to illuminate this turnabout in the tale, I propose at present to adopt a Barthesian narratological approach, which distinguishes five codes in the narrative text.[7] Two of these codes are responsible for "narrative suspense, for the reader's desire to complete, to finish the text" as Robert Scholes explains;[8] these are the proaieretic code or code of actions, and the hermeneutic code or code of puzzles which "plays on the reader's desire for 'truth', for the answers to questions raised by the text."[9] The three other codes refer to what Susan R. Suleiman has noted as the "potential considerations of the relation between the text and its context,"[10] creating in this case a specific socio-cultural context for "A Story from Worms"; these are the connotative,[11] referring to the linking together of the various connotations of "wealth" and "marriage"; the cultural, referring to the Jewish religious concept of a pious woman; and the symbolic, based on the opposition between the holy and the profane.[12]

Taking these distinctions into consideration, I will now posit two

---

[7] Roland Barthes, S/Z, trans. Richard Miller (New York: Hill & Wang, 1974).

[8] Robert Scholes, *Semiotics and Interpretation* (New Haven: Yale University Press, 1982), 100.

[9] Ibid.

[10] Susan R. Suleiman, "Introduction: Varieties of Audience-Oriented Criticism," in *The Reader in the Text: Essays on Audience and Interpretation*, ed. Susan R. Suleiman and Inge Crosman (Princeton: Princeton University Press 1989), 12.

[11] Barthes uses the term "semic," but I prefer the more familiar term "connotative," adopted from Scholes.

[12] The terms "holy" and "profane" are adopted from Theodor H. Gaster's book, *The Holy and the Profane: Evolution of Jewish Folkways* (New York: William Morrow & Company, 1980).

hypothetical readers for "A Story from Worms": the naive reader, associated with the proaieretic and hermeneutic codes; and the sophisticated reader, associated with the connotative, the cultural, and the symbolic codes. This formulation clarifies the distinction made by Christine Brooke-Rose in her comment on a type of American folk tale,[13] that the overdetermination of the hermeneutic and proaieretic codes shifts the focus of interpretation onto the connotative, cultural, and symbolic codes. In other words, overdetermination is the unnecessary repetition of information, for the sake of a naive reader who must be told everything. Such repetition serves to raise questions and underline issues whose resolution depends on the sophisticated reader's access to the other, more general codes, referring as they do to the wider socio-cultural context. In the case of "A Story from Worms" it is the naive reader, following the closely delineated path of the narrative, who accepts the conventional norms of Jewish piety, while it is the sophisticated reader, whose interpretive powers are shifted onto the larger context, who challenges the explicit moral lesson stated at the story's end.

In "A Story from Worms" information from the proaieretic code does indeed repeat itself. There are two instances of murder, as well as repetitions of the ring's loss and the pious wife's generous act in lifting up the she-demon's hair, which are repeated through the narrative techniques of first "showing" and then "telling." Along with these narrative repetitions comes the repetition of information in the hermeneutic code, bringing the solution to the riddles of the ring's loss, the murders of the two brides and the husband's daily disappearance. A primary example is the appearance of the she-demon before each of the three brides: the she-demon solves the mysteries of the ring and the murders with her words: "You arrogant one! Why do you lie next to my bridegroom, who sanctified me in marriage in a tree...? I have already killed one [/two] who lay thus with my bridegroom." The reader and the first bride learn simultaneously about the solution to the ring's loss, which is a form of "telling"; yet for the reader this also constitutes a repetition of the earlier "showing" in the park. The informing of the second and third brides about the previous murders again constitutes a form of "telling"; yet while for them it establishes new infor-

---

[13] Christine Brooke-Rose, "The Readerhood of Man," in *The Reader in the Text*, ed. Suleiman and Crosman, 128. Brooke-Rose also distinguishes between the encoded (naive) reader and the actual (sophisticated) reader. Both because definitions of these two terms (encoded and actual) are problematic (as Brooke-Rose herself points out), and because the focus of the present paper is on the socio-cultural context, this is not the place to enter into that discussion.

mation, for the reader it is overdetermination heaped on overdetermination. What is more, while the murder of the first bride constitutes a dramatic instance of "showing" ("the beauty grabbed the bride and choked her, and left her lying dead next to the bridegroom"), the subsequent "telling" about the murders ("And she killed this bride also"; "I have already killed two") further overdetermines this reader as subcritical or naive.

In contrast to this naive reader, whose simplicity justifies the retelling of various actions in the tale, the sophisticated reader of "A Story from Worms" can bestow additional meaning on the repeated sequence of actions through the use of three other codes: the connotations of "wealth" and "marriage" from the connotative code; the reference to the concept of a pious woman from the cultural code; and the opposition between the holy and the profane from the symbolic code. Throughout the story a preoccupation with wealth is evident; Rabbi Zalman is said to be wealthy, and the third bride uses a popular rephrasing of a Talmudic statement in saying that "a poor person is like a dead person."[14] Accordingly, it comes as no surprise that the son's first two brides are the daughters of wealthy community leaders; only out of desperation does his mother finally turn to the poor maiden. This desperation is evident in the elaborately courteous language of her request, when she says, "If I may permit myself to ask, if the thing is possible, that your daughter would take my son as a husband." Thus the rich Rabbi's wife is suitably humbled, repeating the humbling of the two rich brides, who died not only because of their sexual rivalry with the she-demon, but also because of their arrogance in repulsing this she-demon: "This is not true! He is my bridegroom ... so go on your way," as the first bride says.

It is almost superfluous to remark upon the centrality of marriage manifested in the three marriages of the Rabbi's son. What is important to add is that marriage is portrayed in this tale primarily as a social institution for preserving family and wealth, to prevent the situation in which, in the words of the Rabbi, "our memory will be erased from the world, and our wealth will be scattered and fall into the hands of strangers." This conversation between the rich Rabbi and his wife also determines the marriage model prevalent in this story, that of a wise wife and a passive husband,[15]

---

[14] The source of this statement is in the Babylonian Talmud, Tractate Nedarim 64b: "Four are thought of as dead: [the childless], the poor, the leper and the blind" (my translation).

[15] For a discussion of the model of the active wife and the passive husband in Jewish culture and literature, see Daniel Boyarin, *Unheroic Conduct: The Rise of Heterosexuality and the Invention of the Jewish Man* (Berkeley: University of California

for it is the wife who suggests a solution to the situation and who immediately acts upon her words. This initiative and determination are echoed in the actions of the son's pious wife, who releases her notably mute and passive husband from the demonic marriage.

The cultural code in "A Story from Worms" refers specifically to the Jewish concept of a pious woman. The rich Rabbi's wife says of the third bride that "I wish and hope that her devoutness, piety and poverty will be before God's eyes, Blessed be He, and she will remain alive." The she-demon spares the third bride twice because of her piety, first saying, "Dear child, thank your piety and devoutness that you are speaking piously to me," and then saying to the Rabbi's son that "because she did this piously, because she spared my beautiful hair so it would not hang down to the floor, this will be in her favor." Lastly, the narrator explains that the third bride "clung to her husband, and her husband clung to his wife, because she was a very modest woman."

Finally, the opposition between the holy and the profane is introduced by the mysterious hand's appearance in the tree. In Jewish folklore the forest in general and trees in particular are the acknowledged domain of demons; as Joshua Trachtenberg writes, "demons frequented uninhabited places, deserts and forests and fields ... and consort[ed] in the shade of trees."[16] In "A Story from Worms" the narrator specifically notes that "there were many trees" in the city park, thereby establishing it in this story as analogous to a forest. With the appearance of what becomes an unexplained hand, the urban park thus becomes for the sophisticated reader a parallel to the forest in which, at the story's end, the she-demon lives and to which she takes the Rabbi's son each day. Danger may thus lurk even in apparently innocent places, as the intrusion of the profane, demonic presence turns the familiar city park into a sinister place, threatening the holiness of the young boys even in their innocent respite from religious studies.

This blurring of the spatial boundaries between the holy and the profane takes on an added dimension later in the story, with the use of the term "a beautiful creature" (*ein shoyn mentsh*) to describe both the she-demon and the pious wife. The use of this term regarding the she-demon occurs from the viewpoints of the son's three brides, when the narrator

---

Press, 1977), particularly 68–73.

[16] Joshua Trachtenberg, *Jewish Magic and Superstition: A Study in Folk Religion* (Cleveland and Philadelphia: World Publishing Co. & The Jewish Publication Society, 1961), 32, 34. He also notes that "the belief that demons dwell or assemble in trees was also strongly held among the Germans" (276 n25).

relates that "she saw a beautiful creature approaching the bed,"[17] while it is the rich Rabbi's wife who describes the poor maiden as "a beautiful creature." The repeated use of this epithet underlines the blurring of the distinctions between the demonic and the human feminine. In this way the opposition between the sexual, jealous she-demon and the pious, modest human is qualified, suggesting other sides to them both that will indeed emerge during the story's development.

The implementation of Barthes's five codes in my reading of "A Story from Worms" therefore brings out the following aspects of the tale:

1. The text can be seen as a series of repeated actions and situations, emphasizing puzzles to be solved.
2. Narrative repetitions are embedded within a system or network of social relations and divisions in the German-Jewish community: wealth, the centrality of piety to female character, and the belief in demons and their intrusion into the human realm.
3. Two types of readers are posited: the naive reader, who accepts social norms; and the sophisticated reader, who challenges them.

In the light of these principles, I will now offer a detailed reading of two sections of "A Story from Worms," those in which the creation and the breaking of the demonic bond are narrated. The first, near the beginning, narrates the accidental demonic marriage:

> There were many trees in the park, and the Rabbi's son looked for the student behind all of them until he reached a hollow tree. There he saw a hand stretched out towards him. The Rabbi's son thought this was the student he was looking for, who had hidden in the tree, and he began to shout: "Anshel, come out, I have found you." But when the Rabbi's son pulled on the hand, it would not come out of the tree. So he took a gold ring from his own hand, put it on the hand stretched out from the tree and said: "Because you do not want to come out of the tree, I sanctify you to me in marriage." Thus he took out his anger, because he thought that it was his friend Anshel, for whom he was looking. The moment he had sanctified the hand in marriage, the hand disappeared along with the gold ring.

---

[17] Specifically, in the episodes of the first and third brides the term used is "a beautiful creature," while in the episode of the second bride the term "beautiful figure" (*shoyn bild*) is used.

The second, near the end, relates the demon-wife's defeat:

> The she-demon woke up with a great and bitter cry, and said: "My dear husband, I must die. When your dear wife was here she touched my shame [*meyn vushen*].[18] And when someone touches me, I must die. Therefore, my dear husband, because she did this piously, because she spared my beautiful hair so that it would not hang down to the floor, this will be in her favor. Here, my dear husband, on my hand is the gold ring with which you sanctified me in marriage. I return this to you. Go home through the hole, the hole will disappear, and we will be parted forever." This he did. He returned home, the hole disappeared and he remained at home. He said nothing to his wife, and his wife said nothing to him.
>
> He remained at home for three days and then held a great feast for the entire community. Neither his wife, nor his father, nor his mother knew the reason for the feast.

"A Story from Worms" can be summarized here within the framework of the proaieretic (action) and the hermeneutic (puzzles) codes: because an interdiction is violated, the demonic bond is formed; and because of the third wife's piety, the bond is broken. In the first section the Rabbi's son performs several traditional functions of the fairytale hero as analyzed by Vladímir Propp:[19] he receives and violates an interdiction; he is deceived by the villain (the she-demon) and submits to her. The Rabbi's son violates two specific interdictions (which do not explicitly appear in the story):[20] the prohibition against entry into the demons' domain and the prohibition against taking the marriage benediction lightly. The mistake made by the Rabbi's son in identifying the hand as that of his friend provides a further opportunity for his deception by the she-demon, while the immediate disappearance of her hand and the ring validates the demonic marriage.

In the second section it is the pious wife who performs four traditional functions of the fairytale hero as analyzed by Propp: the struggle between

---

[18] The phrase "my shame" (*meyn vushen*) refers to the she-demon's hair, also alluding to the importance in Orthodox Judaism, till today, of covering a married woman's hair. In addition, the use of the term "shame" in an expansion of its sexual connotations can also refer to pubic hair.

[19] See Vladímir Propp's classic discussion of functions, in *Morphology of the Folktale*, trans. L. Scott (Austin: University of Texas Press, 1968), 25–65.

[20] As Propp explains (ibid., 27), the violation of an interdiction does sometimes exist without the explicit statement of the interdiction.

the hero and villain; the villain's defeat; the correction of the initial absence or lack; and the hero's return home. Evident therefore in "A Story from Worms" is the division of the heroic role between the Rabbi's son and his pious wife. In the first section he is the hero, but in the second it is she who struggles with the shedemon and wins, thereby affirming her own exclusive sexual relationship with the Rabbi's son. The human wife's discovery of her husband's trysting-place could potentially bring her into confrontation with the demon, but her piety prevents disaster. For although her human touch brings about the she-demon's death, the generous act of lifting the she-demon's hair off the floor saves the human couple and restores the lost ring.

In this way a narrative analogy of actions and solutions is established between these two sections, which emphasizes the danger of demonic involvement with the human realm, as well as the importance of piety in correcting the harm thus inflicted. Read in this way, "A Story from Worms" comprises an example of a moral Märchen (fairytale), which "can be used to express a 'social charter' outlining norms and values."[21] The moral lesson is stated quite explicitly in the closing statement: "Thus the poor maiden arrived at wealth and honor because of her great piety and because of her modesty. Therefore should each and every person act thus." To the naive reader this lesson is obviously about a Jewish maiden and her reward for adhering to the norms of piety laid down by Jewish tradition.

Yet by employing the additional codes, the sophisticated reader can understand this lesson in a more subversive manner, as a sign of a threefold victory: that of an active wife over a passive husband (connotative); that of a poor but pious woman over the wealthy religious class (cultural); and finally that of a clever woman over the demonic female (symbolic). Shifting the focus onto these codes (because of overdetermination of the proaieretic and the hermeneutic codes) involves, in Barthes's conception, a use of the ironic, which both "expresses" the proaieretic and the hermeneutic codes "at a distance" and "absorbs" their "naiveté."[22] In the terms of the present discussion, an ironic distance is thus established in "A Story from Worms" between the naive and the sophisticated readers' respective understandings of the narrative events. This distance serves to underscore the former's limitations and misconceptions.

I propose that in "A Story from Worms" the primary source of such irony is to be found in the differences between the naive and sophisticated

---

[21] Alexander, "Theme and Genre," 57–58.
[22] Barthes, S/Z, 139.

readers in their filling in of gaps of information. Perry and Sternberg have explained that "the literary work is composed of fragments that must be linked and pieced together during the reading process: it establishes a system of gaps that must be filled in."[23] Taking as a starting point this explanation, I will show that in this tale the fictional characters' (usually unrealistic) explanation of events within their own world is accepted by the naive reader, and is contrasted to the sophisticated reader's accommodation of the textual world to the competing models suggested by the connotative, cultural and symbolic codes. In other words, the differences in the filling in of these gaps result in a highlighting of the "naiveté" and lack of understanding on the part both of the fictional characters (who very often presume a mantle of authority and knowledge) and of the naive reader, while at the same time they highlight the sophisticated reader's more comprehensive explanations for the same events.

In the case of the two sections discussed previously, the Rabbi's son is presented as lacking vital information, unable to fill the hermeneutic gap created by the disappearance of the mysterious hand and by the loss of the ring: "The Rabbi's son thought this [hand] was the student he was looking for, who had hidden in the tree." The naive reader receives the information about the ring's loss simultaneously with this fictional character, and remains limited here to the character's viewpoint. But with access to the symbolic code, the sophisticated reader can fill this gap by understanding the significance of the son's entry into the park as an intrusion into the demonic realm. This reader can causally accommodate the ring's loss as the move from the holy realm (participating in Jewish religious studies) to the profane realm (the park). What is more, such a reader can legitimately question the son's (possibly even homosexual) motives for reciting the marriage benediction to what he thought was his male friend's hand. In this way the ironic nature of the story is first established, as the sophisticated reader is privy to more information than are the unwitting fictional character and his naive counterpart in the reading process—information which places the responsibility for ensuing events squarely on the shoulders of the naive, though certainly not blameless, Rabbi's son.

In the second section it is the pious wife who lacks vital information, unable to fill the hermeneutic gap created by her husband's remaining at home. The Rabbi's son—along with the naive and the sophisticated readers—knows immediately about the breaking of the demonic bond, for

---

[23] Menahem Perry and Meir Sternberg, "The King Through Ironic Eyes: Biblical Narrative and the Literary Reading Process," *Poetics Today* 7 (1986): 276.

the she-demon has explained to him that she must die, and returns the gold ring with the words "Go home through the hole, the hole will disappear, and we will be parted forever." The pious wife, however, is not immediately cognizant of the dissolution of this demonic bond, nor of its direct relationship to her own actions in lifting the she-demon's hair off the floor. This is not only because the pious wife has left the trysting-place before either her husband or the she-demon awoke, but also because the silence between the human couple continues for three days. Ironically then, it is the pious wife's generous act, representing as it does her continued submission to the pact with the she-demon, that leads in the end to its unexpected dissolution.

Both the naive and the sophisticated readers shift their viewpoints here, as they discover the trysting-place along with the wife and the dissolution of the demonic bond along with the husband. Such "real-time" narration heightens the dramatic tension, as well as returning the narrative viewpoint from the pious bride back to her husband. It is the sophisticated reader, however, who can explain the ensuing silence as a direct result of the demonic bond, for neither the Rabbi's son nor his wife inform anyone of its dissolution (and of its prior existence) until the trial period of three days has passed. The perception of the silence in this way points to an intertwining of the hermeneutic and symbolic codes, since such silence (a lack of information) originally comes about because of the son's move from the holy to the profane.

A central claim of this essay is therefore that the intertwining of the hermeneutic and symbolic codes comprises a pivotal issue in the reading of "A Story from Worms." This aspect of the tale can be fruitfully approached if we highlight various "junctions of meaning" in the text, which reveal the process of the discovery and filling in of gaps of information. Two such junctions will be discussed here, the first relating to general (particularly male) knowledge and ignorance, and the second relating specifically to the pious wife's knowledge of the bond between her husband and the she-demon. In order to look closely at each junction, central sentences from the text will be quoted below (representing many others that repeat the same information):

A. Knowledge and Ignorance
1. The students returned home and told the Rabbi the tale (shemu'ah).
2. The Rabbi listened and said: "Go call my son, and tell him not to make himself sad; I will give him something expensive" ... and the ring was forgotten.

3. A long time after these events the Rabbi's son grew up and became a respected person; one heard his learning spoken of far and wide.
4. He said: "To my sorrow I fell asleep, and I do not myself know."
5. Many people said that the bridegroom had killed the bride.

Rabbi Zalman's response to the boys' adventure centers on property loss and on an attempt to calm his beloved son. With the son's return home the other fictional characters and the naive reader as well are calmed, as indicated by the sentence "and the ring was forgotten." For the sophisticated reader, however, a hermeneutic gap is created here, since within the framework of the symbolic code the Rabbi's response is surprising. Indeed, two questions can be posed: why does Rabbi Zalman not address the *circumstances* of the ring's loss; and what does the Rabbi really know about his son's deeds, since the Yiddish word *shemu'ah* (tale/tall tale/fable) contains a semantic element of rumors and gossip. What is left open is an uncertainty about what exactly the Rabbi was told. His lack of interest in the circumstances of the ring's loss or in the possibility of a demonic presence ultimately places the responsibility on him for the death of the two brides. For if the Rabbi had taken care to annul the marriage (as was done, we recall, in the historical analogue), the very first bride might have survived. Rabbi Zalman's silence is therefore an interweaving (partially causal) of the hermeneutic and symbolic codes.

The son's similar lack of knowledge is emphasized in the fourth sentence on the list, when he says, "To my sorrow I fell asleep, and I do not myself know." This confession of ignorance stands in contrast to the learned commentary that a Jewish scholar is expected to give on various occasions, including at his wedding feast. What is more, the son's lack of knowledge about his first bride's death results in a mistaken and dangerous hypothesis: "Many people said that the bridegroom had killed the bride." Rabbi Zalman and his son are therefore presented in the story as lacking in basic information, which is both ironic and sinister because they represent Jewish scholars in general: the Rabbi is the head of a Yeshivah (a Jewish religious school), while it is said of the son that "one heard of his learning spoken of far and wide."

In the rest of the sentences in list A, the main point is the shared sin of Rabbi Zalman and his son. In this manner a double irony is created. First, every reader, even the most naive one, now knows more than either of the two rabbinic scholars. Second, there exists an ironic gap between the fictional characters and with them the naive reader, on the one hand, and between the sophisticated reader on the other. While the characters and the naive reader raise and accept mistaken hypotheses (the hand is the hand of Anshel, the bridegroom is a murderer), the sophisticated reader raises hypotheses which include access to other codes (the hand does not belong to the human realm; the son's rash act is actually a transgression of the holy). This intertwining of the hermeneutic and symbolic codes is revealed therefore in the naiveté of Rabbi Zalman and his son, whose sins in sustaining the profane (the son's disregard of the sanctity of the marriage benediction, and the Rabbi's disregard of the demonic presence) turn them into simpletons.

At this point, it should be noted that in addition to the evident stratification of German-Jewish society by wealth, there is another hierarchy defined by religious scholarship. Thus the reputation of the Rabbi's son as a learned man brings him the offer of a prestigious marriage. Ironically, then, it is a woman—traditionally outside the Jewish religious and scholarly establishment—who becomes the focus in the second junction for the transmission of knowledge:

B. The Pious Bride's Knowledge of the Demonic Bond
1. The Rabbi's wife said: "I come because of this: you surely have heard what, because of many sins, happened twice to my son."
2. [A beautiful creature] said to the bride: "You heard, but nevertheless you dared again. Therefore I will kill you also."
3. The bride heard this, became very frightened and said: "Dear mother, I have spent my days in the poorhouse and did not hear that his two brides died."
4. When the beautiful she-demon heard this, she said: "But this you must do in order for him to be our husband: each day he will disappear from before your eyes for one hour and will come to me."
5. But wives always wish to know more than is necessary for them.
6. The good woman searched for her husband and thought: "I will risk my neck, I wish to know where he is going. I will follow him and I will risk my neck."

The sentences in list B raise a central question: what is the true nature of the pious bride's character? The first answer to this question is revealed in sentences 1–3. The pious bride's answer to the shedemon is rather surprising, for we already know that she and her mother know the story (confirmed by the rich Rabbi's wife in the first sentence quoted), and what would she be doing by the bridegroom's side if the first two brides had not died? Thus her answer to the she-demon is a lie, but a cleverly defensive one. It emphasizes the pious bride's social as well as economic marginality (which would naturally limit access to information), thus making her seem innocuous, a victim; the she-demon is appeased, and she sees the pious bride as an ally rather than an enemy.

Sentences 4–6 reveal another answer. Here the pious wife's desire to discover her husband's destination comprises another surprising response, as her pact with the she-demon (quoted in the fourth sentence) had previously made clear the secret and the danger involved with her husband's disappearance; since she has explicitly agreed to share him with the she-demon, what is left for her to know? Such ambiguity about the extent of the pious wife's knowledge continues with the narrator's statement that "wives always wish to know more than is necessary for them." This clearly points out, even for the naive reader, a contradiction in the pious wife's character that is difficult to reconcile with her piety extolled throughout the story, for in folklore curiosity is deemed a negative characteristic.[24] To the sophisticated reader this hermeneutic gap again reveals the other side of the pious wife's character, that of a clever, even deceitful, person who answers the she-demon in her own language, and breaks their agreement when curiosity gets the better of her.

In this way the pious wife takes on characteristics usually associated with a she-demon (cleverness, deceitfulness, cunning), thereby further blurring the distinction between them, a blurring first introduced when each is described as "a beautiful creature" (*ein shoyn mentsh*). There is, however, another side to this blurring that should be noted. The pious wife's generous act (of lifting the she-demon's hair off the floor) elicits a similarly generous response on the part of the she-demon: before her death she releases the Rabbi's son from their bond. Once again there is an alliance between the she-demon and the pious wife, only this time out of piety. To the naive reader it may seem at first that this instance of female solidarity, affirmed by the pious wife's generous act, continues the male fantasy of being sexually shared by two wives.[25] Yet for the sophisticated reader such solidarity ultimately undermines this fantasy. This is not only because confirmation of the female alliance through the she-demon's generous reciprocity itself leads ironically to the dissolution of the demonic

---

[24] See Zfatman, *The Marriage of a Mortal Man and a She-Demon*, 55–56 n27. For a more general discussion of this motif, Zfatman refers to Stith Thompson, *Motif-Index of Folk-Literature*, 6 vol. (Bloomington: Indiana University Press, 1966), No. Q341 and H1219.8.

[25] This discussion of female solidarity and masculine fantasy was proposed by Sheila Delany. I would like to thank her for this reading.

bond with the male partner. It is also that such female solidarity underlines the ambiguous nature of the human wife, who retains characteristics of both piety and cunning, deference and self-assertion. For it is her defensive lie to the she-demon and her curiosity, as much as her piety, that contribute to her victory over the demonic realm, thereby shedding an ironic light on the story's moral that she "arrived at wealth and honor because of her great piety and because of her modesty."

This, then, is the particular fascination of the Yiddish folk tale "A Story from Worms." Its simple moral lesson fails to resolve narrative ambiguity about the extent and possession of knowledge, or the issues of poor against rich, women against men, and social outcasts against the religious establishment. The use of narratological codes makes possible the unmasking of this folk tale. It overturns the conventional "rags to riches" story in which a poor maiden attains wealth and marriage through her piety, replacing it with the tale of a clever heroine whose victory resonates even today.

Ben-Gurion University of the Negev

Appendix: A Story from Worms (Mayse fun Vorms)

Let us tell what happened many years ago. There was a respected Rabbi in a city still called Worms, an ancient community from the time of Jesse.[26] This Rabbi, who was called Rabbi Zalman, was very wealthy and headed a great Yeshivah,[27] in which one hundred respected students studied day and night. This same Rabbi had an only son, a respected student, and his father and mother loved him dearly because of his good deeds.

One day the holiday of Lag ba-'Omer arrived,[28] and the students went

---

[26] Apparently this refers to King David, since his father was named Jesse. According to local tradition Jewish settlement in Worms had already begun during the time of the First Temple, built by King David's son, Solomon. See Zfatman, *The Marriage of a Mortal Man and a She-Demon*, 119. In historical fact, the settlement of Worms dates from the beginning of the eleventh century; see Fritz Reuter, *Jewish Worms: Rashi House and Judengasse* (Worms: Jüdisches Museum im Raschi-Haus: 1992), 28.

[27] Yeshivah: a Jewish religious school for boys and young men.

[28] Lag ba-'Omer: There are traditionally two main reasons for the celebration of this minor Jewish holiday. One is that a plague was active among the disciples of Rabbi Akiva (d. 135 CE), and on Lag ba-'Omer it ceased; thus this day is also called "The Scholar's Festival" and became a holiday, especially for rabbinical students in the Middle Ages. In addition, it is also considered a celebration of the Jewish rebel-

out to enjoy themselves. In the city of Worms there was a park called "Havel Park," a place known to all the city's inhabitants. On Lag ba-'Omer the students went to play in the park and they took the Rabbi's son with them. They played a game called "Hide and Seek" which is played in this way: one person bends down on his knees while the others hide, and then the one who has bent down looks for the others until he finds all those who have hidden. The students played for such a long time that it became the turn of the Rabbi's son to bend down. All the students hid, he began to look for them and found them all. But he did not find one of them, Anshel, and he searched for a long time.

There were many trees in the park, and the Rabbi's son looked for the student behind all of them until he reached a hollow tree. There he saw a hand stretched out towards him. The Rabbi's son thought this was the student he was looking for, who had hidden in the tree, and he began to shout: "Anshel, come out, I have found you." But when the Rabbi's son pulled on the hand, it would not come out of the tree. So he took a gold ring from his own hand, put it on the hand stretched out from the tree and said: "Because you do not want to come out of the tree, I sanctify you to me in marriage." Thus he took out his anger, because he thought that it was his friend Anshel, for whom he was looking. The moment he had sanctified the hand in marriage, the hand disappeared along with the gold ring.

When the Rabbi's son saw that the hand had disappeared, and with it the ring, he became very frightened because the ring was very expensive, and he was afraid to return home to his father and mother. He returned to his study companions, and was surprised to find Anshel with them. He said to him: "My dear Anshel, give me my ring." The student said: "I did not see your ring, and I know nothing about it." Again the Rabbi's son asked: "My dear Anshel, give me my ring, that I put on your hand when you hid in that tree." Again the student answered: "I bring all this study company as witnesses that I was not hiding in that tree but in another place." So the ring was lost.

The students returned home and told the Rabbi the tale. The Rabbi listened and said: "Go call my son home, and tell him not to make himself

---

lion against Roman occupation of the Land of Israel, led by General Bar-Kokhba (132–35 CE). The Maharil of Mainz (note 4, above) discusses this holiday at great length in his works, describing the custom of the students to go for trips outside of the city, and to play at different games. To this day it is customary for Jewish children to go out into the forest, light bonfires and play with bows and arrows. See Julian Morgenstern, "Lag Ba'Omer—Its Origins and Import," HUCA 39 (1968) (in Hebrew): 81–90; Yom-Tov Levinski, *Encyclopedia of the Jewish Way of Life and Tradition* (Tel-Aviv: Devir, 1970), 296–97 (in Hebrew); *Encyclopedia Judaica* 10:1356–75.

sad; I will give him something expensive." They called him and he came home, and the ring was forgotten.

A long time after these events the Rabbi's son grew up and became a respected person; one heard his learning spoken of far and wide. There was a community leader who lived in Speyer, and he asked the Rabbi from Worms if he would agree to wed his son to his daughter. Because he had heard about the son's great studiousness, he would add a great sum to the dowry. So the betrothal contract was signed, and it brought great joy.

When the time for the wedding came, many people gathered in honor of the event, as is customary at the weddings of the rich. They rejoiced greatly, held the wedding and set up the marriage canopy. When the feasting ended, they led the bridegroom and the bride to the bridal chamber in great joy, as was customary.

The bridegroom had just lain down in bed when he fell into a deep sleep, but the bride remained awake for a long time. As she lay awake, she saw a beautiful creature approaching the bed, dressed in clothes of gold and silk. The creature said to the bride: "You arrogant one! Why do you lie next to my bridegroom, who sanctified me in marriage in a tree?" The bride said: "This is not true! He is my bridegroom, I have only just now stood with him under the marriage canopy, so go on your way."

Upon hearing this, the beauty grabbed the bride and choked her, and left her lying dead next to the bridegroom. After midnight the bridegroom awoke and wished to talk to his bride, as was customary. When he saw the bride lying dead by his side he started up in great fear and woke everyone. When they came to the bridal chamber and found the bride dead, they asked the bridegroom what had happened. He said: "To my sorrow I fell asleep, and I do not myself know." The bride was buried, the joy in the house turned into mourning, and everyone went home. Many people said that the bridegroom had killed the bride.

Three years passed, and the Rabbi's son was unable to find a wife. In spite of his father's great wealth and his own great learning, no man could be found who would agree to give him his daughter.

This continued for a long time, until a rich community leader, a relative of the young man, said to the Rabbi from Worms: "It is my wish to give him my daughter, because we are of the same flesh and blood, and although it happened once, I hope it will not happen again." They arranged the betrothal contract, and set up the wedding and the marriage canopy. When the bridegroom lay with his bride they locked the room, and everyone left. The bridegroom fell into a deep sleep, but the bride lay awake and was very frightened. When she had thus lain there a long time, a beautiful figure in a golden dress approached the bed and said to the bride: "You arrogant one, I have already killed one who lay with my bridegroom, and this was not enough for you?" She killed this bride also. When the bridegroom awoke, he found his bride dead. He began to shout until everyone came and he said: "To my sorrow, my bride is dead." They buried her, and again the wedding turned into great mourning.

So ten years passed, during which the Rabbi's son could not find a wife, and he was already thirty years old.

Once on the Sabbath of Repentance[29] the young man's father sat together with his mother, and the Rabbi said to his wife: "My dear wife, what shall we do? We have an only son and great wealth. But if a wife is not found for him, our memory will be erased from the world; our wealth will be scattered and will fall into the hands of strangers. Who would be willing to give him his daughter?" So they talked in sorrow and in tears. The Rabbi's wife said: "My dear husband, if I am not mistaken, no community leader will give him any daughter. I know a poor Rabbi's wife, a widow, from a very good family. She has an only daughter, a beautiful creature, and she lives in the poorhouse. Who knows, my dear husband, perhaps I will go to her and give our son to her daughter, and I wish and hope that her devoutness, piety and poverty will be before God's eyes, Blessed be He, and she will remain alive." The Rabbi said to his wife: "You have spoken well, go immediately and speak with the poor Rabbi's wife and see if she will agree to give her daughter to our son."

Immediately the rich Rabbi's wife, the young man's mother, went and knocked on the door of the poorhouse. The poor Rabbi's wife saw the rich Rabbi's wife knocking on the door, ran to her daughter and said: "My dear daughter, why is she knocking on the door?" Her daughter answered: "My dear mother, perhaps she wishes to give us a present of jewelry!" So they let her enter, greeted her with honor, asked her to sit down and said to her: "Madam, dear Rabbi's wife, why have you come here?"

The rich Rabbi's wife said: "I come because of this: you surely have heard what, because of many sins, happened twice to my son. If I may permit myself to ask, if the thing is possible: would your daughter wish to take my son as a husband? Who knows, perhaps her piety will commend her, and she will remain alive. Then an end will come to your poverty and your daughter's poverty." The poor Rabbi's wife turned to her daughter and asked: "My dear daughter, you have now heard what the rich Rabbi's wife says. Is it your wish to do this? I do not wish to force you, I do not wish to give you away. If you wish, you can remain with me." The daughter answered her, saying: "My dear mother, we are indeed poor, and a poor

---

[29] Sabbath of Repentance: The Sabbath between Rosh Hashanah (the Jewish New Year) and Yom Kippur (the Day of Atonement).

person is like a dead person. I will do the thing in this way: the Rabbi will write that if I die, he will maintain you in his house until your dying day—then I will marry his son and risk my life." Thus once again a betrothal contract was signed.

Quickly the rich Rabbi's wife made expensive clothes for the poor maiden. From the moment she put on the new clothes no one recognized her because of her great beauty, and she did not have to beg anymore. Previously she had dressed in rags and without jewelry, and now, when they dressed her beautifully, everyone who saw her testified to her beauty. They held the wedding with a few guests, and did not have a great celebration, for they thought: "If she remains alive, then we will celebrate." They set up the marriage canopy and afterwards led the bride and bridegroom to bed, as was customary. Everyone left and locked the room. The bridegroom fell into a deep sleep, and the bride lay awake in great fear.

Midnight arrived, and again a beautiful creature wearing a dress of pearls, with golden hair, approached the bed and said to the bride: "You arrogant one, I have already killed two, why are you lying next to my bridegroom? You knew, but nevertheless you dared. Therefore I will kill you also." The bride heard this, became very frightened and said: "Dear mother, I have spent my days in the poorhouse and did not hear that his two brides died. Therefore, dear mother, if he is your bridegroom—I will get up, and will let you lie by his side." When the beautiful she-demon heard this, she said: "Dear child, thank your piety and devoutness that you are speaking piously to me. But this you must do in order for him to be your husband: each day he will disappear from before your eyes for one hour and will come to me. Therefore speak not at the risk of your neck, because God loves you." The bride answered that this was God's will. Then the she-demon disappeared.

Not a half hour passed before the bridegroom awoke in great fear and searched for his bride. When he found her alive, he was very happy. Day had hardly dawned when everyone came into the room, to find the bridegroom and bride lying side by side. The father-in-law and mother-in-law and the bride's mother were very happy, and for the first time there was great joy at the wedding. The poor maiden became very rich, and everything was done at her bidding. She clung to her husband, and her husband clung to his wife, because she was a very modest woman. They had three sons.

But wives always wish to know more than is necessary for them. Daily she released her husband for one hour, and did not know where he went, for she saw him enter his room and disappear. The good woman searched for her husband and thought: "I will risk my neck, I wish to know where he is going. I will follow him and I will risk my neck." She searched for the key to his room and opened the room, but did not find him there. She searched for him everywhere in the room. Under the bed she found a large stone, which she moved from its place. In front of her a large hole was revealed, and in the hole there was a ladder. She thought: "Dear God, should I climb down? My husband surely did." She deliberated for a long time about what to do. Finally she climbed down and reached a large forest.

In the forest she saw an elegant house of stone and entered it. She was astonished to see a room made of stone, and in it a table set with beautiful dishes, but no one was sitting there. In the room was an entrance leading to another room. She entered the other room and was surprised to find her husband lying on a silken bed together with the beautiful she-demon. Both of them slept, held in each other's arms. The she-demon had golden hair, which trailed down from the bed to the floor. When the wife saw this, she felt sorry that the elegant hair was hanging down to the floor. She took a chair, stood it near the bed, and placed the hair on it. Afterwards she returned the way she had come. She returned the stone to the hole, locked the room and returned the key to its hiding-place. She told no one in the house about this.

The she-demon woke up with a great and bitter cry, and said: "My dear husband, I must die. When your dear wife was here she touched my shame. And when someone touches me, I must die. Therefore, my dear husband, because she did this piously, because she spared my beautiful hair so that it would not hang down to the floor, this will be in her favor. Here, my dear husband, on my hand is the gold ring with which you sanctified me in marriage. I return this to you. Go home through the hole, the hole will disappear, and we will be parted forever." This he did. He returned home, the hole disappeared and he remained at home. He said nothing to his wife, and his wife said nothing to him.

He remained at home for three days and then held a great feast for the entire community. Neither his wife, nor his father, nor his mother knew the reason for the feast. When all the guests had eaten and drunk, and the time came for grace after meals, the Rabbi's son rose and said: "My dear people, I will not let you say the blessing before I tell you why I held this feast. My dear father, here is the ring that I lost in the tree. At that time I sanctified a she-demon in marriage, because I thought it was the young man I was searching for. It was the she-demon who murdered my first two brides, and my dear wife released me from her." So he told the tale in full. Afterwards his wife rose from her place, because she had heard him, and told what had happened from the first night of the wedding to this very day, and unloaded everything from her heart. Thus the poor maiden arrived at wealth and honor because of her great piety and because of her modesty.

Therefore should each and every person act thus.

So ends "A Story from Worms."

Contributors

DANIEL BOYARIN is Taubman Professor of Talmudic Culture and rhetoric at the University of California, Berkeley. His Ph.D. is from the Jewish Theological Seminary of America; he has been a fellow of the National Endowment for the Humanities, the Guggenheim Foundation, and the Institute for Advanced Studies in Jerusalem. His many books and articles center on talmudic and midrashic studies, including gender and sexuality in rabbinic Judaism. His most recent works are *Dying for God: Martyrdom and the Making of Christianity and Judaism* (Stanford, 1999) and *Border Lines: The Partition of Judaeo-Christianity* (University of Pennsylvania, 2004).

MICHAEL CHERNICK is the Deutsch Family Professor of Jewish Jurisprudence and Social Justice at Hebrew Union College-Jewish Institute of Religion in New York, where he teaches Talmud and Jewish law. He edited *Essential Papers on the Talmud* (1994) and is author of *A Great Voice That Did Not Cease: The Growth of the Rabbinic Canon and its Interpretation* (Hebrew Union College, forthcoming 2008).

SHEILA DELANY is Professor Emerita at Simon Fraser University. She has published widely in Chaucer, medieval cultural studies, and gender studies. Her most recent books are *Impolitic Bodies: Poetry, Saints, and Society in Fifteenth-Century England* (Oxford, 1998), which won the Society of Canadian Medievalists prize, and an edited collection, *Chaucer and the Jews* (Routledge, 2002).

SUSAN EINBINDER is Professor of Hebrew Literature at Hebrew Union College, Cincinnati. She has been a fellow at the Davis Center for Historical Studies at Princeton and at the National Humanities Center in North Carolina. She is author of *Beautiful Death: Jewish Poetry on Martyrdom from Medieval France* (Princeton, 2002) and is currently working on *God's Forgotten Sheep: Poetic Responses to the Fourteenth-Century Expulsions of Jews from France*.

SONIA FELLOUS works at the Institut de Recherches et d'Histoire des Textes at the CNRS in Paris and teaches religious history at the University of Paris IV-Sorbonne. She was the 1994 Laureate of the Académie Hillel, and her doctoral dissertation won the 1996 prize of the Association Zadoc Kahn. She is author of

Les manuscrits hébreux enluminés des bibliothèques de France (Louvain and Paris, 1994) and *Histoire de la Bible de Moïse Arragel: Quand un rabbin interprète la Bible pour les chrétiens: Tolède 1422–1433* (Somogy, 2002), and has edited *Les relations judéo-musulmanes en Tunisie du Moyen Age à nos jours* (Somogy, 2003).

CHANITA GOODBLATT is a senior lecturer in Foreign Languages and Linguistics at Ben Gurion University of the Negev in Beersheva, Israel. She specializes in Christian Hebraism of the English Renaissance and in modern Israeli poetry. She has coedited *Tradition, Heterodoxy and Religious Cultures in the Early Modern Period* (Ben-Gurion University Press, 2006).

WILLIAM CHESTER JORDAN is the Dayton-Stockton Professor of History at Princeton University and former director of the Davis Center for Historical Studies there. His major work relating to the topic of this collection is *The French Monarchy and the Jews: From Philip Augustus to the Last Capetians* (University of Pennsylvania, 1989). He is also author of *The Great Famine: Northern Europe in the Early Fourteenth Century* (Princeton, 1996), which won the Haskins Medal of the Medieval Academy of America in 2000; *Ideology and Royal Power in Medieval France: Kingship, Crusades, and the Jews* (Ashgate/Variorum, 2001); and *Europe in the High Middle Ages* (Penguin/Viking, 2003).

TOVA ROSEN is Professor of Medieval Hebrew Literature at Ben Gurion University of the Negev, Israel. Her recent publications are *Unveiling Eve: Women and Gender in Medieval Hebrew Literature* (University of Pennsylvania, 2003) and *Gazelle Hunting* (2006, in Hebrew); she is currently working on editions of the poetry of Samuel ha-Nagid and Moses Ibn Ezra.

BRUCE ROSENSTOCK is associate professor in the Program for the Study of Religion at the University of Illinois, Urbana-Champaign, and also a Humanities Computing Specialist in its College of Liberal Arts and Sciences. His most recent publication is *New Men: Conversos, Christian Theology, and Society in Fifteenth-Century Castile* (University of London, 2002).

ELLIOT R. WOLFSON is Abraham Lieberman Professor of Judaic Studies at New York University and author of many studies in the history of Jewish mysticism and philosophy with special focus on hermeneutics and gender theory. His *Through a Speculum That Shines: Vision and Imagination in Medieval Jewish Mysticism* (Princeton, 1994) won an American Academy of Religion award and a National Jewish Book award in 1995. His most recent book is *Luminal Darkness: Imaginal Gleanings from Zoharic Literature* (Oneworld, 2007), and he is currently at work on three monographs on various aspects of Kabbala.

www.ingramcontent.com/pod-product-compliance
Lightning Source LLC
Chambersburg PA
CBHW070249230426
43664CB00014B/2454